Dave Rudabaugh
Border Ruffian

F. Stanley

David G. Thomas, Editor

Copyright © 2024 by Doc45 Publishing

All Rights Reserved

This book, or parts thereof, may not be reproduced in any form,
including information storage and retrieval systems,
without explicit permission from Doc45 Publishing,
except for brief quotations included in articles and reviews.

Doc45 Publishing, Las Cruces, N. M.
books@doc45.com

To obtain books, visit:
doc45.com

YouTube Channel
youtube.com/c/Doc45Publications

ISBN 978-1-952580-12-3

000p

DOC45 PUBLISHING

Mesilla Valley History Series

La Posta – From the Founding of Mesilla, to Corn Exchange Hotel, to Billy the Kid Museum, to Famous Landmark – by David G. Thomas

Giovanni Maria de Agostini, Wonder of The Century – The Astonishing World Traveler Who Was A Hermit – by David G. Thomas

Screen with a Voice – A History of Moving Pictures in Las Cruces, New Mexico – by David G. Thomas

Billy the Kid's Grave – A History of the Wild West's Most Famous Death Marker – by David G. Thomas

Killing Garrett, The Wild West's Most Famous Lawman – Murder or Self-Defense? – by David G. Thomas

The Stolen Pinkerton Reports of Colonel Albert J. Fountain Investigation – David G. Thomas, Editor

The Trial of Billy the Kid – by David G. Thomas

The Frank W. Angel Report on the Death of John H. Tunstall – by David G. Thomas

Water in a Thirsty Land – by Ruth R. Ealy, David G. Thomas, Editor

"Dirty Dave" Rudabaugh, Billy the Kid's Most Feared Companion – by David G. Thomas

Mesilla Valley Reprints

When New Mexico Was Young – by Harry H. Bailey

Dave Rudabaugh, Border Ruffian – by F. Stanley, David G. Thomas, Editor

List of Images

1. Notice to thieves, thugs, fakirs and bunko-steerers 4
2. Plaza at Old Town Las Vegas 70
3. Rudabaugh and Billy the Kid being brought in to Las Vegas 86
4. Drawing of Las Vegas jail 92
5. Dave Rudabaugh, headless in Parral 113
6. Rudabaugh's head on a pike in Parral 114

Table of Contents

Introduction by Editor 1
Foreward 5
1. Kansas 7
2. The Kinsley Robbery 21
3. The Affair at Royal Gorge 39
4. Las Vegas Days 51
5. With Billy the Kid 71
6. The End of the Line 101
Bibliography 117
Appendix A – Rudabaigh's Confession 121
Appendix B – Trial Testimony – Territory vs David Rudabaugh, Murder 125
Appendix C – Rudabaugh's Death Photos 151
Index 153

Doc 45

Buenas noches boys,
A social call no doubt –
Do we talk it over,
Or do we shoot it out?

I'm Doc 45,
Toughest man alive.
Hand over those golden bills
Or I'll dose you up with dirty leaden pills.

Introduction by Editor

The author of this book, Father Stanley Francis Louis Crocchiola, writing under the pen name F. Stanley, states in his Preface:

> *"In other books I used to apologize for my mistakes. Come to think of it, why should I! I tried; that's more than my critics did. I investigated to the best of my ability, often going both sleepless and hungry in order to attain the facts.... I expect to be crucified as a result of this work by readers who consider themselves authorities on the West, but I will continue my research until they come up with something better, which perhaps wouldn't take much. If there is no comment for the work; let there be a wee bit for effort...."*

As Father Crocchiola suspected, his work does contain errors – but primarily because new information about Dave Rudabaugh is available today that Father Crocchiola had no access to while he was writing his book. In supplying supplementary details to the text of Father Crocchiola's book (in brackets), I have relied on the research I conducted for my book, *"Dirty Dave" Rudabaugh, Billy the Kid's Most Feared Companion.*

I have also added Appendices A, B, and C. Appendix A gives the complete text of Rudabaugh's amazing confession to the Kinsley Train Robbery. Appendix B gives the complete transcript of Rudabaugh's trial for killing Las Vegas County Jailer Antonio Lino Valdez. Appendix C gives the story of the death photographs of Rudabaugh taken in Parral, Mexico. These photos were first published in Father Crocchiola's book. They appear on pages 113-114. For the footnoted sources of the supplemental information, I refer you to my above named book. Father Crocchiola's book had no index. I have added one.

Stanley Francis Louis Crocchiola

Father Crocchiola was born of Italian, Catholic, immigrant parents October 31, 1908, in Greenwich Village, New York.[1] His father was Vincent Crocchiola and his mother was Rose Lovico. They knew each other as children in their home town of Palermo, Italy, but only married after they had arrived in the United States. Vincent and Rose had eleven children. The tenth child was Louis, Father Crocchiola's birth name.

Louis Crocchiola's interest in writing developed while attending DeWitt Clinton High School, an all-boys school in Lower Manhattan. In his junior year, he was selected as editor of the school newspaper, after having numerous articles and poems published in the paper. As an outgrowth of his interest in writing, he decided to be a school teacher. His family pastor, however, told him that the teaching field at that time (1927) was too full to offer much opportunity, and convinced him that he should join the priesthood.

Louis' father was *"very much against"* his son becoming a priest, but nevertheless, Louis had made up his mind.[2] He enrolled in Catholic University in Washington, D.C. On February 10, 1938, he was ordained in the Order of the Atonement, a branch of the Third Order of St. Francis. As was traditional on ordination, Louis had the option of taking another name or adding additional names to his birth name. He chose to add "Stanley" and "Francis," becoming Stanley Francis Louis Crocchiola.[3] His pen name F. Stanley comes from "Francis" Stanley, not "Father" Stanley as many readers have supposed.

Three days after his ordination as a priest, *"doctors found two spots on my right lung. They gave me five years if I didn't go to a drier climate."* [4] He had tuberculosis.

After two years struggling to get assigned to a diocese in the Southwest, Stanley was appointed assistant pastor of Our Lady of Guadalupe Church in Taos, New Mexico, in 1940. Over the next 12 years, he served in various parishes in New Mexico. In 1952, he was transferred to Texas. He served in sundry Texas parishes until his retirement, January 20, 1984. Stanley died February 5, 1996, in Amarillo, Texas.[5]

During his life, Stanley published at least 190 books. In an interview in 1969, he said he *"hoped to do five hundred [books] before I die."* [6] Stanley financed his books himself, often going into debt to pay the printing costs. Concerning his Rudabaugh book, Stanley said he twice lost the completed manuscript: *"I started over and wrote [it] again, because I always felt – don't quit, don't quit."*

Rudabaugh's Early Life

Rudabaugh's early life is obscure. Apparently, the only U.S. census in which he or his family appears is the 1875 Kansas State Census for Spring Creek Township, Greenwood County.[7] That census is extremely sketchy. The census lists only the first initial of each person's given name (!), age, sex, race, value of real estate (not filled in), value of personal property, place of birth, and place came to Kansas from. There are other fields on the form which were not completed by the census taker.

The census lists:

A. Radenbaugh, 46, Female, White, Ohio, Iowa, (implied birth date, 1829)

D. Radenbaugh. 21, Male, White, Illinois, Iowa, (implied birth date, 1854)

Z. Radenbaugh, 19, Male, White, Ohio, Iowa, (implied birth date, 1856)

I. Radenbaugh, 15, Female, White, Ohio, Iowa, (implied birth date, 1860)

J. Radenbaugh, 14, Male, White, Ohio, Iowa, (implied birth date, 1861)

Stanley identifies these persons as Anna (Rudabaugh's mother), David, Zeth (may have been Zadek), Ida (possibly), and John. Where he obtained their given names is undocumented and thus unknown. They were all born in Ohio, except David, who is shown as being born in Illinois. Stanley mistakenly gives Zeth's birth place as Illinois. A diligent search of census returns, newspapers, and military records produced no further record of Rudabaugh's mother or siblings, with the single exception of a newspaper report that Rudabaugh's two brothers were living in Dodge City at the time of Rudabaugh's trial for the Kinsley train robbery.[8]

Stanley says that Rudabaugh's father was James Redenbaugh and that he served in Company D, 103rd. Illinois Infantry during the Civil War. The Federal database of Civil War soldiers lists no James Redenbaugh in Company D. It does list a James Rodenbaugh in Company G, 103rd Infantry.[9] That is probably the individual Stanley is identifying as Rudabaugh's father. Rodenbaugh's brief service record says he joined October 2, 1862, and was discharged January 15, 1863. He served as a musician. Stanley says he was killed during the Civil War, but I could find no confirmation of that.

In his sworn confession to the Kinsley train robbery, Rudabaugh gives his surname as Rodenbaugh, so that is almost certainly the way the family spelled their last name. Because he is universally referred to as Rudabaugh by historians, that is the spelling Stanley uses.

Stanley's Footnote Philosophy

Stanley's attitude and approach to footnotes was eccentric:

"Most people find footnotes a bother.... Footnotes really do not tell anymore than what the author just got through saying.... Time is the test of a man's research."

"Rather than annoy the reader with little numbers after certain references... take my word for it that the facts are gleaned from [the source given at the end of a quote]." [10]

The abbreviation o.c. in his footnotes means *opere citato* (in the work cited).

– David G. Thomas, Editor

Notes:

1. Mary Jo Walker, *The F. Stanley Story*, (New Mexico Book League and The Lightning Tree, 1895), p 20; *Cimarron News*, Feb. 6, 1987.
2. Walker, p 21.
3. Walker, p 23.
4. Walker, p 23.
5. https://www.findagrave.com/memorial/121280168/stanley-crocchiola, accessed Jan. 5, 2023.
6. Walker, p 30.
7. 1875 Census, Spring Creek Township, Greenwood County, Kansas, ancestry.com, accessed Aug. 5, 2022.
8. *Dodge City Times* (KS), June 29, 1878; *Weekly Commonwealth* (Topeka KS), June 27, 1878..
9. https:// www.nps.gov/civilwar/searchsoldiers-detail.htm?soldierId=DFAE5BCADC7A-DF11-BF36-B8AC6F5D926A; https://www.fold3.com/image/293442249; accessed Aug. 5, 2022.
10. Walker, p 58.

NOTICE

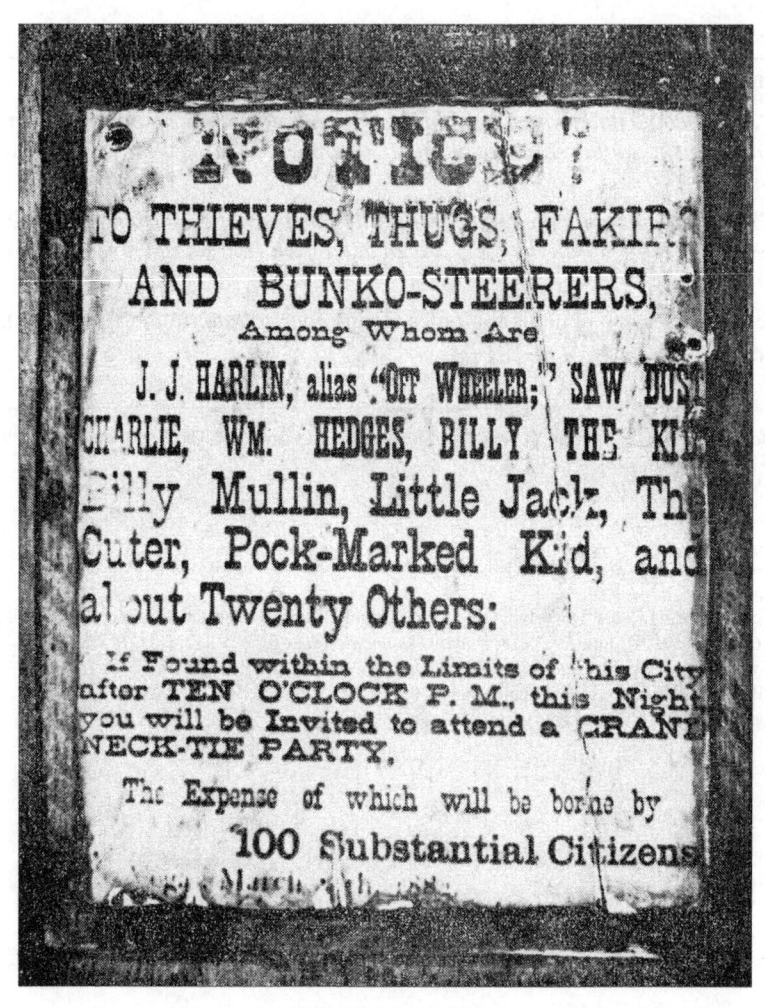

TO THIEVES, THUGS, FAKIRS AND BUNKO-STEERERS,

Among Whom Are

J. J. HARLIN, alias "OTT WHEELER;" SAW DUST CHARLIE, WM. HEDGES, BILLY THE KID, Billy Mullin, Little Jack, The Cuter, Pock-Marked Kid, and about Twenty Others:

If Found within the Limits of this City after TEN O'CLOCK P. M., this Night you will be Invited to attend a GRAND NECK-TIE PARTY.

The Expense of which will be borne by

100 Substantial Citizens

Notice found nailed to board in the saddle room of the Tom Linnekohl Ranch near Dalhart, Texas. Courtesy of Mr. O. Jordan.

Foreword

We will make no attempt to explain the adverse conditions under which this book was written. They would stump even Ripley. The manuscript has been in New York, New Jersey, California, Kansas, and a number of other states, It was lost twice, scattered by the wind in New Jersey, gone over by nephews and nieces whose propensities to emulate Leonardo da Vinci were more than compensated for by the choice of colors. The tabulating machine to number the interruptions by phone, both door bells, daily visitors, other duties – has yet to be invented. Yet the job is done. It can't be compared to anyone else's simply because no one else has attempted a book length study of Dave Rudabaugh any more than they have of Jim Courtright, Clay Allison, Dave Mather and a few other infamous characters known to readers of Western Americana.

In other books I used to apologize for my mistakes. Come to think of it, why should I! I tried; that's more than my critics did. I investigated to the best of my ability, often going both sleepless and hungry in order to attain the facts. No patron has come along the way. I had to rough it alone. I expect to be crucified as a result of this work by readers who consider themselves authorities on the West, but I will continue my research until they come up with something better, which perhaps wouldn't take much. If there is no comment for the work; let there be a wee bit for effort. There have been many friends along the way to offer encouragement and open archives. Mr. Bliss, once associated with the famous Huntington, and the Huntington Staff in San Marino; the staff at the Bancroft Library; the American School of Research Library at Santa Fe; Mrs. Alberta Pantele of The Kansas Historical Society; Mr. Blackburn and the Staff in the Census Office at Topeka; the New York Public Library; Mr. Willis Tilton of Topeka; Mr. Fred Rosenstock; Mr. J. J. Lipsey; Mr. Paul Galleher; Evelyn Shuler; Mrs. Troy Smith, all the University Librarians from Massachusetts to California and numerous city librarians especially at Denver, Socorro, Raton, Albuquerque, Woodward, Canadian, Amarillo – recognized my need for help and encouraged me to keep going to the bitter end. The librarian that brought me the hamburgers; the one that brought me the coke; the other that brought the sandwich those times when I refused to take time out to nourish the body for time was of the essence, thanks. All the others who in any way helped, my sincere gratitude.

I have not set out to prove anything. I merely give you Dave Rudabaugh because no one else has. It took stamina perhaps more than I really had, but in the final count, a book emerged, or rather evolutionized, from the set-backs, pains, tears, hardships such as never before encountered. This has been a challenge not to my stamina, but to my nerves, considering the front and back door bells, visits to hospitals, phone, people coming in for personal attention, sentences left in mid-air and lost forever because of a hundred interruptions a day.

The book may not be literary, but it is at least factual. In the long run, truth survives. I expect no thanks. I do not even expect to be listed in booklets dealing with Southwestern Americana any more than I ever hope to live to see one note of encouragement from any university, book critic, newspaper review, but I will not lose faith in what I am trying to do for Southwestern Americana, the collector, research student because of the lack of recognition. I am confident this book will stand the test of time. Perhaps I am fighting a losing battle, but I am fighting nevertheless. This, those who are prepared to tear apart, scoff, detract, will be forced to admit. If enough mud is flung they might eventually build me a niche. I am not looking for a place in the sun but for a place on the bookshelves of those who respect the truth and cherish it. Unembellished, it may not be a best seller, or even a seller at all, but we hope it may prove a definite contribution to Western Americana, if only a crumb. To all the librarians, court clerks, county clerks, collectors, writers, who made this book possible, my sincere thanks and appreciation. I have used both McCarthy and Bonney for Billy the Kid to satisfy both factions.

    F. STANLEY
    October 31, 1960
    Dumas, Texas

Chapter 1 | Kansas

"My name is Dave Rudabaugh and I was born in July, 1854." Thus spoke the star witness for the State of Kansas when testifying against his former friends. All eyes focused on this smirking figure, now out of character, for Dave Rudabaugh was loyal to the core. Of average height, not over five eight, prone to be lean rather than corpulent, his punctiliousness for those he favored or who befriended him was a creed, a point of honor known to all and definitely not what they expected of him at this given moment.

The year 1854 will go down in history as one of vehemence, bluster, barn burning and violence. Turmoil seemed to be the rule rather than the exception. This was true even of Illinois, where Rudabaugh was born. A product of turbulence, agitation and restlessness, the family meanderings prepared him for violence, disorder, antimony that ignited and exploded the day he recognized it as a heritage bequeathed to a widow too weighed down with her brood to allow her time to go berserk. There was very little time for schooling in the world of Dave Rudabaugh, whose tender years seem to have been taken up with peregrinations not of his own choosing but proved his undoing. He called a number of states home during his childhood; none really making any difference, for the talk was the same everywhere about slavery, free-soil, and the activities of the border ruffians.

His birthday was Bastille Day or Bonaventuremas, depending on the psychoanalysis of environment that molded him or failed to mould him. Saint or sinner; violence or peace. Francis of Assisi looked upon a little babe presented to him for his blessing and he said: "Good will come of him." The child was called Bonaventure. This was on July 14, the day known to many as Bastille Day and to those up on their outlaw history as the day Pat Garrett gunned down a horse-thief and cattle-rustler in the home of Pete Maxwell at Fort Sumner, New Mexico. The child in Illinois gave scant notice to birthdays, always but another day in the lives of the poverty-stricken. His may not have been a charmed life but it proved fascinating viewed in the light of his times. All in all he had little cause for regret and it is doubtful if he would have lived it any other way had he been born in more comfortable circumstances.

The family was so constantly on the move David had little chance to meet gentle folk. His lot was to be with the shiftless, passionate, unconventional, hard-drinking ruffians who used the slavery question as an excuse, not a cause. In Kansas, night riders were on the prowl, hunting, raiding, killing as they rode, never really understanding why they did these things and they challenged the right of any man to question the right or wrong of their night-riding. Pro-slavery factions became increasingly embittered at the boldness of the abolitionist faction moving with its propaganda into circles definitely separated from puritanical transcendental hogwash that served New England well but was entirely out of place where squatters and snakes cursed the relentless sun. The night riders amazed even the Indians, ruffians were nervy enough to call savages.

"No sooner had President Pierce signed the Kansas-Nebraska bill than companies of Missourians pushed into Kansas and seized upon extensive tracts of the best lands, not waiting, in some cases, for the Indians to get out of the way. A convenient simplicity marked their proceedings. The laws of preemption, literally interpreted, required the erection of cabins and periods of actual residence; but the exigencies are unfriendly to restrictive and dilatory technicalities. At all events, they must not be allowed to imperil great public interests. The squatter should simply notch a few trees in evidence of occupancy, or arrange half a dozen rails upon the ground and call it a cabin, or post a scrawl claiming proprietorship and threatening to shoot intermeddlers at sight seems to have been all that was considered absolutely essential."

"These energetic first-comers were mostly amateur immigrants men who bestirred themselves in the interest of slavery rather than at the solicitation of personal concerns, who proposed to reside in Missouri, but to vote and fight in Kansas should necessity arise for such duality...." (Spring, *Kansas*, p. 26)

Little is known of Dave Rudabaugh's father. Had Rudabaugh not been with Billy the Kid few, if any, would be concerned with the man, much less the name. Various spellings are offered; clerks at the trial in Kinsley wrote Rudabaugh; the *Las Vegas Optic* called him Radabaugh; he signed his name as Raudenbaugh, Radenbaugh, Radabaugh, Rudenbaugh [in his confession to the Kinsley train robbery, he signed his name Rodenbaugh – see Appendix A]; the census-taker referred to the family as Radenbaugh; the War Department used the spelling Redenbaugh [it was Rodenbaugh]. Most writers have kept the name Rudabaugh. Dave's father seems to have been James Rudabaugh, a private of Co. D, 103rd. Ill. Inf. from Fulton county [This is wrong – the entry for Rudabaugh's father is James W. Rodenbaugh, Company D, 103rd. Ill. Inf.]. He was killed early in the War Between the States [there is no record of his death either during or after the Civil War]. One other Rudabaugh (to use the familiar spelling) from Stephenson county was also killed during the war. Little is known of him. Of the other three named Rudabaugh who served in the war, one died in 1909; one in 1911; one in 1919. None of these three could have been Dave's father since the [1875] census lists Dave's mother as a widow when Dave was in his early teens [he was 21]. [Rudabaugh's his mother is not identified as a widow, only as female. There is no father listed with the family.]

Dave's mother's name was Anne. She was born in Ohio in 1829 and married in her native state. Following the marriage the family moved to Illinois, where Dave, the first child, was born. Zeth, two years younger than Dave, was also born in Illinois [the census says Ohio]; five years later came the first girl listed as "I" (possibly Ida). She was born in Ohio; John, born the first year of the war, was also born in Ohio. It seems evident that when the father enlisted, Mrs. Rudabaugh went to live with her kinfolk. After the war she moved to Iowa. The Rudabaughs did not come to Kansas until after 1870. Mrs. Rudabaugh never remarried.

This background will have to serve. It is all we have to go on. Schooling, early years would be pure guesswork. When the Rudabaughs moved to Kansas they squatted on Spring Creek Township land. The post office was at Eureka in Greenwood county. The first settlement in Greenwood county was made in the spring of 1856, not by settlers from Missouri as one would suppose but by colonists from Mississippi who had hoped to win Kansas over to the pro-slave cause and to counter moves made by the New Englanders. The first settlers founded the Land Township and Madison. These were D. Vining, Austin Norton, Fred Norton, Anderson Hill, Wesley Peersons, Mark Patty, Myrock Huntley, E. R. Holderman, William Martindale and others. In July of that year they were joined by Josiah Kinnaman, Archibald Johnson, Peter Ricker, Adam Glaze, John Baker, Wayne Summer and William S. Kinnaman. Spring Creek Township census lists the name but once; then silence. By the time Dave moved to Dodge [City] in search of employment, the family no doubt back-tracked to Ohio. Whatever schooling Dave had in Kansas was at Eureka. [Rudabaugh's written confession to the Kinsley train robbery shows that he was extraordinarily well-educated for his upbringing. The confession is a masterpiece of exposition.]

Eureka is located in the center of Greenwood county on land once owned by David Tucker and Levi N. Prather, and, to the eternal credit of the Eureka Townsite Company, the first building laid out was a school house made of planks and logs. In this building were held for several years "all meetings, religious, scholastic and political, and here the Eureka Debating Society rubbed their wits on the great questions of the day, while the walls yet ringing with the voice of the singing master. At this time (1857) no enterprising merchant had established a corner grocery, and stores of all sorts had to be brought by ox team from Kansas City, a distance of 140 miles. The nearest post office was near Burlington, in Osage county, and mail for Eastern friends had to be sent by the chance hand of overland travelers. The first post office in the county was at Pleasant Grove, and was supplied once a week from LeRoy, Coffy county. Late in 1858 the postal authorities allowed the residents of Eureka an office of their own on condition that they did their own route carrying. This continued for several months until supplanted by the official pony rider. The post office at Eureka, the first in the county, was opened by Edwin Tucker in 1858."

"The first store opened in Eureka was a result of a determination on the part of the settlers to combat the reflux tide which was draining the country of settlers, for a natural part of the reaction after the giant struggle of the war was inimical to new settlements. At this time, James Kenner, who was living on a farm about four miles north of Eureka, was deputed to carry on business for one year, with the understanding that if it interfered too much with farming, the store should, at the end of one year, be turned over to Edwin Trucker. A stock of goods was procured and brought to town, but it was not until about the 1st of April, 1866, that a cabin could be secured large enough to accommodate them."

"At the expiration of one year, Judge Kenner turned the stock over to Tucker who ran a store for about six months and then sold out to two newcomers, Hitchcock & Farris. After a year these two sold out to Rizer & Co.... The first doctor was named Reynolds. He drowned in 1866. The first lawyer did not arrive until 1868 (named Lillie). That was the year the blacksmith McCartney arrived but the carpenter did not come to Eureka until 1867. His name was Hawkins. The first hotel was not built until 1868. The first school was taught by Edwin Tucker and when this burned down in 1861, children attended school at old Fort Montgomery. The *Eureka Herald* was not founded until 1866. S. G. Mead was the proprietor and editor. Other papers were the *Censorial*; *The Greenwood County Democrat*; *The Sun*; *The Republican*. The first church was the Christian Church established in 1862...." (See Andreas, Greenwood County, Vol. 1, *History of Kansas*, pp. 1891, 1214)

Spring Creek Township was not founded until shortly before the Rudabaughs came to live in Greenwood county. The family lived at Eureka a short time before settling at Spring Creek.

"Greenwood county suffered considerably during the war period. It was the scene of violence from all quarters. It suffered especially because its people were divided on the slavery question and brought personal and property damage against each other. It was exposed to the attacks of hostile Indians and both the Southern and Union guerrillas. Its villages were sacked and burned on a number of occasions. In 1861 a rough fort was built at Eureka and named in honor of Colonel James Montgomery of the Tenth Infantry. It was erected by the home guard Bemis and was occupied by them during the entire term of the war...." (Frank Blackmar, *Cyclopedia of Kansas History* Vol. 1, pp. 792-795)

The *Wichita Morning Eagle* for October 9, 1955, gives this account of Fort Montgomery:

"It was built as a community project in 1861 under a 'home guard' set up because the community feared raids from bands of unfriendly Indians as well as ruffians crossing the border from Missouri who were pro-slavery sympathizers. Later, however, the fort was used at intervals until about 1868 by the 15th and 19th Kansas Volunteer Cavalry regiments and the 9th Kansas Volunteer Militia for various purposes, including scouting expeditions. The fort apparently was built wholly of volunteer labor. Several historians describe it as being of logs chinked with Greenwood county gumbo. The shingles were of the 'shake' variety. (Shake shingles were narrow and thick and were hewn from logs by a device called a 'river.' Later a shingle-making machine was developed.) The floor was of puncheon, logs split and smoothed and then laid split side up as closely as possible to make a smooth floor. The only 'boughten' materials used were a few window sashes, hardware for a door and a few nails. Many wooden pegs were used in its construction."

"The 'shake' shingles, even if they were made of walnut, were never very satisfactory. All native lumber must be used before it dries if it is going to be nailed at all. These 'shakes' would warp and dry out in the hot summer sun until they would turn neither water nor snow. The floor, too, was not so good. Many small animals and even rattlesnakes made their homes under the floor. The fort was surrounded by breastworks of logs piled high and mounded over with dirt. A stockade was built of poles driven vertically into the ground as close together as possible."

"Commanders of the First Company were Captain Leander Bemis, who lived about six miles north of Eureka, and Lieutenant H. G. Branson, who lived on Fall River. Edwin Walter, an early-day teacher in Eureka, reported that the company had a swivel (small cannon) that chambered a ball weighing three or four pounds. No one seems to know what became of the swivel. Royal Wolcott, in his *History of The Shell Rock Township*, reports that the guns were issued by the government to the settlers even before the threat of Civil War. He mentions that the home of Randall Brown in Shell Rock Township was used as an arsenal for dispensing these guns. The history says too, that these guns were never returned to the government and that he used the barrel of his for making a stem for a post auger."

"Eureka had a Quantrill scare in 1863. Lawrence had been raided in August and the settlers, as well as the military, were fearful that he would make his way to Eureka. He was known to be working southeast. State militia headquarters at LeRoy were issuing alerts to intercept him, Two companies were hastily recruited in Greenwood county but they served only a few weeks. The men in these companies apparently drilled with guns issued from Randall Brown's house. One company was ordered into active service by Major J. B. Scott at LeRoy on October 7, 1863. It was active only five days and was mustered out November 13, 1863. The company recruited at Eureka was ordered into active service by the same officer on October 12, 1863, and it, too, was active only five days. (It was mustered out on the same day as the one above.)"

"On July 4, 1868, S. G. Mead started a publication known as the *Eureka Herald* in old Fort Montgomery. (Eureka had thirteen houses and forty residents at the time.) Nearly every issue of the paper had some complaint about the building. On one occasion, rattlesnakes under the floor scared the wits out of the copy girl; another time snow fell through the roof until everything was covered with several inches of snow. No paper was issued that week. In the winter of 1868, Mead found that the logs in the breastwork around the fort made very good and easy to get fuel so he dug them out. At one time he reported that if the bullets ever whistled through Fort Montgomery as the winds did last week, we wonder where a soldier would have found a safe place. The February 19,

1868, issue stated that the editor (Mead) found a building (for his paper) and the building would be torn down."

The fertile valley along Fall River as well as a fresh flowing spring induced a Mr. Tucker and four others to locate on the spot and inaugurate the Eureka Townsite Company. Tucker not only became the president of the company but a self-elected one man chamber of commerce to bring in new settlers and new business. He entered politics to become Greenwood county's first representative, senator, banker, real estate agent, founder of the first public school and well known figure in political circles.

Eureka, the town where the Rudabaughs did their shopping when they first came to Kansas, had an unusual beginning. All the families united in building the log schoolhouse. The interior was partitioned off as living quarters during the night; classrooms during the day. All the settlers pitched in to build the town's first home; then the next, until all the families were moved out of the school. Later on the log-cabin school was torn down to make room for a stone structure. Dave Rudabaugh's younger brothers and sisters attended this school. Tucker explained that the reason for a school before any residence was built in Eureka was that if children took to farming they usually neglected their education. A school would encourage farmers to send their offspring for at least the fundamentals and elements of learning.

A post office was established as early as 1858. This proved a rather nominal affair causing the mail to be dropped at Pleasant Grove and picked up for Eureka only if anyone from the latter place happened to be in Pleasant Grove on business. Occasionally the postmaster at Pleasant Grove asked roving cowboys to carry the mail to Eureka, especially after it piled up for several weeks. By 1860, the town boasted eight houses. Most of the time was spent in farming the land about the tiny village. Eighteen Sixty was the year of the Great Famine. Half the farmers about Eureka moved elsewhere.

"The Rebellion springing forth in the following year effectually retarded the growth of the whole State until the fall of 1865, when emigration again began to be turned in this direction. Each successive year since then has marked a more rapid increase in our development and population. It was not until the spring of 1867, however that the second town company was organized, the original one having fallen into oblivion in the 'fatal year' (of the famine). An occasional building was erected at great cost of time and money, individuals being compelled to haul the materials for their construction from Lawrence, a distance of about one hundred and thirty miles."

"In February, 1870, less than a year ago, there were about twenty-five houses on the town site. At that time the great flood of emigration that has run uninterruptedly into Southern Kansas set in, the Indian Trust lands below town being opened up to actual settlers, and Eureka, in striving to keep pace with the advance of the surrounding country, has added some two hundred houses to the twenty-five of ten months ago.... The first regular mail service into Eureka was a weekly mail from Burlington, established something over two years ago It was followed in a short time by a semi-weekly over the line from Emporia. These mails were all carried on horseback, or buck-board, until June last, when a tri-weekly was established between Eureka and Emporia, and the first stage was driven into our town. Six months ago this was the only public mode of conveyance to and from our town, and today Eureka is the most important point for stage connections in the whole state, there being daily lines over four different routes, and tri-weeklies over three others, all connecting at Eureka."

"The Kansas Stage Company recognizing the importance of this point, have made it their headquarters, and placed here one of the company, General W. D. Terry (one of the very best stage, or any other kind of men we have ever had the pleasure to make the acquaintance of) to give their affairs his personal supervision and attention. Other routes about being projected by the company, among which is one destined to become the most important stage line in the state. This is a route running south (through Howard, Dexter and Arkansas City), and eventually through the Indian Territory and into Texas. With a most sturdy, industrious and intelligent class of citizens in and about her, a rapid settlement of the country in all directions, an advantageous location, geographically, and the near prospect of having the junction of two of the most important railway lines in the west, Eureka is destined to become, at no distant day, one of the most flourishing and influential towns in Kansas...." (*Eureka Real Estate Pilot*, February 1871)

Dave Rudabaugh was not a year old when John Brown, wild-eyed, Puritanical, defiant, slave-hating, stormed into Kansas and settled at Osawatomie. He was not a self-seeking man any more than Dave Rudabaugh. Both were propelled by rashness, equivocation, imprudence; machines browbeaten by compulsion and drawn by blood as a moth to a flame. Fascination ruled their lives inducing them to pursue a single evil or a single good because it epitomized all the sinning or all the good of humanity. The life of any one individual man weighed against the interests of the inexorable cause, was as light and trivial as dust on the hummingbird's wing. Peaceful methods were not the answer in a land divided such as John Brown found it any more than the Border Ruffians taught Dave Rudabaugh. Up and down the length and breadth of Kansas, the one thing all seemed to have in common was violence or violent talk. Rascals from Missouri preyed on the settlers; marauding Indians gave them no rest; insects attacked the crops with all the zeal of the Israelites moving in on Mammon; Southern sympathizers now avoided the house of one they formerly called a friend and marked the dwelling for future destruction. Garrett Smith stood up and addressed the Kansas Convention in words that might have been spoken by Brown or Rudabaugh: "You are looking to ballots when you should be looking to bayonets; counting up voters when you should be mustering armed, and none but armed emigrants...."

The sack of Lawrence is taught in every history class not only in Kansas but the whole nation. John Brown made his march from Osawatomie ostensibly to aid the mourning townspeople but in reality to put the fear of the Lord into the heathen Palmyrans who insisted on making a slave Territory of Kansas. The affair at Dutch's Crossing; the Pottawatomie Massacre were incidents Dave Rudabaugh heard over and over again on his frequent visits to Eureka. Border Ruffians looted, pillaged, burned, killed as they rode to Palmyra, Black Jack, Prairie City. Slavery had long since ceased being a cause. The quest for booty was now a habit. Brown's attack on Black Jack gained him twenty-three prisoners and a store of commissary supplies which he packed off to his camp on Middle Creek.

Five miles from his camp, in the center of the hamlet known as St. Bernard, lived a successful merchant who let it be known that he stood on the side of slavery for Kansas. His store was lined with shelves full of dry goods, drugs, clothing, firearms, shoes, hardware, sweets, and tobaccos. This man must be punished. Brown armed his men with Sharpe's rifles, bowie knives, rifles, pistols as he drilled them for the raid on St. Bernard. It took but a moment to overpower the merchant and to sack the store. The little army returned on the following day for what they left behind. When they forced themselves into a room occupied by a young woman, she called them the most vicious men she had ever beheld and felt she would be more at ease in the company of barbarians. She insisted that they were Border Ruffians because they were as desperate and vicious in actions as well as looks, worse than an untutored Indian in utterance, actions and sentiment. She defied them to justify the attack on St. Bernard.

Turmoil everywhere – Whitfield, Westport, Lexington, Independence – the Ruffians along the Missouri border engaged in a campaign of extermination for all settlers in sympathy with the abolitionist movement. Everywhere one encountered men, guns, horses and whisky. The Bloomington Rifles, Lawrence Stubbs, Blue Mound Infantry, Wakarusa Boys, Prairie City Company, and so many others, ready and willing to kill anyone and everyone interested in freeing slaves, Two hundred and fifty men placed themselves under the command of General Coffee and Colonel Whitfield.

Governor Shannon, partial neither to Brown's army nor Coffee's army proclaimed them both illegal. He sent Colonel Summer, with fifty federal dragoons, to disperse the mobs and to free Pate from the terrifying grip of old John Brown. Pate grateful for Summer's timely arrival, mounted a stump and began a speech declaring that anyone who came from Brown's came with both skin and scalp, deserved to be acclaimed. Summer, purple with rage, yelled at him: "Not a word out of you, sir. Not a word. You have no business here. The governor told me so." Summer was able to talk Coffee and Whitfield into returning to their respective towns without incident, but he was wary of the few freebooters who remained. Summer found free-hooters particularly distasteful because they favored both parties and used the political situation to cover their raids.

Meantime, New England raised thousands of dollars for the express purpose of placing a bible and a rifle into the hands of the terrorized settlers. Colonies from Maine, Massachusetts, and Connecticut migrated to Kansas with the blessing of Henry Ward Beecher. This tremendous influx of Yankees into Kansas alarmed the pro-slavery faction. These latter could not but help feel that these settlers were being pushed into Kansas by abolitionists interested in political control for the North. It was resolved to patrol the great national waterway of the Missouri against all traffic directed to further the cause of antislavery groups. Masked men and men with blackened faces boarded steamers seized consignments of free-state merchandise and turned back anyone unable to explain satisfactorily the reason for homesteading in Kansas. One such raid uncovered four thousand dollars worth of Sharpe's rifles. A group of immigrants from Chicago encountered no difficulty until they landed at Lexington where their Sharpes were taken from them. They were processed again at Leavenworth and relieved of two bushels of revolvers, pistols and bowie knives. All such firearms fell into the hands of the Border Ruffians. Not only were the Chicago settlers refused admittance in Kansas; they were told to make their way back the best way they could, without provisions, sidearms or proper clothing. The fact that a heavy rain began just as they started back failed to melt the hearts of the Border Ruffians. The *Squatter Sovereign* newspaper suggested that the citizens of Leavenworth band together and hang a couple of boatloads of abolitionists as the only solution for the peace all Kansas desired. Try as they might the Border Ruffians could no more prevent settlers from entering Kansas than they could order the Missouri to stop flowing. Nor was the Missouri open to all accessible routes. The Chicago emigrants decided that they had struck their tents in Illinois. Patiently they waited as settlers from Ohio, Illinois, Indiana, Wisconsin, and New England invaded Kansas by sheer force of numbers. They latched on to one of these groups and four hundred camped near Nebraska City. This alarmed Governor Shannon who called out the militia "to take the field with the whole disposable force in the Territory."

General Smith meantime succeeded Summer as commander of the military. The so-called Northern Army was found to be in a deplorable state akin to the half starved little army that marched on our nation's capital shortly after World War I. Smith agreed that food would prove more serviceable than bullets. These were the settlers who founded the towns of Plymouth and Holton. Those refusing to identify themselves with either community went on to Topeka. After this came James Redpath and one hundred and thirty men. Colonel J. E. Johnston was sent to investigate this army but found it to be composed of honest-to-goodness immigrants.

Colonel P. St. George Cooke thought that in arresting John Brown, peace would come to Kansas. Brown was an outlaw and should be treated as such. The crafty agitator succeeded in eluding him and laid plans for the march on Harper's Ferry. Rumor of war between the States persisted and vigilance tightened. U. S. Marshal Preston searched the wagons of another immigrant train and confiscated Hall's muskets, Sharpe's rifles, revolvers, sabres, bayonets, ammunition, powder and saddles said to have been stolen from the Iowa State Arsenal by one Robert Morrow for use in Kansas. Lawlessness and marauding was rather the rule than the exception. The sad state of affairs proved too much for Governor Shannon and he resigned with the parting retort: "It is easier to govern the devils in hell than the people of Kansas." Secretary Woodson, who succeeded him, declared the Territory to being a "state of open insurrection and rebellion." And well he might when a Border Ruffian could openly bet six dollars that he would have the scalp of an abolitionist within two hours.

"General John W. Reid, with two hundred and fifty men, took in hand the business of destroying Osawatomie, the headquarters of Old John Brown. He approached the town about dawn, under pilotage of Rev. Martin White, whose experiences two weeks before (John Brown had threatened his life) had not served to promote the passive virtues. On the outskirts of the village, the expedition met Frederick Brown, whom the divine shot. The entire force available for the defense of Osawatomie was only forty-one men, seventeen belonging to John Brown's band, and the remaining twenty-four divided between the companies of Dr. W. W. Updegraff and Captain Cline. These two score men, equal to nothing more than a resolute show of fight, took post near the town and the line of Reid's approach, among the trees and underbrush that skirted the Marais des Cygnes. When the enemy came within range, they opened fire and caused some temporary confusion. The Missourians unlimbered a field-piece and belched grape-shot at the thicket, which crashed harmlessly above the heads of the concealed riflemen. Tiring of the inconsequent bombardment, they charged and brought the skirmish to an abrupt conclusion. Only one practical course then remained for the handful of men in the thicket, and that was to get out of the way with all possible dispatch. This they did without standing upon the order of their going, and scattered here and there after an every-man-for-himself fashion. Six free state men were killed, including assassinations before and after the fight, and three wounded. Reid's loss was probably not more than five killed – in his own account of the affair the number is put at two and a few wounded. Only four cabins escaped the torch, so completely did the raiders accomplish their mission...." (Spring, o. c.)

Kansas was indeed a dark and bloody ground. Whether Dave's father had settled here for a time before moving back to Illinois is disputed, but he certainly kept posted as did the rest of the nation regarding events and people during these trying years. There was no middle ground in Kansas. The bee hive was ever active and causes became an obsession. Violence was a part of living. Barn-burning, arrests, blood-letting, confiscations were as prevalent in broad daylight as the darkest night. Governor Woodson stormed at Colonel Cooke, giving him no rest until he went to "invest the town of Topeka, and disarm all insurrectionists or aggressive invaders against the organized government of the Territory, to be found at or near that point, retaining them as prisoners, subject to the order of the marshal of the Territory. All their breastworks, forts, or fortifications should be leveled to the ground."

These were the days of sounds and fury. Six-shooters, rifles, cannon, marching feet, fast moving horses, up and down the length and breadth of the land – none of this was lost on the growing boy moving back and forth from Ohio to Illinois, to Iowa, to Ohio, and finally Kansas. He probably knew how to use a six-shooter before he learned to use a pencil. It certainly was part of the education of the frontier youth of his day. A far cry from the primo-genitor of the family whose occupation seems to have been that of ship or helm-builder [Rudabaugh's father's service record shows him to have been a musician], which is what Rudabaugh means in German. There would be no need for helms in Kansas or New Mexico but Dave Rudabaugh found plenty need for bullets. There were no toy guns for the growing boy. He worked the family acreage, plowing, toiling from dawn to sunset whenever he was not in school and the mother found plenty of chores before and after school for the oldest of the fast growing family.

He must have rebelled from the very beginning for he detested farming and the lot of the farmer. He learned to ride early in life and was an expert horseman. A frontier lad of seven who couldn't handle gun or horse showed little promise for the future. At that tender age he could very well find himself playing the role off family breadwinner since Indians still roved about, testing their skill as takers of scalps. At twelve he was a man or nearly a man. At fourteen he was a hired hand. At sixteen he was expected to take care of himself. In fact, at sixteen Rudabaugh seems to have been very much on his own. His mother had little or no influence over him. In his entire career as a train robber, highwayman, outlaw he never once made reference to his family [The *Weekly Commonwealth* of June 22, 1878, reported that Rudabaugh's two brothers were living in Dodge City, Kansas, at the time of Rudabaugh's trial for the Kinsley train robbery].

Life was made even more exciting with the ever expanding commerce of the prairie known to all as the Santa Fe Trade. Santa Fe become the Mecca to be visited at least once during a lifetime. Looting, plunder, bloodshed, stealing, marshals, barn-burning, arrests, fires, bullets, booty, rustling, forts and forays, Indians, all had their place and were part of the heritage of the frontier but a dream was always safeguarded for the first ride into Santa Fe where senoritas, fandangos, faro tables, cantinas evoked joys superior to any experienced in the States. This was the way of life of the Border Ruffian. Rudabaugh lived with blood, sweat and tears from the time he could talk. There were times he tried seriously to make himself a useful citizen as an express messenger, bartender, cowhand, manager of a ranch, but he had to be where life was exciting and he was part of the excitement. He belonged to that breed of men who cut one path for themselves as if it were their destiny and they could steer no other course – Courtright, Black Jack Ketchum, Butch Cassidy and so many others who made their choice the day targets ceased being an answer to boredom. Perhaps their dexterity with a six-shooter made them feel above the law or became a law in their hands. Pity is the word for such men; we are too prone to call it glory. They were products of their times; only in this light can they be understood. They must be judged by their generation rather than glorified by ours. Retrospect rather than dimension comes closer to the truth when examining the whys and wherefores of their deeds or misdeeds.

The embargo on Missouri river traffic failed to halt the influx of settlers in to Kansas. The Border Ruffians could hardly be everywhere at once nor were they potent enough to ebb the flow of empire. Some of the Border men were sincere in their convictions as slave holders and their fight for Kansas as a slave Territory; others were indifferent, selling their guns to whichever side offered the most profits. These latter were eventually classified as the real Border Ruffians. They burned homes, barns, stole horses, fired on men, women and children indiscriminately, eyes glued only to the final outcome in terms of profit. They often selected a leader who promised to permit plunder and that unchecked. They were loyal to him as long as it proved profitable. Also, they were quite certain to claim the land of the farmer they manager to scare off. They employed guerrilla tactics most of the time, operating in bands of fifteen to twenty, and sometimes with as few as three or four. To bullets and fire they added the elements of surprise and intimidation – brain-washing, we call it today – and knew a week in advance the name of the next victim.

Rudabaugh studied Border Ruffian tactics in order to stage the Kinsley train robbery [the planner and leader of the Kinsley train robbery was fellow robber Mike Roarke – see Appendix A]. He reasoned that if worked all over Kansas prior to the war it ought to work for robberies, rustling and gunplay after the peace. Turmoil, hate, suffering bloodshed, barn-burning, cattle rustling, horse stealing, gun fighting, Indian scares, free-and-slave bitterness, plunder, rapine, killing, none of this stopped because Lee surrendered to Grant. The progress of the railroad and the sudden rise of cattle drives help perpetuate the Border Ruffian although the name changed to gunslinger, rustler, outlaw. The excitement of the cattle drive and the mushrooming of end of track towns held such attractions for such as Dave Rudabaugh who longed for the return of Border Ruffian days of pre-war Kansas.

"The conditions of Kansas settlement were neither Eastern nor Southern, but distinctively Western; conditions that made no appeal to cotton-belt planters or New England townsfolk, but which hardy farmers of the wide median region live in a straw tent, to shake with chills and fever, to burn buffalo chips, to forage for rabbits and berries, to endure, build, and prosper such pioneering had the essential breath of freedom. A Boston woman, lucky in possessing a cabin of 'shakes' near Lawrence, its inner walls pasted over with newspapers, was appalled by the fierce western winds, which shook the frail edifice till it seemed about to fall; by the prevalent typhoid, malaria, and digestive ills; by the rough fare of bread, milk and small game. The want of good wells, the crowding of invalids in rooms half-freezing, half-roasting, the abundance of vermin, were dismaying. At night she listened to noises which slowly lost their power to terrify. 'Far across the river, in my wakefulness, I hear the whoop of the Indian, or the echo of the rifle; or quite as often, the sound of hungry and quarreling wolves.' Already immigrants were finding that cattle, corn, wheat, potatoes, pumpkins, and beans, on small holdings well tilled, were their best reliance. It was not the land for the slaveholder or his antagonist the anti-slavery agitator." (Nevins, *Ordeal of The Union*, Vol. 2, pp. 383)

April 26, 1869, a day long remembered in Kansas. Crowds gathered to take a first look at the Wakarusa Picnic Special, Santa Fe's first venture in the Sunflower State, as it puffed along to end of track. Railroading and trail driving were now ready for courtship, the bands publicized all over the Southwest. On April 13, 1871, two men from Newton, Massachusetts, staked out a claim and built a shack laughingly dignified with the sobriquet Newton, a contrast to the said New England town known for its beautiful homes and conventional manners. They hoped for the end of the rainbow they failed to find back East. Friendly with Tom Peters and his railroad gang they knew exactly the route of the Santa Fe. In six weeks Newton was a town of two thousand people. By the time the grading gangs arrived the town broadened out to include six thousand. Twenty gambling tents were making things lively on Main Street. One tent boasted accommodations for six hundred patrons. Financial reverses and other unforeseen difficulties precluded the possibility of the railroad moving out of Newton for some time to come.

"There was hardly a wilder place at which to stop. Cowboys, dry and cash-heavy after weeks on the trail, milled through saloons and bawdry houses; Mexican gamblers, overland from Santa Fe, resplendent in their silk shirts, slashed velvet breeches and crimson sashes... helped blend various colors in a colorful town.... Cattle began to come up the trails from Texas to be loaded onto ears. Newton boiled with business and sin. Ministers held services in saloons, being rewarded with a drink and the privilege of taking up a collection from the faro and monte players. One such saloon preacher was the Rev. M. M. Haun, a tall Methodist. He preached regularly in the Golden Rule at 515 Main Street, using a beer barrel for a lectern. His sermon concerned the wages of sin, which, he intimated, would shortly be paid in full to most of his congregation. At the conclusion of the homily, two cowhands went through the crowd, hat in one hand, gun in the other, accepting offerings. Mr. Haun expressed his appreciation, politely refused a slug of raw whisky, and left...."

"Free whisky by the barrel was set out at election time. At the first polling, eight men were shot dead and seventeen wounded.... Meantime, small farmers, called nesters by the cattlemen, were pushing slowly west, putting up fences, breaking the sod, forcing the cattle drives farther from midwestern markets. Then followed the railroad, which carried them, their tools, stocks and furniture out from Kansas City, Independence and St. Louis. These migrants did their share of Indian fighting and grimly rebuilt fences the buffalo tramped down, but many a settler saw his first crop pounded out of sight by the thundering herds.... (Marshall, Santa Fe, *The Railroad that Built An Empire*, pp. 53-54)

Rudabaugh, senior, was in Kansas but a short time before moving to Illinois where he again made a move with very little success. Border Ruffian tactics were not for him, much less his growing family. Whether he was killed in the war, or died at home as a result of wounds, his brood was no better off than the Israelites in quest of the Promised Land. The advance of the railroad encouraged the Border Ruffian to carry on, changing his cause but not his course. Cattle drives were a source of encouragement to both the railroad and the Ruffian. End of track Kansas proved the end of the track gang. Cowboy, gambler, demirep, Ruffian, gunslinger, outlaw and nester lifted its face to the sun, a delegate with a full vote at the convention of contributing factors to American border life. The sounds of cowboys hurrahing Hays City, Newton, Caldwell, Dodge carried to the ploughboy at Spring Creek Township near Eureka and beckoned him to the source. He hired him-self out in order to earn the price of a horse, gun and saddle. He turned his back on farm and family forever [following his release from custody after the Kinsely train robbery, Rudabaugh returned to his family home in Spring Creek for awhile – he likely did so other times].

Just when the urge for the excitement of the cattle drives spirited Rudabaugh away from the Eureka area is not recorded but about this time he became the friend of Doc Holliday. Oddly enough he did not associate with Dutch Henry, Bat Masterson and Wyatt Earp until Holliday introduced them after the Kinsley robbery. When Earp and Masterson sought out Rudabaugh they were not certain who to look for until Holliday briefed them at Fort Griffin, on the fringe of the South Plains of Texas. Rudabaugh's life as a cowboy was short lived. Either he felt out of place or insecure, or was attracted by the even wilder life of adventure of the buffalo hunter. The fact that Doc Holliday was quite friendly with Rudabaugh long before Webb, Masterson and Earp came into the picture leaves room for speculation that the pair may have met some few years before the Fort Griffin days.

Holliday did not do any gambling at Fort Griffin until after the New Year of 1875, a rather important year in the life of Dave Rudabaugh as will be seen later. Holliday was two years older than Rudabaugh and often invited him to learn the technics of his profession but the younger man was already too involved in rustling and robbing to accept Holliday as his teacher, Nor was Rudabaugh inclined to favor the clean clothes, groomed look, polished manners, patience and other amenities necessary for success. He learned to love gambling but refused to accept it as a steady diet.

The depression of 1873, as well as poor health, induced Holliday to try Fort Worth as a place of business, for he seems to have been a competent dentist, and as a spot where he could improve on his fame as a gambling man and a steady drinker. Since Holliday did not wear sidearms until he came to Fort Worth, it is quite probable that friend Rudabaugh taught him how to use a six-shooter [there is absolutely no evidence for this assertion, and it is untrue]. The dentist seems to have had little concern for firearms during the two years he lived the dual life of dentist and gambler, for on New Year's Day of 1875 when he decided to shoot it out with Austin, the saloon-keeper, his aim was so bad, despite the many shots fired, that the *Dallas Herald* rather laughed it off as two men mistaking that holiday for the glorious Fourth. Austin's aim was no better. By the time Doc Holliday latched on to Wyatt Earp he had no peer as a pistol shot. Had Dave Rudabaugh a Boswell he might have marked the occasions when the outlaw came to know Bob Robertson, Cal Polk, Bill Moore, Lon Chambers, Clay Allison, Tom Emory, King Fisher, John Culp, Billy Wilson, Mike Roarke, Ed West, Charles Bowdre, Ben Thompson and others known for their dexterity with liquor, cards, and guns. The town holding the most fascination for Rudabaugh was Dodge City.

In July, 1877, when Dave reached his twenty-third birthday, about two hundred thousand head of cattle, attended by two thousand cowboys, grazed almost in view of the frontier town. Despite the presence of these latter the town had comparatively few killings, Freighters, railroad men, gamblers, dance hall girls, camp followers, drummers, con men, harridans, politicos, skinners, packers, frontier lawyers, country doctors, buffalo hunters, range men, nesters, hired killers, prospectors and drifters produced a rather odd assortment conducive to anything but gentleness and the art of gracious living. It was not how much they drank, but the gut-rot they were able to down hour after hour without the necessity of medical care or the need of the drink if only for sobering up purposes. Everyone from Mayor Jim Kelley down to the stable boy encouraged party life in the interest of good business. But the wide open town refused to tolerate cattle rustlers and train robbers. Complaints had reached Mayor Kelley office that the Roarke-Rudabaugh gang was making life miserable for trail bosses and stage lines. "You must hunt down Rudabaugh and Roarke," he told Wyatt Earp, "and bring them to justice. The prosperity of Dodge City and the mayor's peace of mind depend on it." Earp, himself a controversial subject; insisted that it was while on this search for Rudabaugh, ending in failure as it did, a friendship began with Holliday that was to last till death. Although Earp outlived Holliday by many years, he never forgot that first meeting. How much Mayor Kelley and the Santa Fe Railroad really paid Earp to find Rudabaugh is a secret he took to the grave with him. His statements to Stuart Lake are to be taken with a grain of salt. Perhaps he realized only traveling expenses since Masterson and [John Joshua] Webb, not Earp, eventually brought Rudabaugh to trial.

"Rudabaugh was about the most notorious outlaw in the range country," Earp remarked in his reminiscences to Lake when he caught his ear, "Rustler and robber by trade with the added specialty of killing jailers (actually he was really accessory after the fact. Rudabaugh never killed a jailer in his life, although he did make unsuccessful attempts as we shall see) in the breaks for liberty at which he was invariably successful whenever he was arrested. He was the same Rudabaugh who ran later on with Billy the Kid, down in the Pecos country. After a series of hold-ups, word came that Rudabaugh and Roake were in Texas and as I was a deputy U. S. Marshal (questioned, or at least disputed. Earp does not seem to have been anything more than a bounty hunter at the time, or at best sub-deputized by his brother who was the actual marshal) I was offered ten dollars a day and expenses if I'd get them. I left after I promised (Mayor) Kelley that I'd come back to Dodge City. Dave Rudabaugh's trail had been cold for several weeks when I took it up, but he had been reported last at Fort Griffin, Texas, some four hundred miles from Dodge. So I struck for Doan's Crossing and the Brazos. John Shanssey was about the first man I met at Fort Griffin. The last time I saw him was when he fought Mike Donovan on the Fourth of July, 1868, in the prize ring at Cheyenne. Shanssey was running a saloon and a gambling house and from him I learned that Dave Rudabaugh's gang had left Fort Griffin; but he didn't know whether the outlaws had headed across the Staked Plains for New Mexico or south toward the Rio Grande...." [Nothing in Earp's story about Rudabaugh is true. In 1868, Rudabaugh was 14. He was NOT riding with a gang in Texas, much less leading one. The veritable evidence shows that Rudabaugh until some time after 1875, was living on a farm with his 46-year old, single mother and three younger siblings, two brothers and a sister.]

Earp started south from Dodge to Commission Creek, where E. E. Polly ran a stage stop for Lee and Reynolds. Polly, an ex-soldier from Fort Hays and Fort Dodge, kept an ear to the ground for news of Rudabaugh and his gang, but could give Earp no information. Earp rode on to the dugout of A. G. Springer near the site of Canadian, Texas, and after paying the old skinflint for a meal, learned nothing more than Polly told him. He went on to Fort Griffin. The area around Fort Elliott was familiar to Earp for it was at old Mobetiee that Earp ran into difficulties with Sheriff Fleming and gambler Jim Mcintyre. Doan's Crossing, north of the site Vernon in Willbarger county, was Earp's next objective. This was the principal ford across the Red River along the Dodge Trail. This has been dubbed the Western Trail by some authors. When Earp came through, in his hunt for Rudabaugh, the picket house with the buffalo robe doorway was still standing. Corvin Doan was fairly certain that Rudabaugh and Roake were at Fort Griffin for they had paid the toll at the Crossing but a few weeks before. Indeed they had often used the ford whether for rustling purposes or not was of little concern to Corvin F. Doan who kept a toll gate not an information center. Earp eventually arrived at Fort Griffin. Fort Griffin, like Fort Dodge, was a magnet luring freighters, gamblers, camp followers, bartenders, merchants, con men, rustlers, which could be said for about any post during those frontier days. Established on July 31, 1867, it was manned by four companies of the Sixth Cavalry under the command of Bvt. Col. Sturgis.

"Some of the frontier towns in the Southwest rivaled in notoriety such as Dodge City, Abilene.... The most noticeable of these was Fort Griffin, or 'The Flat', near the banks of the Clear Fork of the Brazos, nestled the adobe huts and small frame shacks of the town. A more desperate and lawless class of people never collected at a western town than was to be found at this frontier village. The post surgeon at Fort Griffin in May, 1872, said that a short distance from the post was a camp of Tonkaways and a settlement of 'Squatters.' Prominent among them was a saloon-keeper called 'Tol Bowers,' a noted desperado who killed a citizen named Cockerall without being tried by the military authorities. He further stated that the Tonkaways in their drunken brawls kept the settlement in constant terror. So turbulent were the lawless characters in this notorious settlement that robbery was frequently perpetrated in open daylight, and at night the 'Flat' was an inferno of ribaldry, lewd women, drunken gamblers, and designing thieves. It was a common sight to see both men and women in a 'state of beastly intoxication....'" (Rister, *The Southwestern Frontier*, p. 251)

Shanssey knew very little of Rudabaugh and told Earp so. But he knew a man who was quite friendly with the robber who by this time had become more of a shadow than a reality to the lawman. Shanssey, like the others, was passing the buck. Earp hoped for nothing more from the man he would be introduced to than he had obtained from the others along the line. Now the question arises: How reliable was Earp? The saloon he makes reference to is the Bee Hive and it was owned by Shaughnassy, who might very well be called Shanssey. Holliday was not in Fort Griffin in 1877 nor was Earp a police official in that year and the *Dodge City Times* of July 21, 1877, refers to him as the "ex-officer." Earp had served as a policeman in Dodge under Marshal Larry Deger from May 17 to September 9, of 1876, and again from July until November, 1877, under Marshal Ed Masterson. He was a city official not a government marshal or deputy marshal. As a city policeman he had no jurisdiction outside of the city limits. Is it possible that his brother Virgil took after Rudabaugh and Wyatt, whose fictional exploits have dazzled the world as truth, appropriated the real marshal's doings as his own because he was the oldest of the Earp boys who pretty much ran them his own way? At face value, no one disputes that Wyatt chased after Rudabaugh because Raine and Lake told us he did, their source being the venerable Buntline Special owner himself. But none of the pieces seem to fit [because the story is not true]. Nevertheless Wyatt Earp continues his narrative:

"When Shanssey and I were discussing the chances of locating Dave Rudabaugh, we were sitting in a small room where the ex-boxer kept his strong box and from which he commanded a view of the bar, gaming tables and dance hall. He called to a young man sitting at a nearby table. This was Doc Holliday. When Shanssey told Holliday what I wanted, he said he would learn of Rudabaugh's whereabouts if I'd give him time. Within the next week or so I saw a great deal of Doc Holliday, and learned much of his family and his earlier life. Whatever attachment may have existed between us at the time was entirely one sided. If I encouraged intimacy it was only because I wanted information about Dave Rudabaugh...." (Lake, o. c. pp. 191-198 inter.)

By the time Holliday was able to report to Earp, Rudabaugh was already on his way to Fort Davis. Earp wired the marshal in that area to hold the rustler for him but the lawman wired back that Rudabaugh had already left. No doubt Rudabaugh was making the round of frontier posts in quests of government horses and mules to be re-sold to the Kiowas, Comanches or Comancheros (what few of these were left after the slow down of the buffalo trade), or to be taken to New Mexico and Colorado for re-distribution after the re-branding.

Earp next tried Fort Clark only to learn that Rudabaugh had moved on to Fort Concho. From here Earp, again too late, rode on to Fort McKavett where he learned that the post sutler had heard Rudabaugh remark that he was going back to Fort Griffin. By the time Earp got to Fort Griffin the elusive rustler was on his way to Wolf Creek, the gang's hide-out. Earp once remarked that he collected a thousand dollars on Rudabaugh. No doubt Kelley kept his promise and paid the ten dollars a day and costs even though Earp failed to produce the badly wanted rustler and robber. Holliday, Earp, and several others drop out of the picture until we meet them all again in Arizona. Meantime events are shaping up that throw Webb and Rudabaugh together. One might say that Webb was to Rudabaugh what Holliday was to Earp, Kingfisher to Thompson, McIntyre to Jim Courtright. One might add that Holliday was never as loyal to Earp even at the OK Corral as Rudabaugh was to Webb. Holliday welcomed lead as the answer to a destroying disease; Rudabaugh dodged lead as the answer for a fuller life he wished to live to the last exciting moment.

Chapter 2 | The Kinsley Robbery

Dave Rudabaugh may have been a product of his times but at closer range he stands as a gargantua in the land of giants. Discarded for such contemporaries as Wyatt Earp, Bat Masterson, Billy the Kid, Dave Mather, Doc Holliday and Curly Bill, he emerges now as an unknown quantity if only because curiosity touching these others has been satiated. He is brought to light for a moment as a "killer of jailers" which, of course, he was not, a companion of Billy the Kid and then relegated to the background as a lesser satellite standing in awe of the more popular desperadoes whose feats of daring and (mis) adventure hardly approach, much less, equal those of Dave Rudabaugh. He was no gunslinger as we understand the term, but he could hardly have associated with such men if unhandy with a gun. Billy the Kid never dared talk to him as he did to Charles Bowdre, Tom O'Folliard or even Pat Garrett. While there are occasions when he soars above them all, he never made pretensions as a killer of men, a robber, rustler or desperado. Masterson, the Kid, Earp and Holliday respected his trigger finger enough never to challenge or question his courage and aim. Highwayman, rustler, train robber, bartender, gambler, deputy, horse thief and hangman he moves about as silently as an Apache to outwit the best lawmen of his time forcing them to acknowledge that for sheer spunk, courage, audacity and prowess Rudabaugh deserved a better fate than a nod or two from students of Western folklore.

Of his love life, if he had any, little or nothing is known. He may have been attracted to women but they certainly were not to him. No doubt he wanted it that way since he was not about to change his ways for any of them. He was an opportunist. Each time he broke out of jail he proved it [he only broke out of jail successfully once – December 3, 1881]. He had no use for bunglers. This answers why he turned "State's Evidence" in the Kinsley robbery, why be killed Allen [this Allen is John J. Allen – Stanley gets him confused with James "Jim" Allen regularly] and why he told Billy the Kid to surrender to Pat Garrett. In the end, it messed up his own life just at the time he thought he had it made. Judge B. Prince proved a prophet when he remarked to a lawyer in Santa Fe as Rudabaugh was leaving the court room in chains: "That man will never hang."

Rudabaugh was no bit player in the history of the lawless West. Journalists of his own day were rather inclined to regard him as the central figure, the hub, web, fulcrum, magnet drawing others to him like flies to honey. When men like Holliday, Earp, Curly Bill, Billy the Kid and Johnny Ringo are suffering a bad case of the jitters (their admirers to the contrary not withstanding), Rudabaugh stands aloof, calm and unassuming, smilingly awaiting the outcome. He is as unruffled robbing a stage as he is in jail. [On the contrary, contemporaneous newspapers often remarked on his nervousness. "Radabaugh was brought up in irons and showed a restless, uneasy condition of mind when he was taken from the cars." – *Las Vegas Daily Optic*, March 7, 1881.]. He speaks no word; he leaves no blood; he covers up his trail and disappears into the shadows.

Such tactics exasperate the biographer who is drawn into too many dead end streets and byways – that is why he was left alone in favor of the more boisterous who knew how to shoot off their mouths as well as their guns. Despite his Border Ruffian methods Rudabaugh had one quality that made him outstanding among the desperadoes of his day: He was loyal to a friend. Loyalty to [John Joshua] Webb forced Rudabaugh to seek out Billy the Kid. Jim East was not the only lawman to remark: "If ever Billy the Kid was afraid of a man that man was Dave Rudabaugh." Rudabaugh had little admiration for McCarthy (or Antrim or Bonney) who pushed the wounded Bowdre out the door to gun down Pat Garrett before he died, and who selected a convenient moment to ride to the rear when he suspected a trap, thus exposing his "Pal" O'Folliard to the bullet meant for him. The Kid knew better than to leave Rudabaugh behind, when in flight, after a skirmish with the law. When they were cell mates at Santa Fe the Kid was always careful not to arouse Rudabaugh.

The Dodge City newspapers were inclined to refer to Rudabaugh as a Border Ruffian because he not only played the part; he lived it and looked it [no contemporaneous newspaper ever called him a Border Ruffian]. Unkempt in dress and looks during these early years of his career as rustler and outlaw, he seemed uncouth even to the hussies of the bagnio sisterhood who could ill afford to be particular. He was putty in the hands of dancehall girls. "A fool and his money are soon parted." He said that to himself time and again but like poor Oliver, he always "asked for more." Being broke was the least of his worries as long as cattle roamed the range, stages raised dust, railroads kept puffing West, gaming tables left uncovered, freight wagons loaded and unloaded. Despite his untidy appearance he seemed well liked by the brotherhood of rustlers, highwaymen and gunslingers.

The bartender at the Long Branch thought him polite and well mannered. He was always welcome at the Alhambra, the Gay Lady and other like spider-parlors. He had an even temper and never caused a rumpus at a gaming table, nor did he ever attempt to prove he was "the fastest gun in the West." He was fast enough on the draw and possibly a better shot than most, with enough sense not to invite proof and courageous enough to face trouble when it tagged him. He was very much like Clay Allison in this respect. Excitement fascinated him to the extent that he felt lost without it. It has been said of him that he had the look of a man who enjoyed sleeping in his clothes. A man constantly on the dodge could look no other way. There were times when he looked very dashing but he lived too close to nature for prolonged visits to barber shops, bath houses, haberdasheries. No one friend, enemy, lawman, outlaw ever referred to him as a coward. Earp, Masterson, East, Garrett, all admired his courage, loyalty and devotion to friends. It is puzzling that he should turn against his associates in the Kinsley affair, and he seems out of character [on the contrary, he always confessed and named his confederates when in legal jeopardy – the smart move]. When the incident is studied, and one terrible mess from the start, Rudabaugh is very much in character in washing his hands of would-be train robbers who were nervous about the whole thing from the very start.

Briefly he is described as five feet eight inches tall, weighing (in his prime) one hundred and sixty-five pounds; hazel eyes, brown hair that curled at the tips when dry; weather-beaten face; square-jawed. When out rustling or robbing, he usually let his beard grow several inches but shaved it off if he intended visiting the dance halls. He always wore a mustache. Contemptuous of physical labor, nevertheless he was inured to hardship and willing to risk his chances as a rustler ever mindful of the prize as a freebooter, robber and horse thief. As customary with Border Ruffians, he had a hardened insensibility to suffering, neither in himself nor in others. He was imbued with a spirit of adventure tantamount to road fever. No one place or person could ever hold him for long. Despite the many things that might be said in his favor he was no paragon.

Considering the respect men like Webb, Masterson, Earp and Holliday had for him, or his exploits, it is surprising Ned Buntline, Beale, Street & Smith, or other dime novel publishing houses made no attempt at glamorizing him, or at least his daring deeds. He was responsible for more stage robberies, horse thefts and cattle thefts than any other of like ilk addicted to lawless ways [not true]. Every stage line owner in Kansas, Colorado and New Mexico would have relished the hanging of Dave Rudabaugh. What Dodge City liked about him was his spunk. Up to the time of the Kinsley robbery, newspaper editors wrote him off as a petty rustler, highwayman and frequenter of dives [Rudabaugh is never mentioned in the newspapers until after the Kinsley train robbery]. It was rumored in Dodge that he could ride like the wind and hit what he aimed at. After all, he had years of practice in his constantly changing world. Civil War veterans, trail drivers, railroad gangs, tent-town dwellers, end-off-track hoodlums, stock yard men, buffalo hunters, freighters, skinners, bushwhackers, tradesmen, drummers, dancehall girls, gamblers, lawmen, Indians, ruffians, marshals, horse thieves, frontier lawyers, nesters, gunslingers, cattle buyers, soldiers, circuit riders, con men, they were his passing parade. The iron horse bellowed and puffed and panted under the weight of so many strong boxes it carried back and forth across the nation, causing Rudabaugh to wonder. Perhaps it would be just as easy to relieve a train of this load as it would a stage. If horses could be halted, why not a train?

Dodge City – no lover of Western Americana can afford to by-pass the Queen City of frontier Kansas. Every desperado of note, and many of lesser fame, dwelt a moment in Dodge, if only as a passing shadow or the fleet touch and go of the relay racer. The story of this city begins with H. L. Sitler. He reasoned that since so many people were making money selling hay, wood, cattle, oats, water, lumber, merchandise to a government building a string of forts all over the Southwest, he might as well join the crowd and turn the tables on these scavengers, who loved to overcharge, by building up a nest egg of his own. The spot he selected was near the newly established post known as Fort Dodge. He stacked sod under the shade of a solitary cottonwood and called it home. A government teamster, with an eye for ready coin as well as the next, he contracted to supply the garrison with firewood, saving his profits for a cattle herd he had always hoped to own.

As he suspected, freighters took to stopping at his shack, and they spread the word to buffalo hunters, drummers, prospectors and all sorts and condition of men. Tent saloons covered buffalo grass. Other shacks defied the elements and stood their ground. Charlie Myer decided on a business in hides, and his trading post became the most popular gathering place in the fast growing shanty town. A year later Buffalo City lifted its head in challenge, for the railroad crews had arrived. A. A. Robinson, chief engineer for the A. T. & S. F., considered this as good a spot as any for a townsite, calling the place Dodge in honor of the colonel, or the post, or possibly both. [Dodge City was founded in June or July, 1872.]

The first train was welcomed in September, 1872. Meantime, new horizons were opening to the southwest in the Texas Panhandle country. Moody, Goodnight, Springer, Plummer, Studer, Young, Hext and others were having remarkable success with whitefaces. Longhorns were on the way out. British capital stepped up the program considerably. Cattle barons lorded over large spreads known as the Spur, Rocking Chair, Turkey Track, Matador, Laurel Leaf, Anvil, transforming the solitary plains into a veritable cattle empire. Ranchers explored the possibilities of Morgan creek, Horse creek, Wolf creek, Commission creek, the Canadian.

A new army supply line was established in Nations Territory. While Camp Supply had been established a few years before, it was dormant until ranchers flooded the northern plains of Texas. All these draglines were but spokes in the wheel whose hub was Dodge City. If freight, feed, lumber, tools, food and saloons were the framework, then rustlers and desperadoes were the furniture. One complemented the other. Those latter furnished the excitement. The railroad proved a boon for the cattleman. Herds as far south as Corpus Christi were driven north to fatten on Kansas grass as they awaited shipment to market. Indians in Nations Territory resented the railroad because trail herds by-passed their toll gate.

The Kansas-Pacific Railroad facilitated matters by building loading pens at Abilene. In exchange for its cargo of beef the train unloaded dance hall girls, gamblers, settlers, prospectors, lawyers, merchants, hardware and a volume of dust. Saloons and sporting houses vied with con men in separating the cowboy from his money. Such places in Dodge operated on a twenty-four-hour basis. Texas street boasted twenty saloons, ten dance halls, a lunch room, a general store and twenty gambling halls. The rest of the town, whether it was Abilene, Dodge, Caldwell – end of track and end-of-cattle-trail towns followed the same pattern – proved quite dull in contrast. Cowboys were allowed the run of the place just as long as they spent freely, drank heavily and had one last farthing to throw across the counter. In some houses women made certain that they left with empty purses and empty dreams. There was always the promise that they would be waiting next year when the boys drove in a new herd.

None of these proceedings were lost on Dave Rudabaugh, which may have explained why he had no entanglements as did Doc Holliday, Wyatt Earp and others who sought to emulate Don Giovanni. The cowboys themselves did much to add to the excitement by hurrahing the town with Rebel yells, pistol shots and tricks such as we see today in convention parades, They were particularly fond of cornering a dude, with whom they carried on mirth and merriment for hours at a time. Sometimes the dude turned the tables and blood was spilt. Professional gunmen often rode with the cowboys and arrival meant seeking out a faster gun. Sort of a contest like our modern boxing matches and sometimes just as dirty, or crooked. The honest-to-goodness gunman (if he could be called that) never took advantage of an unarmed man, nor did he ever shoot in the back. Ethics among killers!

More money than one would be apt to spend today was spent for bullets to be used in target practice. A fast gun meant hours and hours of drawing, shooting, drawing, shooting, until the gunman felt confident enough to offer the challenge. They schooled themselves in various types of draws, worked at perfecting gunbelts, studied weights of lead, guns, powder, improving their gunsights, and even caused much murmuring among Cyprians who accused them of loving their horses and their guns more than chosen escort. Percentage wise, all these towns boasted good citizens and those in quantity. Law and order would never have conquered Dodge had it been all bad. The lines were drawn. No gunslinger ever married into the bluebloods or four-hundred of the frontier in Rudabaugh's day. Bluebloods and redbloods were not cast in the same mould. Gambler sought out gambler; gunslinger haunted gunslinger; rustler rode with rustler; horse thief consorted with horse thief.

No one looked for Dave Rudabaugh among the snooty coat and cravat group. The slow parade of the herds to the railhead; the riotous entry of uninhibited cowboys appealed to the young man from Spring Creek Township. He was often seen mingling with the hands, and there were choice remarks on how uncomfortable they felt in their store-bought clothes. But how else could you impress a calico queen? They slickered up for fun at the hoe-dig. They named the honky-tonks they hoped to visit. Bartenders watered down the whiskey over against these visits. Hired fiddlers played and played as if they knew the last coin hadn't been shaken down. Gaming tables never wanted for players. Sombrero, bottle, spurs, revolvers, pistols, ankle-turning, whirling, jingling, clanking, flapping, bobbing only the fiddlers were bored. The dancing partner was more like a sparing partner and an armful. Although she smiled she was calculating to the last note of music how much she could get out of this one before turning on the charm that invited the next spender. He might be half-horse, half-man, but she never ceased being all woman until his pockets lay flat against limb and muscle. After all, business was business. Never let it be said that she wasn't gainfully employed.

By what authority did Bat Masterson feel obliged to hunt down Dave Rudabaugh after the Kinsley robbery? Ford county definitely was not Edwards county. Perhaps Masterson merely sought to prove that Rudabaugh could be caught, or he was trying to live down an embarrassment that gave Dodge a good laugh at his expense. When asked later why he crossed county lines in pursuit of Dave Rudabaugh and his gang he merely shrugged his shoulders. It was illegal but nothing was done about it. A wise lawyer might have played this up to obtain the release of all the men taken into custody or at least have made it an issue at the trial. Neither Earp nor Masterson merit the great hullabaloo of our times that seeks to canonize them any more than Rudabaugh or Webb, who have not as yet jumped into Hollywood's crystal ball.

The man who did more for the West than Earp and Masterson combined was Charlie Rath. Take David's name from the Psalms and very little holds together; forget Rath in speaking of Dodge and the story isn't half told. Rath, Wright, Lee, Reynolds were the four pillars upon which Dodge rested. Charlie was part white, part savage, and all business. He belonged to the frontier breed of men who succeeded the trapper, plainsman, frontiersman and hunter. The buffalo hunter and hidesman inherited many of the characteristics of the Mountain Man. No traps were necessary to the buffalo hunter; only a good Sharpes or a Henry rifle. Rath was once married to an Indian squaw, a common practice among Mountain Men, Carrie, a white woman, was content to be recognized as his legitimate spouse, which indeed she was, and made it a point of telling you so. She had hoped to make a society blueblood of Charlie as long as he insisted on operating a mercantile store in Dodge and could afford the many niceties that suited her taste. He was happier when he operated the sutler's store at the post, and Robert M. Wright was his partner.

The rise of the cattle industry, the new demand for buffalo hides, the advance of the railroad, sent Charlie scampering off to the Texas Panhandle, where he negotiated for the sutler's trade at the newly created Fort Elliott on the Sweetwater. Next he explored the possibilities at Camp Supply near the site of Woodward, Oklahoma. He called on the prominent citizens of Dodge to interest them in a Fort Griffin-Fort Dodge highway. He founded Rath City in the Texas Panhandle; pounded out the Rath Trail; built up a freighting empire between Dodge and Fort Griffin. This necessitated the employment of drivers, clerks, skinners, hunters, blacksmiths, and others to keep his multiple interests in the black. He was not a drinking man, but a several-times-married man who thought he understood women, until he ran to the privacy of his office in the general store and raised doubts. He once remarked that he was never happily married. His wives were always trying to dress him up, straighten his cravat, keep him spotless as befitted a man of means, and they how to take care of his strongboxes. Carrie indoctrinated him in the social graces but he was too much of a nomad to learn or care. He gave her the magnificent home in Dodge, with all its furnishings; several thousand in cash and settled an allowance on Charlie, Jr. Bertie, the daughter, received even more than her brother. No one in Dodge was surprised at the divorce; only that it was so long in coming.

Next Charlie took to wife one Emma Nesper of Philadelphia. A son born of this marriage was named Morris. Emma shook her head over Charlie's failure to come up to her expectations both as a husband and as a merchant. Gunslingers were not the only ones who filed down their gunsights. She eventually left him. Rumor has it that he finally threw his hands up in disgust and went back to the squaw woman. Bald, disillusioned, broke, he sought her tepee, and ended his days in obscurity, cared for by the only woman in his life who placed no value on possessions or the lack of them. No doubt her blood was red without the alchemy of blue.

It was this man who took Rudabaugh under his wing when he first went to Dodge and gave him a job as a rider in his outfit [there is no evidence for this]. It was while he was with the Rath freight and hide wagons that Rudabaugh came to know the Panhandle country, Camp Supply, Fort Elliott, Mobeetie, Commission creek, Wolf creek, Fort Griffin, Adobe Walls, Dodge. Thrown in with skinners, hunters, freighters, plainsmen, ranchers, drivers, he soon learned the names of the various trails, creeks, hamlets, outposts. He also learned the ways of rustlers, and the code of gunfighters. He accustomed himself to the odor of thousands of buffalo hides drying in the sun, and tolerated the stench of skinners when they sat next to him at camp chow. He knew Billy Dixon and the Comanche attack on the hunters at Adobe Walls. There was just one woman in the broken down post at the time – one woman but a thousand smells – drying bones, skins freshly cut from the animals, buffalo chips, buffalo wallows, but she squared her shoulders, as pioneer women were wont to do, and she saw her dreams rather than the filth, curses, Indians and raw prairie. Had Rudabaugh waited but a few more days before moving on with the load of hides he might have been next door to immortality at least in Hutchinson county. She could look at all those men (Masterson among them), turn her nose up to the air and wonder when they last took a bath – if ever. When did she? Hollywood would have to be deodorized if smells matched talkies. What would she look like on the screen – or even Adobe Walls itself?

The Rath wagons rolled on to Fort Elliott, where men rested at old Mobeetie for the "whisky break;" equivalent to our coffee break, only it lasted for a couple of days and took in gambling and women. Wolf creek, Commission creek, Camp Supply, and on to Dodge became familiar ground. It is quite possible that he may have gone out with the crew of men, young as he was, sent out by Rath & Wright, Lee & Reynolds, to stake out the Fort Griffith Trail.

The spring of 1876 found Rath riding at the head of his contingent, a compass on the horn of his saddle, directing them south in the march of commerce over the plains, as they slowly changed the course of frontier empire. No obstacle stood in the way of the hardy breed. Chasm, canyon, quicksand, stream bowed to superior power. The Rath Trail was a monument to the buffalo hunter, and lasted just as long. Today, Double Mountain still guards the south central plains and the secret of Rath City, which long ago ceased being even a ghost town. It must have been quite a place if you go in for that sort of thing and can blot out hides, buffalo entrails, half dried bones, and the dust. Rath's Mercantile Company in Dodge was as well known in Dodge as the Wright House, Gay Lady, Long Branch. Because the movies or TV have failed to do it justice doesn't mean that it wasn't popular among the cowboys, gamblers and other Dodge citizens.

One day three men walked in. They were well mannered, glib of tongue, and smooth operators. When they left the clerk realized he was short one hundred dollars worth of merchandise. Indignant because he had been imposed upon and hurt because it was the Rath Mercantile Company, he sought out Sheriff Masterson, begging him to bring back the merchandise or the culprits, unless they were willing to give the one hundred dollars. When the officer caught up with them they lacked the proper amount to meet the price of the goods. They offered a gold watch which was to be sold to make up the deficit. The watch proved to be the property of Sheriff [Robert] McCause of Edwards county. Dodge had a laugh on Bat Masterson for days. Piqued at the unpleasant outcome,

Masterson asked around until he learned that three men answering the description of the ones he sought had been seen in the vicinity of the Van Voorhis ranch near Spearville. He mounted, hell bent for leather, to make them assuage his hurt pride. The posse approached the trio, pistols in hand, ready to pump lead at the least sign of resistance. They disarmed two of the men, but the third broke away and prepared to offer a fight. Singling out Masterson as the leader, he asked why he and the two others were set upon. His language was choice and strong. Masterson gathered from the tirade that the man was a law enforcement officer. Tempers cooled and Sheriff McCause introduced himself and his two deputies. If Dodge had laughed before, now it would howl. The sheriff got his watch back and the two became friends. How this incident missed the probing eyes of Masterson's biographers is hard to understand. It helps to explain why he felt obligated to Edwards county whether McCause was sheriff or not. It was from this time on that he counted as many friends in McCause's jurisdiction as in Ford county. Incidentally, the three suspects were caught and they were properly taken care of for all the embarrassment they had caused the sheriff. However, they only blamed themselves for having stayed in the vicinity too long. Dodge had no more laughs at Masterson's expense.

Whether or not Masterson became a fighting, gambling dandy, he was part of Dodge, more so than his brother Ed, who never lived to enjoy his twenty-seventh birthday, because two cowboys loaded with gutrot had unsteady trigger fingers. All Dodge was at the funeral. Ed dead had more friends than Ed living. Even Dave Rudabaugh had to admit that Ed was the first citizen to have such an impressive send off. Bat and Dave had nothing in common save perhaps the love of the gaming table. It is not known that they were on speaking terms. The train robbery made a difference. Masterson credited Rudabaugh with courage and knew that the robbers would never be brought to trial until Dave made it possible either with a direct confession, assumption of all the blame or as state's evidence. [The six train robbers were Rudabaugh, Michael Roarke, Dan Dement, Edgar J. West, Thomas Gott, and J. D. Green. Rudabaugh and West were arrested February 1, 1878. Gott and Green were arrested March 15, 1878. Roarke was arrested and Dement killed October 20, 1878. See page Appendix B for the complete text of Rudabaugh's confession.]

With all that dust on Front Street, Dave couldn't understand why Bat enjoyed going about like a well-dressed dude from a picture book. The saloons on Front Street were attractively decorated and admired around the clock. They never closed. Besides the fixtures and furnishings the patrons enjoyed cooled beer, free lunch made up of such delicacies as Swiss cheese, Limburger cheese, pickled herring, caviar, liverwurst, rye bread, crackers. Water? I believe the bartender had some behind the bar to rinse glasses. It may have been there for a week or so. When you wiped these glasses clean, even breathing on them to give them a shine, who cared?

Whisky was better than Listerine. Any bartender will tell you it still is. Masterson had Rudabaugh pegged as a rustler but not a train robber. Frankly, he didn't think he had it in him. A number of things could be said in favor of Kinsley, one being that it was one of the few towns in Kansas refusing to involve itself in a county seat war. Founded in 1873 by thrifty New England Yankees, it was almost throttled out of existence by angry elements that seemed to have allied themselves with Border Ruffians. The Easterners missed the hills, river, lakes, brooks, trees, flowers, green ever so green countryside. Here they encountered pestilence, crop failures, dust, tornadoes, drought, baked earth, beetles, bugs, treeless plains and silence. The New Englander is not known as a quitter. Doggedly, they held on. Then came the promise of the railroad and things began to look up. It was almost as if they were "back home." Here was East Lynn on the plains of

Kansas. It was too snooty for the trail driver, gambler, gunslinger, up-stairs girl. They by-passed it for Dodge, and Kinsley settled back to enjoy a rocking-chair, staid existence. Until Rudabaugh came along and shook it into publicity.

Camp Supply, in present Woodward county, Oklahoma, was ninety odd miles southeast of Dodge. Established in 1868 during the Indian Wars, it became exactly what the name implied, the supply depot for the garrisons in Kansas and the cantonments in the Texas Panhandle. The rise of the buffalo trade, advance of the railroad, success of the cattle drives, settlement of the north plains area and Nations Territory, singled out Camp Supply as a landmark. The land between Camp Supply and Fort Elliott was often referred to as Rustler Paradise. Horses stolen in Kansas were sold in Colorado and New Mexico; live stock taken in Texas was sold in Colorado and New Mexico after brands were changed. While the Cattleman's Association failed to solve the problem it did curtail it to some extent. "The ranchers," said the late Lewis Nordyke, "had only a determined plan to organize frontier cowmen in a unified and unrelenting war on cattle rustlers. They had by letter, word of mouth and advertisements in the few newspapers, invited all stockgrowers in sparsely populated northwestern Texas to gather at Graham to consider a means of joining forces...." (*Great Roundup*, Page 18)

That was on February 15, 1877, when Rudabaugh and Mike Roarke were gaining notoriety as rustlers, horse thieves and hold-up men. They were responsible for the theft of payrolls belonging to the end-of-track crews [there is no evidence for this]. By his own admission Rudabaugh testified that he first became acquainted with Roarke (also spelt Rourke, Rourk, Roark) in August of 1876 [1877], shortly after his twenty-second birthday. Roarke introduced him to a. cowboy named Daniel Dement. All three were on the Rath payroll at one time or another and were well acquainted with the Rath Trail [Roarke was a professional civil engineer – neither were on the Rath payroll]. They were seen together so often in Dodge that gamblers, Cyprians and bartenders referred to them as the Trio. The Rand, McNally Atlas for 1876 lists the population of Dodge as 225. Kinsley was listed as having twenty-five. Any town not reporting its population was given the number 25 either to indicate that the real number was unknown or that at least that many should be around.

The Dodge-Camp Supply Trail crossed the Cimarron, Beaver creek, Buffalo creek, Sand creek, Rabbit Ear creek (better known as the North Fork of the Canadian). Cowboys, freighters, stage drivers, circuit riders, hunters, prospectors were interested in watering spots and wooded areas because sometimes not only the lives of the horses and steers depended on knowing this but also their very own. South, and flowing from the west, was Wolf creek, familiar to the soldiers from Fort Elliott, Camp Supply, Fort Dodge and the cowboys working at the Turkey Track, Anvil, Laurel Leaf, Rocking Chair and Moody. How many cattle the Trio lifted from these spreads would be pure guesswork but it would not be wrong to place them in the thousands. The judge at the trail robbery trial did not concern himself with their deeds as rustlers; it might have been quite revealing if he had.

About a year later Thomas Golt [Gott] joined the gang, J. D. Green and Ed [Edgar J.] West did not associate with them as part of an organized rustler band until January 1, 1878, several weeks before the hold-up. Rudabaugh, Roarke and Dement might have succeeded had they not taken on Green, West, Golt. Dave was not in favor of having them but Roarke insisted. Rudabaugh never forgave him, which partly explains why one so loyal to his friends as Dave Rudabaugh testified against these at the trial. It was not to save his skin as some suppose [it was to save his skin!]. A man as adept at breaking out of jail as he was had no fear of the sentence neither at Kinsley, Las Vegas nor Santa Fe.

A number of writers of Western outlaw deeds are of the opinion that Golt was as infamous as Billy the Kid, Dave Mather, Sam Bass, Jesse James and Wes Hardin. No doubt men like Rudabaugh, Golt, West, Miller will prove a change of diet from the time worn characters like Billy the Kid, the James Brothers and other run-to-earth characters of gunbelt days.

January 16, 1878. The rustlers rested about the camp fire after a highly successful raid on a herd near the site of Canadian, Texas. Wolf creek proved the best hideout to date. Ever since Roarke first mentioned the possibility of a train robbery at this very spot last August, this spot became headquarters by mutual consent. Golt fell in with the idea from the very beginning. Rudabaugh stuck to the "steady as she goes" policy arguing that he knew rustling but nothing about hijacking a train. The original plan was as daring as it was bold. The train was to be held up at Dodge. Golt thought the ripest time would be after Christmas or the New Year when life in the queen city of the Kansas plains would be at low ebb and everyone too sluggish after a wet celebration to form a posse.

Christmas came and went but no robbery. Perhaps the would-be robbers themselves were not up to it having imbibed with the rest of the merry makers. The same thing happened on New Year's Day. It was next decided to stage the hold up on January 7th. When the time arrived to gather together, Green absented himself on other business and the robbery was called off for the third time. Rudabaugh was fit to be tied. He had ridden in from Wolf creek. The others calmed him down for they had come in from Wolf creek also and they couldn't understand why he should take exception. They all made a useless ride.

Early that evening it began snowing, falling heavier as the night wore on. With or without Green they doubted whether they could have held up the train or even that it would arrive at Dodge that night. Roarke rode off to the west; Golt took a room in Dodge, and was soon joined by West; Rudabaugh and Dement braved the storm and rode all that night, making camp at dawn some twenty-five miles south of Dodge. A week later Roarke drifted in to the hideout on Wolf creek. West, penniless in Dodge, decided to join the gang in the Panhandle where the rent was free. Dave had already spent the week at Wolf creek wondering how he got mixed up with such nincompoops.

They decided to make a fourth try. Back in Dodge Jack Wagner and Alf Walker had already punctured Ed Masterson and Charles E. Bassett replaced him as marshal. The Senator, Rudabaugh called him, because his face was clean shaven and he went about in neat, clean attire. Roarke said he didn't want to tangle with Bassett who was considered an expert shot, and most likely to suspect him if the robbery did take place. After consultation it was decided that Kinsley was the place to stage the perfect train hold up. Again they rode to Wolf creek to figure out how to go about taking on the train at Kinsley. By January 22nd, each felt he had his part down to perfection. No one bothered to scout around Kinsley or look over the depot. It seemed so unimportant at the moment. Besides no one handy with sidearms lived there. It was a pushover.

Again, the snow began to fall the night they selected for the hold up [January 27, 1878]. Rudabaugh, having had experience for a short time as an expressman, knew the train schedule for the whole area but no one counted on the weather conditions for that night. They bungled the job from the beginning.

The going from Wolf creek to Kinsley had been very slow especially since they were burdened with a chuck wagon full of provisions. Impedimenta, Caesar would have called it, something under foot to hinder, which is exactly what the word means. It was a rather unusual way to go about holding up a train. Mike Roarke, mounted on a big iron-gray mare, assumed the lead. He was armed with a Sharpes rifle bought at Rath's, and a pistol. Behind him rode Dement, armed with a rifle of the same make, and a Colt's revolver. Golt, who drove the wagon, placed his confidence in a Henry rifle. He was anxious for a brace of side arms but Rudabaugh argued that a man driving the wagon and holding horses for a quick getaway needed both his hands for his work and had no need for pistols. The others would cover him. Green, who rode on the left side of the wagon, had a Sharpes, a Springfield, and two Colts. He bought one of the revolvers at Zimmerman's in Dodge just the week before he and Dave rode in to replenish the larder. Behind him rode West, armed with a Springfield and a Colt. Rudabaugh rode a few feet behind the wagon. He had a Sharpes, and two Smith & Wesson pistols. At Beaver creek they decided to abandon the chuck wagon because it slowed them down, They unhitched the horses, Golt riding one and leading the other. He took his place next to Rudabaugh. They all wore rubber shoes. After dark, the outlaws left Beaver creek and headed north, remaining in the saddle until sun-up.

That night they crossed the Cimarron making camp at the head of Sand creek. At daybreak they took the Camp Supply road to Buffalo creek, where they made camp until noon of the next day. They rode on for a while overtaking the Reynolds stage coming in from Polly's station at Commission creek. They made it a point to engage the rider in conversation, hoping thereby to establish an alibi should anyone suspect them of stopping the train at Kinsley. That night they camped at Mulberry creek in Ford county just below Dodge and five miles south of Pat Ryan's ranch.

Saturday, January 26th, they rode eastward toward Kinsley, halting within ten miles south of the town, making camp in the sandhills. Four hours later they rode to Kinsley two hours before train time. Between the town proper and the water tank was a small house. They knocked at the door and asked the occupant, a laborer for the Santa Fe, if the train would arrive on time. He was rather startled for all of them (except Golt) had their faces blackened [strangely, they only blackened their faces after the attempted robbery!]. Rudabaugh took a pistol from its holster and examined it carefully leaving no doubt in the man's mind. He told them what he knew, closed the door and went back to bed. So he testified at the trial. He was not anxious to put Rudabaugh to the test. He who sleeps the night away, lives to see the light of day. West had asked the laborer how far it was to town. A mile and a half. It was also a mile and a half from the house to the tank. They were saddened to learn that the Eastbound train had already passed. This is the train they were really out to stop. But they knew that another would be by directly.

Dement and West picked this moment to wander off somewhere. This so disturbed Green that he fired a shot to warn them to keep their course along the track. The weather had been threatening for the past several hours and now a light snow made the ground slick. Flakes flew thick and fast with each passing moment. Roarke and Rudabaugh decided to go through with the robbery storm or no storm. The horses were left at the trestle in care of Golt. The others continued on to the depot afoot. Dement and Rudabaugh entered the station. [Andrew] Kincaid, the agent looked up and Rudabaugh engaged him in conversation. Quick to note his blackened face, he gave no response to Rudabaugh's hearty "Good morning." Quickly he opened a drawer and slipped a Derringer into his hip pocket. Rudabaugh went to the railing and stepped inside. Seeing no one else in the room, Dement left. Golt, who had left the horses tied at the depot, saw no necessity to stand in the snow when he could be in the warmth of the agent's room, and entered just as Dement left. Stealthily, inch by inch, Kincaid worked his hand to the hip pocket. Just then Roarke walked in, noted the position of the hand, and sprang for the agent. He took away the gun and handed it to Rudabaugh. Later, when the judge asked the agent what he hoped to accomplish with the little Derringer, Kincaid said that he was going to use it on Rudabaugh who seemed to be the leader of the group. "Of all those participating in the robbery," he testified, "Rudabaugh seemed the bravest. I got the impression that he was the leader. With him dead the others might take to their heels."

When Roarke snatched away the gun he said: "I'll take that." Kincaid was able to identify that voice. Roarke asked him if there was any money in the safe, or the drawer. The agent told him that there was none in the safe but that there had been some in the drawer. It was put on the Eastbound but a few minutes ago. He opened the drawer and invited Roarke to inspect it. Since there was no money, he offered packets of post cards which Roarke rejected with scorn. Looking to the safe he demanded that Kincaid open it. "And be d-d quick about it." The agent said he couldn't open the safe because he didn't have the key. The day agent, named [Fred] Gardner, who roomed at the Kinsley Hotel, kept it in his possession at all times. There was two thousand dollars, in the safe.

Just then the puffing of an approaching train could be heard. The outlaws ran out of the station and almost knocked down W. F. Blanchard, the night clerk at the hotel (the Eureka) who hoped to drum up trade before the travelers learned of the more popular Kinsley. Seeing their blackened faces he suspected their purpose. He ran into the express office to find a gun. Kincaid yelled to him: "Go back. All these men have pistols." Rudabaugh sent a shot in his direction but missed. Meantime the train came to a stop and one of the robbers sprinted around the engine in an effort to grab Kincaid who was bent on reaching the engineer before any of the hold up men could get to him. The agent yelled to him telling him that the train was being held up, and to pull out of Kinsley. But the man wore ear muffs and thought he was just waving a greeting. Getting no response from the engineer, Kincaid continued on beyond the baggage car and called out to Conductor [J. W.] Mallory that the train was being held up. The conductor ran through the train bolting doors as he went.

West and Dement climbed to the cab of the engine and covered the engineer and fireman, ordering them to keep their hands in the air. By this time, several men gathered on the platform of the train. Rudabaugh, Green and Roarke were waiting for the expressman to open the door of the express car. When the door opened, Roarke tried to force his way in. Expressman Brown tried to prevent him but Roarke pushed him back, pulled a gun and demanded the money. Rudabaugh went to the rear of the express car at the front of the coach. Brown threw the lantern he was carrying into the coal box, seized a revolver and commenced firing. This seemed to be the signal for everyone, and bullets flew in every direction. Rudabaugh leveled his gun on Mallory as the conductor jumped off the coach. The outlaw commanded him to join the group on the platform and ordered them all to get back into the coach if they wanted to live.

Brown's first shot missed Green's head by three inches. Rudabaugh ran to the depot and fired four shots is rapid succession to warn all passengers to stay where they were. At this moment the train began to move. Rudabaugh became hopeful for the gang could work better if the train was away from Kinsley. His four shots had made the engineer so nervous that he thought it best to get going. Two miles out of Kinsley the bandits ordered him to stop the train. Suddenly, just when Rudabaugh thought he had it made, Roarke decided to call off the robbery arguing that by this time Kincaid and Gardner must have aroused enough citizens to form a good posse that certainly would out-shoot them by mere force of numbers. Nor was he wrong. Ten men were already on the way and more behind them. Since the men were not organized, none of their efforts proved successful as the outlaws jumped from the train and scattered in different directions.

None of the shots from either side found a target. No doubt Rudabaugh abandoned Roarke (in his thoughts at least) the moment his partner in crime decided to give up the attempt on the train. He was further embittered to see Roarke, Dement and Green far out is front as he made his way to the depot. The awful truth dawned on him: They had abandoned their job even before the posse arrived. There was no other explanation possible. They evacuated to save their own skins, leaving a pal exposed to possible capture or death. To Rudabaugh, this was an unpardonable sin. He would abide his time. He joined them, saying nothing.

The next day found them twenty miles south of Kinsley, at the river, where they washed the gunpowder from their faces. That night they made camp on the prairie near a small lake on the flat. Golt's horse had given out, and he took turns riding with the others. The following night they camped at Bluff creek. Roarke, Dement, Green and Golt went on to Beaver creek. West and Rudabaugh remained in camp another day, then followed the others, pitching their tent on Sand creek on Wednesday night.

Here several men who had been riding to the northeast, approached them. They turned out to be Harry Lovell and some of his cowboys in pursuit of horse thieves who had made off with some of the best stock on the Lovell Ranch. The rancher invited West and Rudabaugh to be his guests for supper. When the posse decided that the bandits had escaped they allowed Engineer [J. M.] Anderson to go on. He brought the train to Dodge at six A. M., tooting heavily in order to arouse the citizens. He had quite a story to tell. Among the ten men who first started after the train at Kinsley were ex-sheriff McCause, C. L. Hubbs, E. A. Noble and N. Billings, all friends of Bat Masterson. The latter took the robbery as a personal insult since it involved many of his friends and decided to do something about it. He was certain that only the blinding snowstorm raging at the time hindered McCause from getting at least one of the bandits. On the other hand, the same could be said for Rudabaugh. The snow covered the tracks of the escaping robbers and the pursuit was abandoned till dawn. At daylight, the posse crossed the river but found nothing. Meantime the second posse under Sheriff [John] Fuller, Clute, Wells and Calamity Bill took the trail into Dodge, where they thought the desperadoes likely to be, but returned empty handed.

Kinsley refused to go back to sleep. At four in the morning, a third posse composed of Robert McComb, G. H. Hubbs, R. J. Berkeley, E. K. Smart, John Dugan, John Reed, Robert McComb, John Culley, loaded a chuck wagon with provisions and ammunition and headed for Medicine river to scout the Cimarron country. There they met a patrol that had been sent out of Fort Dodge under Lieutenant Gardner. It seemed that everybody got into the act. Very few train hold-ups, even in the days of Jesse James down to the last of the notorious robbers under Black Jack Ketchum, ever caused such commotion or brought out so many posses. Gardner had no more luck than the others. Everybody in Kinsley was excited. There was a good-natured laugh over the plight of Agent Kincaid. When he learned that Hubbs, Smart and the others would not wait for dawn to go after Rudabaugh and the outlaws, he ran to the bank, pounded on the door with the intention of asking the night guard for a gun. The guard mistook him for a bandit and told him to throw up his hands. He marched him into the bank as his prisoner but the wily railroad man managed to escape. Fred Gardner (no relation to Lt. Gardner), who slept in an upstairs room, stuck his stocking-cap covered head out the window and demanded to know what "in tarnation the racket was about." Receiving no reply he muttered something about "crazy fools," shut the window and went back to bed.

Fifty men gathered about the depot, all with the solution, and full of speculation as to who the outlaws were. None braved the snow and cold to join the posses, A fellow named Robley kept circulating about astride a bay mare. He had a theory that the robbers were still in town and he aimed to capture them single-handed. After seven hours of this he decided that perhaps they had escaped after all. Superintendant Morse posted a reward of one hundred dollars each for the capture of the outlaws – dead or alive.

Sheriff Fuller appealed to Bat Masterson who seemed indifferent. Actually he was quite interested both because of the reward money involved and as a favor to his friend McCause. Morse's reward was open to all comers; not necessarily lawmen. He excused himself on the grounds that it was a problem for the sheriff of Kinsley, the railroad and the marshal of Kinsley to unravel. He played the part of aloofness so well that the editor of the *Republican* remarked: "The failure of the Ford county sheriff to cooperate with the Kinsley party was, as it appears to us, inexcusable, and the excuse assigned is too thin." The print was hardly dry before Masterson, J. J. Webb, David Morrow, Riley and others collected by the popular sheriff, headed south in quest of train robbers [on February 29, 1878]. Who tipped them off?

How did Masterson know exactly where to go? These questions Rudabaugh pondered and helped settle in his own mind that his companions were not to be trusted. By the time Masterson's party rode out of Dodge the attempt on the train was five days old. Each passing day added fuel to the flame of desire to "get or be gotten" in apprehending the culprits.

Nobody knew where to look or who to look for. Nobody but Masterson. There was a fly in the ointment. The sheriff's informant sent him sixty-five miles below Dodge to Lovell's cow camp. Masterson arrived too late, but he was not discouraged. He had every reason to believe that the camp was not abandoned. The men would be back. He sat and waited. Hours passed. Cautiously, from the east, two riders rode toward camp. Webb rode out to meet them. He wanted to make sure that these were the men wanted; not some of Lovell's cowboys returning to cook a meal. The rest of the posse hid out of sight. Webb kept both hands on the saddle horn where they would be in plain sight of the approaching horsemen. He hailed the riders and engaged them in conversation, directing their course toward the ambush. Once they were within range, Masterson jumped up saying: "Throw up your hands. "West didn't wait for a second invitation. Rudabaugh reached for his sixshooter. Webb took out his own gun, pulled back the trigger, remarking: "I wouldn't do that if I were you." This was the man who would soon change the whole course of Rudabaugh's life.

The rest of the posse closed in with drawn guns and relieved the pair of two rifles, four pistols. Again, the snow began to fall. It was decided to remain at the Lovell camp that night. After a few hours sleep, they set out for Dodge. They camped out one more day and part of the night arriving at Dodge around 6 P. M. in the evening [February 1, 1878]. Quite a crowd gathered in a sort of procession that ended at the jail where they were lodged and put in irons. Captain J. M. Thatcher, the general agent for the Adams Express Company, who had been the armchair strategist and commander in chief of the hunt (a la white collar method from behind a desk) visited the prisoners, taking with him his attorney Harry Gryden, this latter hoping to exact a confession from them by his clever talk. The prisoners had nothing to say.

On Saturday [February 2], Rudabaugh and West were taken out of the Dodge jail and conveyed to Kinsley, escorted by Bat Masterson, J. E. McArthur, Thatcher, H. Zeigler, W. Blanchard, C. Palmer, L. Palmer, Joe German, ex-sheriff McCause, J. Berkeley and Andrew Kincaid. Zeigler was especially happy to be a part of the guard since he was the one that Rudabaugh shot at in order to keep him in the coach and off the platform of the train. His home was in Larned. Kincaid, regarded by all of Kinsley as the hero of the hour, was a native of New York, and was twenty-one at the time of the robbery. He had come to Kansas but two years before for his health. For his part in the affair, the railroad gave him an increase in salary effective as of January 1 and a job with the road as long as he lived. He later transferred to Hutchinson and then Wellington. After the trial no more is heard of him. He had his moment of glory. The rest was oblivion.

The train from Dodge pulled into Kinsley at 4:30 P. M. that Saturday. The townspeople were in a holiday mood, and quite anxious for a necktie party. This was not the last time Rudabaugh was to face people at a railroad station and wonder if the mob would hang him. West and Rudabaugh were shackled together and surrounded by the guards. One little known fact is that there was a third prisoner implicated in the robbery. Or at least some one felt he had reason to implicate him. Masterson arrested him just as the train was ready to leave Dodge. He was at the station. His name was William (Bill) Tilghman. The future lawman protested his innocence but Masterson told him he had no choice. He was twenty-eight at the time, having been a buffalo hunter from the time he was twenty. He once had a contract with another hunter to supply meat for the railroad workers around Dodge and is said to have slaughtered seven thousand buffalo. He missed the famous battle at Adobe Walls by three days. Bat Masterson took him on as deputy in January, 1878.

Some authors doubt this. According to the *Valley Republic* published in Kinsley, Saturday, February 9, 1878, Tilghman was employed as a bartender at the time of his arrest. This is the first time his name appears in print. "William Tilghman, a well known cocktail artist at Dodge, pleaded not guilty and demanding trial. The State asked for ten days' time, which was granted and Tilghman was placed under $4,000 bond to appear before Justice Wiley, Tuesday, February 12th...." (o. c.)

The *Dodge City Times* of a month earlier, suspecting Tilghman as part of the gang that kept Dodge a wide-open town, said: "Bill Tilghman is yet un-arrested. He is a hard citizen, and is said to have more brains than all of them." (Jan., 1879) Tilghman was able to prove to the satisfaction of the authorities that he was in no way associated with the Kinsley affair. Writers seem to over emphasize his part in the arrest of Mysterious Dave Mather when Tom Nixon was killed. Mather did not "vow to drop Tilghman in his tracks" as some writers would have us believe. Tilghman eventually staked out a claim near Chandler in Indian Territory and made headlines all over the Southwest when he single-handedly arrested an infamous outlaw named Bill Doolin. Tilghman was again elected to office as sheriff of Lincoln county, Oklahoma, in 1900. Some years later he became chief of police of Oklahoma City. He served with the film industry in the capacity of advisor on outlaw life. In 1924, he became chief of police of Cromwell, then a boom town in Oklahoma, and was killed by a drunk in the fall of that year. The sad part about the tragedy is that the drunk was a sort of lawman himself. He had sampled too much moonshine liquor as a prohibition officer and went to a cafe where he caused such a commotion that Tilghman was sent for. The prohibition officer saw him coming and sent two bullets his way. Of all those arrested in connection with the Kinsley affair, Tilghman was the only one able to furnish bail. "It is generally believed that Wm. Tilghman had no hand in the attempted robbery," said the editor of the *Dodge City Times* for February 9, 1878. [For a full-length biography of William Tilghman, see *Outlaw Days, A True History of Early-Day Oklahoma Characters* by Zoe A. Tilghman, Harlow Publishing Company, 1926.]

It was decided that since Rudabaugh was the one who stood off the night operator at the railway depot, he should be tried at once. The others could remain in jail until

Monday. Rudabaugh waived examination and was bound over in the sum of $4,000. Since he could not raise bond he was placed in the sheriff's custody. West and the other prisoner were in the same predicament. A fund for Kinsley could hardly be built up this way so it was decided that the prisoners would be less the responsibility of the little city if they were taken back to Dodge. The lawyers asked for ten days in which to build up their case. Meantime the hunt was still on for the other outlaws still at large. Harry Gryden obtained warrants for the arrest of Thomas Golt, who often called himself Dugan; J. D. Green and Dewitt. He asked Masterson to take a posse into Wolf creek country, where they were presumed to be, and effect their arrest. Golt and Green were taken into custody. They remained in jail until the third week of May, posses never relenting in their search for Dement and Roarke.

The State of Kansas vs. Dave Rudabaugh presented a dilemma. Was he to be tried for robbery in the first degree, or was he to be tried for stealing a pistol from Kincaid? In answer to the first, Rudabaugh demanded to know how much was robbed. With regard to the second, Kincaid had heard Roarke's voice and knew that the man who spoke was the one who relieved him of a pistol. Since the State had no case against him Rudabaugh insisted that he be given his freedom. The State rested on the first, but this was struck from the books since there had been no preliminary examination for the offense as charged. Masterson, Gryden, McCause, noting "Rudabaugh's bitterness toward the others and that he accused them of running out on him in their panic at the robbery, induced him to go all the way". Rudabaugh testified that he was promised entire immunity from punishment if he would "squeal;" the therefore, he "squole." Someone said there is a kind of honor among thieves; Rudabaugh didn't think so. Rudabaugh explained that he did not pursue Kincaid and the other man (the hotel clerk) as they seemed to be needing no help to get out of the way. In answer to the question of the judge, "Had you a pleasant home?" Two answered yes. One answered no. Two had mothers living; one a father, who was present. All had brothers and sisters. (*Kinsley Graphic*, June 22, 1878.)

Had the judge questioned more minutely, we might have had definite information as to whether Rudabaugh's father was killed in the war or died a natural death during the war years. The first one to be tried was Thomas Golt (some papers referred to him as Gott) [Gott is the correct name]. The jury was composed of J. E. Crane, A. L. Kendall, G. W. Wilson, J. F. White, W. L. Hunter, Walter Robley, T. J. Carter, S. S. Hart, J. D. Verney, George N. Wear, S. T. Reed, N. L. Mills. The lawyers for the prosecution were Edwards county attorney MacArthur, Capt. J. G. Waters, M. W. Sutton. The attorneys for the defense were B. F. Herrington and A. A. Hurd. The witnesses called were Andrew Kincaid, David Rudabaugh, W. H. Pettibone, J. W. Mallory, James Duffy, Charles Palmer, J. M. Anderson, Thomas Palmer, John Slattery and James Harnmond.

The first of the robbers to be tried was Thomas Golt (the paper uses Gott; we are using Golt for the sake of uniformity). [Rudabaugh, West, Gott, and Green were tried jointly on June 19, 1878, in Kinsley, in one room of the Cuddy Bank Building, which was serving as the Edwards County Courthouse]. He was represented by Messers Hurd and Harrington, who made a determined fight for their client. They first made the motion to squash the information from the files because no preliminary examination had been had and for other reasons. All these motions being overruled, the last resort was an application for a continuance, but the court was immovable, and the stubborn Golt was compelled to face his accusers and prepare to make his defense before the jury. County Attorney MacArthur of Edwards county, County Attorney Sutton of Ford county and Messers Burns and Waters prosecuted. The defense was very hopeful until that repentant sinner, Rudabaugh, the leader of the gang, was placed on the stand. He commenced in a firm, steady voice, and in a clear, concise manner told the court and the jury all about the robbery and who participated [see Appendix A for his confession]. He said that Mike Roarke was to take the lead and act as captain, but when the train ran past the point they had expected to board it, and thus compelled them to follow it up to the depot, Roarke weakened and the scheme was about to fall through. He then took the lead himself and proceeded to carry the robbery into execution. Two men boarded the engine. They were instructed to move on with the train when they heard two shots fired. While the others went to work on the express car, the messenger fired two shots.

The men on the engine supposed this to be the signal and accordingly started the engine, leaving Golt and two others behind. Golt saw the train moving out and looking around him noticed an excited mob gathering. He immediately drew his revolvers and commenced firing into the air causing the crowd to disperse in all directions. He then walked leisurely up the track to the hollow where the horses were hitched, and, finding the rest of the boys there, they all mounted and rode away. Golt was the leader of the party that entered the ticket office and attempted to rob the safe. (This was not the version given by other witnesses). When asked why he did not kill the agent when he refused to give up the money he answered that it was useless since they could not get the money even if they killed him.

After riding out into the plains for some miles, they stopped and waited for the Kinsley posse to arrive, intending to fight it out with them, but no posse came that way, so they rode on. By telling this story and thus insuring the conviction of his comrades, Golt [Rudabaugh] was set at liberty and went East fully resolving to rob no more. [Stanley is confusing Rudabaugh and Gott. Gott, after Rudabaugh's confession, facing conviction and ten years in the state penitentiary, admitted to the robbery and was given five years at hard labor, which he served]. After this testimony, the attorneys for the defense, seeing the hopelessness of their cause, prevailed upon their clients to plead guilty and throw themselves upon the mercy of the court. The jury was discharged without rendering any verdict and the court gave each prisoner the minimum sentence of five years hard labor at the State pen. In passing sentence, Judge Peters spoke for several minutes on the evils of the society of the day and showed how many of the crimes committed could have been prevented had the youth of the country better guidance and encouragement in developing their talents and resources...." (*Dodge City Times*, June 22, 1878)

The judge called on business men and leading citizens everywhere to look into the alarming climb of crimes by young people. Edgar West was described as "tall, low-browed, with black mustache and hair, and looks like a villain." (*Ford County Globe*, February 5, 1878)

Rudabaugh described Roarke as six feet tall, sandy complexion, blue eyes, sandy hair; wore a mustache and an imperial (i.e. a van dyke), weighed about one hundred and sixty pounds, and was thirty years of age. Dement he described as five feet eight inches tall; one hundred and fifty pounds; black eyes; a very thick black mustache; thin face; thirty years of age. West was said to have been a native of Illinois, and an escapee from the Arkansas penitentiary where he had been serving time for armed robbery. His father came to plead his cause. Old and crippled, he was unable to walk without the aid of a cane.

Meantime the hunt for Roarke and Dement continued. On the night of August 13, 1878, they robbed the Kansas City, St. Joseph & Council Bluffs Railroad of five thousand dollars. They boarded the train at Winthrop, Missouri, more successful here than they were at Kinsley. They were not apprehended until the night of October 20th, when they sought to hold up another train. In the gun battle that followed, Deputy Evander Light killed Dan Dement. Roarke surrendered, was taken to the Junction City jail and brought to Topeka, Kansas, to answer for the Kinsley robbery. He pleaded for a change of venue and the trial took place at El Dorado. He was sentenced for five years. Rudabaugh was brought to Butler county to testify against his former pal Roarke. After the trial Rudabaugh was put on a train and told never to show his face again in Kinsley. He rode as far as Newton, got off the train and made his way to Eureka and home. Unhappy and restless there, he wandered to Dodge, where he was given a job as a bartender. He was also employed as a shotgun messenger for the Adams Express Company [not true – he was hired as a Las Vegas city constable]. He hunted up J. J. Webb, who seems to have been responsible for getting him the job [Webb was already a city constable] and the two became staunch friends. The *Ford County Globe* for March 18, 1879, published the fact that Rudabaugh was back in Dodge for a job, but was wrong when it indicated he had gone straight: "Rudabaugh is in town looking for a job, and intends to earn his living on the square."

Chapter 3 | The Affair at Royal Gorge

There are about as many variations of the story behind the violence at Royal Gorge as there are accounts to confuse the reader. Told in a nutshell, one would say it was all thunder; no blood. More blood was spilt in the Maxwell Land Grant War or the Lincoln County War than was ever thought to have been spilt during the Royal Gorge War. This latter turned out to be nothing more than a series of threats and near threats; marches and counter-marches; commands and counter-commands. Narrowed down to actual violence, most of the action called for fists, stones, clubs and talk, although each side seemed to be waiting for the other before rifles and side arms were brought into play. Yet an imposing array of gunslingers, buffalo hunters, lawmen, rustlers could have made it the bloodiest story in all trans-Mississippi history, or at least Colorado history. The incident at Royal Gorge is part of the history of the Santa Fe Railroad. It is also part of the history of Rudabaugh and his friend J. J. [John Joshua] Webb. [Rudabaugh had NO involvement in the Royal Gorge War.] It is better to say that at best a bucket of blood was spilt rather than a stream. This seems startling for a day when spilling blood proved the exception rather than the rule.

Geologists have repeatedly made mention of the Mesozorio era; the age of reptiles; the Cretaceous period and mountain malting movements of millions of years ago when mysterious architects pushed granite and strate skywards to protect sun-baked valleys. Tourists, high school seniors, honeymooners, travelers marvel at such a thunderbolt hurled by the gods to form the geological monument known as the Royal Gorge of the Arkansas. Just a few years ago some high school graduates had a rendezvous with death when the bridge gave way. High winds make it a frightening place to visit. Explorer Fremont once remarked that the Royal Gorge was one of the few places designed by nature to keep man from bridging a gap. Fur trapper, Mountain man, Indian, prospector stood in awe of the canyon. Hunters never failed to write home about it; the westward movement engulfed it; the railroad accepted its challenge. Most of the destruction during the highly publicized display of tempers at Royal Gorge centered about railroad property.

Money may have been passed around in considerable amounts to keep hired guns in readiness but guns did not win the victory for the Royal Gorge. Lawyers ultimately proved once again that the push of the pen was mightier than the point of the six-shooter. Nevertheless, never before in Western gun play history were so many hired guns concentrated in one particular spot, waiting for something to pop so that they could blaze away at each other; one of the very rare instances in which gun toting sought to open a path for the advance of civilization. The Santa Fe and the Rio Grande provided drama in the race for the right of way over the Raton Pass from Colorado into New Mexico; the action was just as intense at Royal Gorge when both these railroads pitted engineering skill against the obstacles placed by nature in defiance of any building program in and about the gorge.

Raton Pass proved just as difficult but it was easier to cut through a mountain than to squeeze through a narrow defile. I, for one, have never been able to go through the old files of the Cimarron papers, with their stories of William Ray Morley (Ray, Jr., for all his football prowess walked with death in his eyes as his father before him), without a sense of foreboding, melancholia, storm clouds gathering, a feeling of panic and fright such as overhangs the story of Beatrice Cenci from the date of her birth to her tragic death. One comes to the conclusion that the successes of life never stack up against the tragedies. Morley of Cimarron – engineer, rancher, stockman, newspaperman, politico, fighter, Maxwell Land Grant agent, thorn in the side of the Santa Fe Ring, leader of the Cimarron Ring, friend of the Utes, Jicarilla Apaches, builder – Morley, who crowded a hundred lifetimes into thirty-eight well spent years. He was the right man for his times; the only voice at Royal Gorge powerful enough to call off a massacre. Had Wyatt Earp, Ben Thompson or even Clay Allison masterminded action at Royal Gorge the story would have been differently told. Using Clifton House at the foot of Raton Pass as headquarters, Morley was able to keep an eye on events in Trinidad, Colorado, and figure each move as the Iron Horse puffed out of Colorado into New Mexico.

Palmer and Hunter of the rival Rio Grande railroad dreamed of making a fortune by locating a townsite at El Moro [Colorado – the name El Moro is a derivative spelling of El Morro, which is Spanish for "Moor"], a Spanish league from Trinidad. This caused some concern in various circles as Trinidad had been promised the railroad center. The townspeople called a meeting and decided that since the Rio Grande failed to honor its promise perhaps the Santa Fe would oblige, especially since the high and mighty Palmer, in his excitement against a competitor, overlooked the importance of filing a plat or a least a profile. This left an opening for the rival railroad. First come; first served. Morley saved the Raton Pass for the Santa Fe. He might have failed had it not been for the old Mountain Man and pioneer, Dick Wooton.

Morley was with J. A. McCurtrie in 1871, when the Rio Grande surveyed the Royal Gorge. Here again the same fatal mistake was made. No one filed the plat. Canon City (Colorado) had ambitions of communication with the outside world and hoped that the Rio Grande would establish at least freight service out of the town in an effort to attract more settlers. The railroad did everything possible to further those ambitions, at least on paper. But, before long the citizens were disillusioned. The track came to a halt at Labran, eight miles short of the town. Freighters did a whale of a business. Canon City was doomed. Business men read the handwriting on the wall, To induce the railroad to move on to the city, the town voted bonds and track was laid to within a mile of Canon City, then veered off in the direction of Veta Pass, establishing townsites as it rolled and ignoring the good will of the citizens of Canon City. Unruffled, these latter founded the Canon City & San Juan Railroad, made surveys and filed them with the Secretary of the Interior. Meantime Leadville came up with some rich strikes and Morley's ears went up like those of a boxer dog on the alert. Like Trinidad, Canon City was now Santa Fe-minded despite the rantings of General Palmer who insisted that this was Rio Grande territory, especially since his railroad came to within a mile of Canon City.

Engineers McMurtrie and [J. G.] De Remer were at El Moro, Miguel Otero tells in his three volume study of the period. McMurtrie received a telegram from Palmer ordering him to rush a crew to the end of track, due east of Canon City, and use all possible speed in building at Royal Gorge. The wire, sent in code, became the property of the Santa Fe engineers. This is not at all surprising as both lines resorted to every trick in the book and a good many not in the book in the push for Raton Pass and the Royal Gorge. Engineer [A. A.] Robinson of the Santa Fe was as much at home with the plans of the Rio Grande as General Palmer himself. In the beginning the crews from El Moro were hired hands. As both sides stepped up the pace they enlisted hired guns. The Santa Fe man from El Moro asked for a train from the Rio Grande people to take him to Canon City. The Rio Grande officials said that this was adding insult to injury. They not only denied the request but also refused to let through all telegrams destined for Canon City. Morley's blood boiled. As he entrained for La Juncta, he formed plans to bring the Rio

Grande to its knees. The Royal Gorge was definitely a challenge. The newspapers got into the act. Editors with a nose for news scented the dramatic in the offering and stirred up mob violence with their editorials. Some papers were for Palmer; others for Morley. Net result: mob violence. Blood and thunder, battle smoke, bodies strewn along the right of way; this and more was fed the reading public by editors with lively imaginations. Too many authors have failed to separate the fact from fiction. A story made the rounds about Morley riding his horse to death in order to beat the Rio Grande that now decided to build into Canon City. The ride was as exciting as that of Paul Revere on the eve of the Revolution, and to Morley, no less important but he loved horses too much to ride any to death. Morley's account of the ride was less pretentious and neither he, or his daughter, who took to writing during the last years of her life, quite agreed that the Otero and other accounts were quite embellished.

A crew, under the sponsorship of the Rio Grande, entrained from El Moro. The Santa Fe had one chance – a slim one, but a possible one to get a crew to the Royal Gorge before the section gang of the opposition arrived. Canon City, still pouting at the Rio Grande, swung its allegiance to the Santa Fe. Pueblo was a good forty miles from Canon City. Morley had a horse at Pueblo. A fine steed he called King William. On more than one occasion, Clay Allison offered double the value but Morley refused to sell. He favored this animal above all the others in his stable. Even after the eventful run Allison kept trying, sending note after note to Mrs. Morley, all bearing the same request that she talk her husband into selling King William. Realizing that no time was to be lost if the Santa Fe was to get ahead at the Royal Gorge, Morley eased the animal along at a, brisk trot, then galloped him, trotted, walked, raced, walked, galloped into Canon City before the arrival of the Rio Grande train and signed on a crew thus winning the right of way for the Santa Fe.

King William did not drop dead within sight of Canon City; Morley did not finish the race on foot as most authors are prone to write. That is all there was to it. King William became a family pet after that ride. He was put to pasture in Cimarron, and later enjoyed the tall grasses of the Datil country where he eventually died of old age, outliving his master by many years. Morley's first words when he reached Canon City were: "The Santa Fe is here."

Hardware stores were able to supply picks, shovels, axes, crow bars, pails, nails, accessories. The Denver & Rio Grande men arrived some thirty-five minutes after the A. T. & S. F. commenced laying track. The Santa Fe men, inspired by Morley's loyalty and courage, worked with a will. This activity failed to alarm the Rio Grande men who rolled up their sleeves and started digging parallel to the Santa Fe men. They shouted across to the opposition that they aimed to beat them to the Royal Gorge. The foreman of the Rio Grande crew asked the foreman of the Santa Fe workers to gather his men and take them back to Canon City. The Santa Fe boss simply told his men to work harder. Then the Rio Grande foreman went in quest of more recruits to swell the ranks of laborers. Not to be outdone, the Santa Fe foreman followed suit. By April 22nd, grading was under way. The Santa Fe organized a pony express to handle communications. Materials came from Leadville for the most part, any anywhere else nails, buckets, axes, picks, shovels and crow bars could be found. Much of the time was spent in cussing each other as they worked. Morley quieted his men; so did McMurtrie lest they advance from cursing to pick, fist and shovel swinging. Both engineers lay awake nights hoping to arrive at a solution to the difficulty. Men were employed to construct rock forts at locations valuable for their strategic military possibilities. Bloodshed was expected momentarily. The wonder was that both crews had come this far unscathed. Morley felt that from the stares, mutterings and threats that built up antagonism on both sides, these stone forts might come in handy. He pleaded with the opposition to let the courts come up with a solution but they were adamant.

Construction continued on the railroad as well as the forts. McMurtrie and De Remer agreed that the final decision certainly rested with the courts, but who was to decide for men bent on destroying each other? The county judge favored the Santa Fe, and an injunction was issued against the Rio Grande which was ordered to stop work and leave the area to the A.T.&S.F. A deputy served the court order and McMurtrie ordered his men to obey it. But not all left. The restraining order said nothing about the fortresses which were well garrisoned and provisioned. Each defender was given arms and ammunition in abundance.

Then followed more writs, injunctions, orders, briefs, decisions, pro and con; now the Rio Grande; now the Santa Fe. The Rio Grande forced the Santa Fe crews out of the Gorge, and the judge held that the Rio Grande acted "in contempt of court." The *Denver Gazette* devoted its columns to exalting the Rio Grande and called the Santa Fe to task for stirring up unnecessary trouble.

The *Rocky Mountain News* echoed the sentiments of the *Gazette*. But the Santa Fe was not without its champions in Denver. *The Denver Tribune* considered the A.T.&S.F. in the right and asked the Rio Grande to fold up and go home. The *Pueblo Chieftain* joined forces with the *Canon City Record* in berating the Rio Grande. Editors and publishers had a ball. They spilt blood by the bucketful, wrote up imaginary gunfights gunsmoke, gore and thunder greeted the reader at every turn of the page. The editors felt that this was an interesting change from Indian raids, silver strikes, rustlers, horse thieves, and the Royal Gorge came in for more than its share of publicity. The extent of the damage in terms of dollars and cents, including the amount expended in hiring gun-slingers, guns, ammunition, provisions, during the Royal Gorge War amounted to one half million dollars, a tremendous sum considering that the value of the dollar was one hundred pennies.

If the Santa Fe succeeded in placing ties during the day the Rio Grande crews destroyed them at night. Nor did the Santa Fe men permit such destruction to go unavenged. Rio Grande tracks were torn up also. Rocks were rolled down from the dizzy heights that walled the gorge on the noggins of the workers below causing both sides to slow up. Rio Grande crews tossed workmen's tools into the river; Santa Fe men used black powder-dynamite on Rio Grande tracks. De Remer enticed many of the Santa Fe workers to the Rio Grande side by the offer of an increase in salary. He built more fortresses and went to Dodge to hire shotgun messengers whose job it was to protect Rio Grande men against Santa Fe boulder-rolling tactics. The leader of these hired guns was J. J. Webb, the erstwhile lawman of Dodge who took Rudabaugh under his wing after the Kinsley trial [not true]. Webb has been variously reported as Chief of Guards for the Santa Fe or the Rio Grande, depending on the whim of the writers. The *Las Vegas Optic*, which should know, places him with the Rio Grande [it reports Webb with the Santa Fe, not the Rio Grande]. The Santa Fe was known to have made several attempts to bribe him for the opposition but he remained steadfast. In one of the rock throwing, club swinging forays between the two outfits, Webb lost a tooth which he had replaced by one of solid gold. This tooth was to prove his downfall. It became his Mark of Cain. With Webb at Royal Gorge was the ubiquitous Dave Rudabaugh [Rudabaugh was never at Royal Gorge during this time period]. It was a strange friendship but a lasting one. Yet it was no more stranger than that of Doc Holliday and Wyatt Earp, although it is doubtful that Holliday would have done for Webb what Rudabaugh did, and visa versa. Earp wasn't that concerned about Doc Holliday. Webb and Rudabaugh were a strange pair, drawn to each other like moths to a flame, suspecting that the end would only spell tragedy for one or the other, or both. In Webb, Rudabaugh found the loyalty he failed to find in Roarke, Dement and Golt [Gott]. A study of frontiersmen and their ways reveals many such friendships especially among trappers, mountain men, cowboys, gamblers, buffalo hunters and freighters. Loyalty was the keynote for such attachments, even if the result meant death. Webb-Rudabaugh; Earp-Holliday; Kingfisher-Thompson; MacIntyre-Courtright are a few such combinations that seemingly have no explanation save that they existed. Of all these, Rudabaugh's end was to be the most violent.

The coffee break is not new; it is merely a revival of an old custom. In those days a man went out to wet his whistle with grog, hard liquor, gut-rot usually watered down or otherwise flavored with dead snakes, mice, prairie dog or anything that would give it body – or even soul. If it didn't have the kick of a mule, it was quite lame indeed. Sometimes cowboys would spot the contents of the bottom of the keg and pepper the bartender with lead. Some boot hills received the barkeep whose only fault was a snake or two in the whisky. Despite such revolting concoctions, the liquor break was always popular. The two most important moments in the life of a bartender were evening and pay day. Most frontier bars were alike in this respect, but the end of track towns made a specialty of frequenting the clip joints after work and on pay day.

At the time Webb and Rudabaugh defended the Royal Gorge, Pueblo, Colorado, boasted the largest gambling house in the nation. It was on Main Street, as big as sin and just as alluring. It was the big brother of a brood of lesser spots none the less notorious and rowdy. Faro banks, roulette wheels, dice tables, poker tables, keno, beer, potent drinks, free lunch all to be found in any one of the noisy resorts. The doors were never locked. The Main Street house employed fifty men and kept everything in operation around the clock. After all the railroad worker's pay was gone, he shook hands with the bartender and promised to return next payday. Meantime, no amount of drinking, carousing, hired guns stopped the push through the Royal Gorge. Judge Hallet ordered both sides to cease work until the decision of the Supreme Court would give one railroad the right of way once and for all. Nature did not intend for two rail lines to squeeze through the chasm. While awaiting the momentous decision, most of the men decided to board a train for a fun fest in Pueblo. They paraded the streets, sang in boisterous glee, skipped from one cantina to the next, guzzled anything and everything like a horde of thirsty long horns fearful of never reaching the next water-hole; they whooped, shouted, wined, dined, climbed and chimed as drunks are wont to do. They raided chicken roosts, took clothes from the lines on which they were set to dry, hurrahed the town and kept the police in a near state of shock and collapse with their frantic antics, and proved too much handling even for the wily cantina owners. They acted like a bunch of wild savages let loose in the land of plenty. Suddenly, the Santa Fe ordered them back to work despite their condition, or lack of condition, and the Rio Grande, not to be outdone, loaded three cars with gunslingers, laborers, crewman and others spoiling for a fight, vomited the load at Canon City and told them to get on the job. As much as Webb and Rudabaugh resented being herded like driven sheep, they complied because it was part of the bargain. Pueblo settled down to comparative quiet as least until the next pay day.

Even today Main Street in the mighty steel city of Colorado wears, or appears to wear, the split personality of charm and challenge. It takes several visits to recognize that it has something new to offer with each visit – never tiresome nor boring – possibly because it has preserved somewhat of its Western flavor without too much ballyhoo, despite the steel mills.

Canon City was no different from any other end-of-track town during the struggle for the deep canyon of the Arkansas. It was parceled its share of rowdies, gamblers, women who catered to hidden desires, land sharks, shysters, con men, thieves, rustlers, highwaymen and the run-of-the-mill hangers-on, who came to life only when loaded to the gills with the collected last drops from cups, glasses, pails and bottles. Every tent town, end-of-track town, frontier-post town and settlement had its skid row, conspicuous in print by their very absence. Skid Row was never as attractive as Front St. with its dance halls, joints and fancy houses. Such places never lacked for women to keep things alive. They later become part of the story of mining and rich strikes. More and more Western magazines are turning to them to re-evaluate the part they played in settling the West, not condoning how they made their living, but admiring what they put up with along the raw frontier. Somehow, such women, perhaps unworthy to lift the first stone, let alone throw it, were in one accord in their contempt for Dave Rudabaugh, who no doubt, was as rough with them as the Border Ruffian was with the people he handled.

De Remer's success in hiring Webb and others to garrison the forts in the interests of the Rio Grande induced the Santa Fe to follow a similar course by inviting in Bat Masterson who hired a hundred men for the showdown. Doc Holliday, Ben Thompson and a number of other notable gunslingers rode with Masterson to the Royal Gorge. Most of Masterson's men found enough to keep them busy at Pueblo. It was as if they had never left Dodge. After a taste of life at Pueblo it was with some difficulty that many could be persuaded to move on to Royal Gorge. Prospects of higher pay, some said, induced Rudabaugh to change his allegiance and espouse the Santa Fe cause. This may be a correct surmise since money was a factor with Dave Rudabaugh. His salary went the way of all flesh at Pueblo, but he had fun while it lasted. He later admitted to some stage hold-ups at this period because he wished to continue the night life at Pueblo [not true; since he never was at Royal Gorge, he never admitted to any holdups there]. It is well known that with all those gunmen in and about the Royal Gorge, horse stealing and cattle rustling hit a new high. With all those desperadoes milling about how could anyone expect anything less? How much Dave Rudabaugh had to do with the over-all picture during these days is pure guess work for he merely mentioned them in passing [he did not] during his trial at Las Vegas and at Santa Fe, admitting to only hold-ups, rustling and robbing in which he was personally involved, without implicating anyone else. Rudabaugh could be very annoying to the Court because of his evasive answers in which he kept the discussion only on Rudabaugh; not his accomplices [Rudabaugh did name his accomplices for the two stage robberies he committed]. Nor were gamblers, Cyprians, bartenders any more helpful. It was no concern of theirs where the money came from once their claws folded it.

Santa Fe placed as many as three hundred men under arms, one hundred of these being turncoats from the Rio Grande due to the higher wages paid by the railroad willing to risk a private war rather than lose the right of way through the Royal Gorge. The Santa Fe won the first round in court; the Rio Grande won the next, a right to build in the canyon, thus making the score one even. Santa Fe lawyers were loud and strenuous in their objections because the floor of the canyon offered barely sufficient room for one set of rails. An amendment to the court order was issued permitting the Rio Grande to use this set of tracks through those places in the gorge too narrow for a double set. The fight now shifted to the beautiful valley above the canyon where the Rio Grande and the Santa Fe had room for parallel lines. Here gunslingers stood like guardian angels over the workers of each side waiting for the opposition to fire the first shot.

The Rio Grande sought an injunction against the rival road's grading west of the canyon. General Palmer had the edge here and he knew it. This time he left nothing to chance nor his lieutenants. He himself filed a plat. Now the court favored the Rio Grande, and the score read: two to one; one even. Smarting under the heavy blow dealt by Palmer, the Santa Fe moved up the San Luis valley, pointed north, then west, in the direction of Denver. Now it was Palmer who sat up and took notice. He worked out a compromise, leading the Rio Grande system to the Santa Fe. Peace was short lived. Robinson insisted that the lease called for the grading of the road to Leadville. Palmer counter-charged that the Santa Fe had agreed to call off all operation of the parallel line from Canon City, Pueblo to Denver. The Santa Fe made use of its tracks to rush crews and materials to complete the work in the gorge. The Rio Grande built more stone forts and garrisoned a spot known as Twenty Mile Post. The court, fearful of bloodshed, ordered a "cease work" decree for both sides, receiving the secret gratitude of the men in so doing for snow storms and slides endangered both their work and their lives. It was bad enough to be in jeopardy of gunslingers without nature taking a hand.

By March 1879, Palmer had worked himself into such a stew that he accused the Santa Fe of breaking the lease, and said that he was taking his railroad back. Dodge, general manager of the Rio Grande, scouted about for a gang of men willing and able to storm the depots and guarantee that the line would be restored to Palmer, even if it meant killing all the Santa Fe station masters, freighters, expressmen, conductors, engineers. They stormed the baggage room at Colorado Springs, but when the Santa Fe men let loose a rain of lead from handy Winchesters, the Rio Grande men agreed that discretion was the better part of valor. They hurried out of rifle range. The only reason there were no casualties was that the Santa Fe gunmen had orders to aim high. Trains ran at the discretion of the engineers who took shotgun messengers along for protection. Stations along the route were filled with gunslingers waiting for the Rio Grande officials to bark out the "shoot-to-kill" order. They seemed a trifle more anxious for bloodshed than the Santa Fe hirelings.

Meantime the courts decided that the Rio Grande had priority rights to the Royal Gorge. With this decision in his pocket, Palmer decided he had the undisputed right to the canyon and took along a number of men to oust the troublesome undesirables of the opposition. Santa Fe wires were cut. Again men on both side took to glaring, staring, daring one another to fire the first shot. Robinson asked the governor of Colorado to order out the militia. The State Guard of Denver, the sheriffs at Colorado Springs and Pueblo were ordered ready to move at a moment's notice. Palmer, who was reasonably certain that the posses raised by both these sheriffs would favor the Santa Fe, asked for more gunslingers.

There are many versions of Bat Masterson's part in the fight for the Royal Gorge, and it is rather difficult to separate the fact from fiction. One story tells of Masterson and his men being surrounded in the roundhouse at Pueblo. After an hour's parley, Masterson is supposed to have sold out to the Rio Grande. Treasurer Robert Weitbrec is reputed to have paid out ten thousand dollars for the switch. Another author places this incident on the same day as the fight at Raton Pass. Either he took the facts for granted or he was too concerned with Bat Masterson. About December 1, 1878, the last spike went in and Uncle Avery rode the first engine over the switchback and down into New Mexico – the first man ever to enter the Territory on a locomotive. With the line now operating down to Willow Springs (present Raton), material, powder and men could be shipped up to the south portal of the tunnel. The headings met – out of the traditional fraction of an inch –

at 3:35 on the afternoon of July 7, 1879. (Marshall, *Santa Fe, The Railroad That Built An Empire,* page 141) The author makes no mention of payola to Masterson.

"And finally it might be feared that the Santa Fe would tap northern New Mexico via Trinidad and rob the Rio Grande of any prospective traffic she was likely to get through the development of that Territory.... As it was, the Santa Fe crossed the divide, gained the cost and became a transcontinental railroad while the Rio Grande still is confined to three states. Small wonder, then, that on February 26, 1878, Strong ordered Robinson in haste to Raton Pass, and to seize and hold the Pass against all opposition. William Morley got together a crowd of men with shovels, and returning had detailed this party at several strategic points through the Pass and were busily grading for the Santa Fe railroad by 5:00 A. M.... To avoid delay, the Pass was surmounted by a 'switch-back,' which was boldly conceived by Chief Engineer A. A. Robinson, and on December 7, 1878, a locomotive traveled over the summit and into New Mexico. The Santa Fe crossed the first barrier of the Rockies over the strategic Raton Pass and the long contemplated entrance of New Mexico had at last been made...." (Bradley, *The Story Of The Santa Fe,* pp 162-182 inter.)

"On April 21, 1879, it appeared that there would be an all out battle between the Santa Fe and Rio Grande forces at Pueblo...." (O'Conner, *Bat Masterson,* page 156.) The author goes on to say that Masterson and fifty gunfighters from Dodge were ready with a Gatling gun, rifles, shotguns, and revolvers. Engineer Robinson testified that there were only thirty gunfighters with Masterson. Morley was able to take the firing pins from the rifles and shotguns unobserved – probably the boys were out celebrating which may account for the reason why Weitbrec's money was more acceptable than gunsmoke.

Engineer De Remer stuck to his guns at Spike Buck Camp, fortifying himself behind a stone construction fifteen feet square, four feet high, and not unlike the structures found near Manzano, New Mexico, known as torreons, save that the New Mexico forts were round and built to withstand the inroads of Comanche and Apache hordes penetrating westward, while De Remer intended his fort to keep out bullets, not cannon balls, as suggested by a recent biographer of Bat Masterson. De Remer sent a note to Robinson demanding that he get out of the canyon or take the consequences, De Remer alerted his men to meet the expected attack. He mounted the rampart and ordered the Santa Fe men to halt. Morley, who headed the contingent, demanded to know by what authority. Pointing behind him to the armed men, De Remer said: "These men and all courts are my authority." Morley looked at the men behind him, then back to the men behind De Remer. He motioned his men back, yelling to De Remer: "You win, we don't want men killed needlessly."

At this juncture word arrived that the courts had ordered the Santa Fe to cease operations and abandon the narrow gauge line. Sheriffs of the counties involved were ordered to seize all Santa Fe property, and to resort to the use of arms if necessary. But first they must try persuasion and peaceful means. In East Denver deputies broke down the doors of the Santa Fe offices and took possession by order of the court. Men armed with rifles boarded Santa Fe trains and converted them into travelling fortresses. Roundhouse were seized, the locomotives still in them. A train load of armed men was dispatched south of Denver to protect Rio Grande interests along the right of way. The sheriff at Pueblo had his hands full. Morley's hired men ran this official out of the depot at gunpoint. He dispatched a telegram to the governor asking for State Militia but was informed that it was a private affair between two railroads, not the concern of the State of Colorado. Unruffled at the rebuke, he swore in more deputies, and headed for the depot.

Firing on both sides was fast, furious and futile. More like a Fourth of July celebration. Guns popping, bullets whizzing, men shouting – but no damage done to either side.

Eventually, the attackers closed in on the dispatcher's office and captured it without bloodshed. Bat Masterson and his men took over the roundhouse. The Rio Grande sent out another train in charge of Hunt, a former governor, who stopped the train at each station and captured it in the name of the Rio Grande Railroad. All the captured Santa Fe agents were placed on the train and guarded by two hundred armed men. Here occurred the only casualties of the war. Two Santa Fe agents who decided to fight it out were killed. Two others were wounded when they refused to surrender. At Canon City, the Santa Fe men defended the depot until they ran out of ammunition. Men on the southbound train, captained by De Remer (who had enlisted the aid of the sheriff and his posse), fought for the Colorado Springs depot. It was at this place that the State Militia stood by to protect civilians and to keep the battle from getting out of hand. They decided that only railroad men and their hired help were to shoot it out.

One can imagine Dave Rudabaugh having a ball while all this was going on. It was like the old days when cowboys hurrahed Dodge as they rode up and down the streets. He got in a good deal of target practice pumping lead into depots, baggage rooms, stations. The grandest part of the whole venture was that he was getting paid for it. Apparently no one was seriously intending wholesome slaughter or many more lives would have been lost.

By the time half of June went by, the Rio Grande went into the hands of receivers. Palmer, Hunt, De Remer construed this action on the part of the courts as prejudice against their road, so they fortified the depot at Pueblo, and defied the authorities. Here was less display of guns but sticks, rocks and fists more than made up for them as the Rio Grande men discovered when they ventured out of the station. A court order was received on June 2 demanding that the Rio Grande return to the Santa Fe all the property confiscated by Hunt on his wild ride. Robinson continued to work at his desk in the upstairs office at the Pueblo depot, keeping two loaded revolvers in view should the occasion arise for their use. Once when the pay car was late several hundred men gathered about the depot and began demonstrations for their pay. This was the work of gamblers, bartenders, dance hall girls and ladies of confused virtue who felt they stood to lose more than the men if no money circulated that week-end. The bartenders had a hard and fast rule: No money; no drinks. Robinson did his best to placate the mob. He promised them that they would have their pay on the morrow – only those who had earned it. The others were wasting their time and his. He said that he had long been aware of payroll padding. This was as good a time as any for the showdown. A bullet whizzed by and lodged in the wall behind him. The engineer picked up his revolvers and defied them: "That's a silly thing," he told them "kill me and nobody gets paid. Who has the authority to sign for the payroll?"

Crowd recognized the wisdom of his words, and confined its violence to threats and curses. Robinson accepted the police protection offered him, and cut through the mob to his hotel. The men were paid off the next day as he had promised, Meantime, the Santa Fe continued to build slowly but surely. By the time August rolled around the tracks were twenty-three miles out of the disputed passage. The Rio Grande had graded eight miles of narrow gauge road that seemed to go nowhere and ended in the wilderness, the tracks being unconnected at either end. The Santa Fe men constructed a fort beyond the Rio Grande line hoping to stop De Remer just as the Rio Grande built one twenty-three miles out of Canon City, making every effort to outwit Morley.

West of the fort, the Santa Fe graded to Leadville hoping to open the road early in the fall. Jay Gould had been watching the progress of both lines and decided to throw his financial aid and his influence on the side of the Rio Grande. Relieved at this turn of events the Rio Grande decided to move into New Mexico, parallel to the Santa Fe. Robinson, Dodge and others argued that this line of action would benefit neither railroad. Was it worth bankrupting the Rio Grande just to get back at the Santa Fe! On December 20, the Santa Fe, Union Pacific and Kansas Pacific worked out a freighting agreement that put a halt to the Rio Grande plans. The armed forces decided there was no further need for their guns so they disbanded to shoot up other towns. Many stayed with the Santa Fe as it hurdled the Pass with the help of old Dick Wooton, and had a time of themselves at the new town of Raton, then on to Otero and finally at Las Vegas, where the story of Dave Rudabaugh continues. Gunsmoke followed train smoke down the line into New Mexico. End-of-track towns from Raton to Albuquerque were not without their bucket of blood, and a "man for breakfast" ceased to be the exception to the rule.

On March 27, the board of directors of both lines held a meeting to settle their differences. The Rio Grande promised to pay the Santa Fe more than a million dollars for all the construction west of Canon City; the Santa Fe promised to discontinue any further attempt into Leadville and Denver. This contract was to bind for ten years. The Rio Grande was able to continue through the gorge unimpeded, and built into Leadville. The first engine to complete the trip was appropriately named the De Remer.

The first train pulled into Leadville in July, 1880. Cooler heads ultimately prevailed. Gunsmoke was not the answer to empire building. The West could be opened to settlement without the aid of roaring guns at Royal Gorge or Raton Pass. Eventually, Raton Pass proved the answer; not Royal Gorge. Raton, Cunningham, Otero, Wagonmound, Springer, Maxwell City, Las Vegas, Glorieta, Lamy, and hundreds of other towns of California convinced the Santa Fe stockholders that the selection over Raton Pass was the wisest along the line.

The first train puffed into Las Vegas on July 1, but the event was not commemorated until three days later [July 4, 1878] to coincide with national holiday. The Glorious Fourth has seen many a "fifth" ever since. Dave Rudabaugh seems to have been on hand for the occasion, although he, like many others, found it hard the next day to remember just what happened. Dan Daley, the engineer; Charles Brooks, the conductor; Miguel Otero, John Dold, Andrew Dold, and a number of other distinguished citizens knew it would be a day long remembered.

The Exchange Hotel in Old Las Vegas, and Close & Patterson's in New Town, were the most popular spots in town that night. The dancing at the Exchange was more dignified. Close & Patterson's was an interesting spot near the site of the Castenada Hotel. No story of Las Vegas can be told without some mention of Close & Patterson's. Rudabaugh spent much of his time here and gave the dance hall girls a rough time. Through its doors passed Bat Masterson, Doc Holliday, Luke Short, Wyatt Earp, Jim Mcintyre, Jim Courtright, Mysterious Dave Mather, Hoodoo Brown, Dutch Henry, Dutchy, Billy the Kid, J. J. Webb, Jesse James (incognito arrived July 23, 1879, to take the baths at the hot springs of the Adobe House [Hotel], later the site of the famous Montezuma [it was nearby, not at the site]), Ben Thompson so many more contemporaries of the more famous – or infamous gunslingers. Carson, Webb, Mather and Rudabaugh were to make New Town [East Las Vegas] the base of their operations as they held up stages from Las Vegas to Canoncito, and continued their activities as rustlers. New Town was to prove Trail's End for many. Unlike Dodge, the Boot Hill at Las Vegas was not to receive as its first customers men from the railroad who died of disease, but men who died with their boots on. For most readers of Western folklore, Dave Rudabaugh first comes to light during these Las Vegas days. They are the most important in his life.

[Rudabaugh robbed a stage only once while living in Las Vegas. On August 14, 1879, he, Joseph Martin, and Joe Carson stopped and robbed the National Mail and Transportation Company's stage four miles south of Las Vegas, near Tecolote. William Mullen and brothers Joseph and William Stokes were convicted of the robbery and sentenced to two and a half years in jail. They were released after Rudabuagh confessed to the robbery and named his two accomplices. They served 16 months of their false sentence. They were in jail in Las Vegas during Rudabaugh's trial for killing jailer Antonio Lino Valdez, and Mullen even testified in Rudabaugh's defense during that trial. See *"Dirty Dave" Rudabaugh, Billy the Kid's Most Feared Companion*.]

Chapter 4 | Las Vegas Days

During World War II, it was my privilege to spend many happy hours with the boys of the Ferry Command stationed at Camp Maximiano Luna up on "the hill," as it was often referred to, between the hamlet of Montezuma and Las Vegas. For many it was their first experience away from home; for most it was their first experience with New Mexico. Some, starved for excitement, would ask: "Doesn't anything ever happen around here? Boy, what a dead place! Give it back to the Indians. How can you stand it here?" It was not always so. It wasn't so now. It was wrong to compare the culture of the Southwest with that of New York, Pennsylvania and New Jersey. The ghosts of Vicente Silva, Dave Rudabaugh, Dave Mather, Billy the Kid, Jim Greathouse, J. J. Webb and others must have often tendered benign, tolerant smiles assuming they are habiting the place where smiles are permitted to hear such talk. A little reading would have convinced the homesick GI's that they were in the heart of what was once the most exciting little spot in all of the West. It all began when New Town [East Las Vegas] (Old Town [West Las Vegas] also came in for its share of night life) sprang into being as an "end-of-track" town catering to gunslingers, gamblers, dance hall girls, Cyprians, frontier lawyers, con men, land sharks, cattle buyers, horse thieves, rustlers, peddlers, drummers and all sorts and conditions of men and women who changed night into day at Close & Patterson's [Saloon]. Also Center Street was quite the place with its row of saloons, brothels, gaming rooms, lodging houses, eating places, dance halls, law offices, smithy shops, corrals and other accruements of frontierville.

There was excitement around the clock, almost to the turn of the century, when Vicente Silva and his Forty Bandits terrorized the country. The boys in the Service would have relished talking to old timers if they were interested in that sort of thing then as they are now with the rise of True Westerns, TV Westerns, Movie Westerns and Western Styles in dress. To have spent all that time in the very warehouse of the frontier and have failed to recognize it! Boys at Highland University in Las Vegas are taking better advantage of their opportunity. History courses saturate them in the folklore of the West, and they are afforded every opportunity to hunt up the few remaining old-timers for term papers. Really there is no need to look further than the city of Las Vegas itself. This was the town (Old Las Vegas) that General Kearny selected to indicate that New Mexico, as a conquered province, was now a part of the United States. Actually, he had no choice. It was the first town in his path on his march from Colorado. From then on it was touch and go – Mountain Men, Buffalo Hunters, Railroad Men, soldiers from Fort Union, soldiers from the post at the very town of Las Vegas itself, cattlemen, gunmen, national celebrities passing through to take the baths at the Hot Springs, royalty from abroad enjoying the fine fountains at the Montezuma.

Moving south with railroad, Rudabaugh was convinced he would be more successful at Las Vegas than at Raton or Otero. Furthermore Webb and a number of other friends were really "in" around New Town. It is "Jim" [James] Allen, a waiter at the St. Nicholas Hotel, who brings Rudabaugh into the picture at Las Vegas. One of the guests at the hostel was James Morehead who enjoying the luxury of being late for breakfast. One day Allen called him down on it, and some harsh words were spoken. "Imagine the nerve of the fellow," Morehead told Miguel Otero later, "Just twenty-three and trying to run the show." Morehead as a drummer (salesman) and a member of the Leavenworth, Kansas, firm of O. R. Morehead & Co. He enjoyed a good cigar and a good game of poker whenever in Las Vegas, Naturally, this latter was not conducive to early rising and Allen's temper mounted.

It was long past nine one fine morning when Morehead came down to breakfast. Allen again reproached him for his laziness. Morehead replied that his living habits were his own and not open to the criticism of any waiter in the hotel. Allen walked into the kitchen, borrowed a gun from the dish-washer and fired at Morehead. The bullet entered the stomach and passed through the left side. Morehead was carried to his room and a waiter went in quest of a doctor. The drummer died that evening at ten thirty. J. J. Webb and Dave Mather, who were connected with the city police force, delegated Dave Rudabaugh to stand across the street from the hotel and report from time to time on the condition of the wounded man. When news leaked out of his death, Rudabaugh went to the marshal's office and told Webb.

Men in cantinas discussed the shooting and agreed that if Morehead died Allen would be invited to a neck-tie party. Report of the death was soon telegraphed and the men poured out into the streets to converge on the jail where Allen was taken shortly after the shooting. Another mob gathered at the hotel. Webb and Mather went there and asked Otero to talk to the mob. They then went to the jail and selected twelve men whose duty it was to protect the prisoner from violence. One of these guards was Dave Rudabaugh. Webb left orders to shoot down anyone attempting to storm the jail. The mob left the hotel and marched to the jail and joined the other voices in demanding the prisoner but no one wanted to make the first move against twelve pointed guns. They dispersed. Justice of the Peace Hoodoo Brown and "Jim" [James] Allen were well known to each other, and the prisoner was certain his friend would find a way out for him despite the bleakness of the outlook.

After a time, when Webb and Mather thought they had it licked, a few of the mob returned and talked to the jailer. Money traded hands. He would look the other way when Allen opened the cell door. Three others in the jail feared the mob would hang them to revenge Allen's escape. They decided to tag along. [This story is based on Miguel Antonio Otero's memoirs, but the evidence from primary sources is that there was NO conspiracy to let the prisoners escape so that they could be killed in being recaptured. The six men who escaped were: Webb, "Jim" [James] Allen, George Davidson, John Murray, William Mullen, and George Davis.] The vigilantes were aware of all this, tracking the fugitives to Aguilar Hill about thirty miles east of Vegas, near Chaperito. The four were surrounded. The bodies were shortly afterwards returned to Las Vegas on a buckboard. [Only Davidson and Allen were killed by the posse. Mullen walked to Las Vegas and turned himself in. Webb and Davis were captured by Deputy Sheriff Pat Garrett November 25, 1880. Murray evidently got away clean.] Brown, Boyle, Mather, Wilson and Rudabaugh voiced a protest but nobody listened. Las Vegas scoffed at the idea of Mather and Rudabaugh speaking of justice for the four criminals. Both were looking upon as mobsters not in the position to say whether the vigilantes were right or wrong.

Of the many men known to Rudabaugh during his Dodge City days who now made Las Vegas their home, H. G. [Hyman Graham] Neill, known to men around Close & Patterson's as the Mystery Man, seemed to have the most influence. Little is known of his early days. He followed end-of-track towns as bartender, gambler and go-between for horse thieves and rustlers. He once owned a road-house near Dodge, said to be the rendezvous for all outlaws, gunslingers, rustlers and murderers hiding from justice. He was known around Fort Elliott on the Sweetwater in the Texas Panhandle and practiced some sort of shake-down racket at old Mobeetie. His life as a buffalo hunter was short lived. He next turned to the hide industry but lost interest in this when profits in handling stolen horses seemed more to his liking. Horses stolen in the Texas Panhandle, Indian Territory, Nebraska, Kansas and New Mexico were often taken to Colorado and Kansas through an underground system perfected by him. He was a slick operator who used most of the tactics known to the abolitionists of an earlier day. He steered clear of the methods of the Border Ruffians which most likely would have been used by Rudabaugh had he been directing the operation. By employing such men as Dutch Henry, J. J. Webb, Joe Carson, Dave Rudabaugh, he was able to continue on unsuspected. They would never "rat" on him since he knew enough to put each one in solitary confinement for life, if not to the hangman's scaffold.

Although a Justice of the Peace [and Chief Constable and Coroner], he walked in shadows. A dance hall girl at Close & Patterson's dubbed him Hoodoo Brown because she felt uncomfortable in his presence [he got his sobriquet "Hoodoo" from being a "charmed" gambler who seemed to possess more than normal "good luck"]. She said he was a jinx, and his shifty eyes convinced her that he was a patron she wanted nothing to do with. She always managed to shift him to another less discerning, less particular associate. All the other girls agreed that he was appropriately named, and thus it remained. With many of like ilk in town it was not difficult to place his name on the ballot and have himself elected Justice of the Peace in New Town. After the murder of Kelliher he managed to escape to Dodge where he was soon in difficulty with the law, for his name appears on the criminal docket for December term of court and Attorney Sutton was hired to defend him. Evidently no one in Las Vegas seemed sufficiently interested in having him extradited to stand trial for the murder of Kelliher. [Hoodoo fled Dodge the day after Kelliher's killing with money stolen from Kelliher. A $200 reward was put on his head. He was found and arrested at Parsons, Kansas, but released on a writ of Habeas Corpus.] Hoodoo came through unscathed and left for Caddo, Indian Territory, where he ultimately became involved in a brawl with a gambler who dispatched him to Boot Hill. News of his death appeared in the *Las Vegas Optic* as well as the *Dodge City Times*.

[This story of Hoodoo's death is false. He went to Mexico, not Caddo, where he lived as "Santiago" Graham. He died November 13, 1910, in Torren, Mexico. His body was returned to and buried in Machpelah Cemetery in Lexington beside his brother, where he has a marker.]

[Russell A.] Russ Kistler, realizing that Otero was doomed as a boom town, moved his press and paper to Las Vegas. As customary with frontier journalists he pulled a number of hoaxes in an effort to save his paper from an early grave. One such stunt was a full-page spread on the violent death of Mysterious Dave Mather; another was the capture of Hoodoo and Dutchy [John Schunderberger]. The vigilantes fell for this latter morsel and milled about the depot to await the arrival of the train. A rope was ready; a tree handy. When they realized that they had been duped, they called upon the editor, who had to do some fast talking for the men were in a hanging mood and Kistler would do as well as Hoodoo. Yet in December he did not hesitate to publish: "H. G. Brown, alias Hoodoo Brown, was killed some weeks ago at a gaming table in Caddo, Indian Territory." The *Dodge City Times* copied this choice bit of news from the *Optic* on December 8, 1880. This time Russ claims to have printed the truth [it was not]. He did not plan to risk another scare, and valued his neck,

The name Caddo was later changed to Concho. It was a stage and freight stop in the wilderness, a desolate place where the government maintained a hospital, school, outhouses for the civilization of the Araphoes and the Cheyennes. It was a gathering place for tribal rituals and for meat rations. Later on the Rock Island built through without bothering about a railroad depot. South and east was Fort Reno, a necessary adjunct when reservation Indians were not always amenable to book learning.

Less is known of Dutchy [John Schunderberger] who also shook the dust of New Town because of his part in the Kelliher affair. The vigilantes could not quite make up their minds about him. He left with Brown and Joe Carson's widow. The name is heard in Dodge, Mobeetie, Hays City, Lincoln, Albuquerque, Las Vegas. No one knew his full name, nor did he ever bother to tell it. Hoodoo Brown hired him as a deputy and he rode often with the posse. Years later when Miguel Otero wrote his memorable three volumes dealing with the history of the area he could find no other name for the desperado than Dutchy. Some authors seem to confuse this Dutchy with Dutch Henry, but they seem to be two different individuals.

A Dodge City paper for July 12, 1881, copied this from the Las Vegas paper: "First we will speak of 'Wild Bill,' whose career is too well known to dwell upon. It is said that he had a notch cut on his pistol handle for each man he killed, numbering twenty-six. He finally met a violent death at the hands of Jack McCall who was hung at Yanktown. Wild Bill's real name was Hickok. He was a native of Indiana, having been in the Western country at the time of his death, over twenty-five years. We next speak of Buffalo Bill, of whom we know little except that he was a desperate man, but within the past few years, his adopted State, Kansas, civilized him. He has simmered down and has finally settled in Nebraska where he was once represented in his district in the Legislature. His real name is Wm. F. Cody and he chiefly won fame as a hunter. Both he and Wild Bill are well known by the old residents of Hays City, Kansas. Cherokee Bill is unknown as a killer and an outlaw, making his home most of the time in Indian Territory. But little is known to the writer of the character of Prairie Dog Dave, except that for a long time he was a 'rounder-up' and a knave. Mysterious Dave is too well known in the community to dwell upon at length. We believe he, too, hails from Hays City, and we don't just know how many men he has killed. 'Fat Jack' was not a bad man; always wore good clothes and belonged to a gang."

"Slap Jack Bill, Fly Spee San and Bull Shank Jack all came to Las Vegas about the same time as the railroad got here, and were soon run in jail on the charge of a train and coach robbery. Cock-eyed Frank is not considered a bad man though he downed his man about two years ago at an Eastern town called Dodge City, but the act was adjudged by the courts of that county to be justifiable. Corn Hole Johnny hails from Texas, and his special forte is three card monte. The homesteaders around Newton, Kansas, will remember him in the years 1871-1872. Slim Jim was shot at Leadville about two years ago. Slit-Nose Red is at present in El Paso getting in his work on tender feet. Six-Shooter Bill, we understand, is doing good work in this line. One-Armed Kelley, who was outlawed from the town of Leadville about six months ago, came to Las Vegas, shot the windows out of Burton's restaurant, and was run in for three months, went to Tombstone, where it was reported that he was handed down as food for worms of the consecrated spot."

"Alkali Charlie, whilst at Canon City, was regarded as an honest youth. He certainly was trying to make an honest living blackening boots; but when he came down to Las Vegas he manifested a desire to be a shootist. He cut a hole in the leg of his boot at the wee small hours of morn, went out on the plaza and fired his pistol several times, literally perforating the front of the Toe-Jam Saloon and reported that some one had shot at him, showing up the wound in his boot. Judge Steele did not think he could get to the joint (jail) as a killer and wisely ordered Alkali to leave town instantly."

"Dutchy [John Schunderberger], who killed Kelleher [Kelliher], after he was dead, slipped out of the country with Hoodoo Brown. Dutch Henry, with a far wider range than all the rest, extending East, as far as Dodge and Hays City, was a bold, fear less bravado, treacherous and inhuman by instinct, and, if we remember right, was captured either at Otero or El Moro about three years ago, and taken to Arkansas where he was wanted. (Dutch Henry deserves more than casual mention. Tall, handsome, blue-eyes, blond, he was the son of emigrants from Switzerland. The family originated in Germany, His name was Henry Born. Tired of farm work Dutch enlisted as a scout under General Custer. When buffalo hunting became the rage, and proved to be profitable also, he asked for, and received, an honorable discharge in order to devote all his time to hunting. He was with Billy Dixon, Bat Masterson and the other plainsmen who were at Adobe Walls at the time Quanah Parker and his tribesmen made a last bid to save the buffalo from extinction. He had been employed for a time by Rath and became quite friendly with Dave Rudabaugh, Wyatt Earp, Doc Holliday, Ben Thompson, Clay Allison, Wes Hardin, Tom Nixon, Dave Mather, Luke Short, Jim Courtright, Hoodoo Brown, J. J. Webb and Virgil Earp. Once a band of Indians, said to be Kiowas, ran off a remuda of his best horses, He appealed to the commandant of Fort Dodge for help to track them down. The officer not only refused to help but demanded that he leave the post. Enraged at the brush-off, he vowed to spend the rest of his life stealing government horses. He found willing hands at Dodge. Dave Rudabaugh was often with him on his forays and learned much in the art of rustling and horse stealing from Dutch Henry [not true]. Hoodoo Brown's station was used as the place of rendezvous. Dutch and his men staged raids on Fort Hays, Fort Dodge, Camp Supply, Fort Elliott, the cantonment on the Canadian, Fort Union, Fort Stanton, the Goodnight Ranch, the settlers in Cimarron, the Maxwell Land Grant, Fort Reno and dozens of other places. Stolen stock was disposed of at Taos, Las Vegas, the Texas Panhandle, Albuquerque, Santa Fe, Trinidad, Rayado, the Verrnejo country, Colorado, Kansas and Nebraska. Dutch was apprehended on one of his forays at Trinidad and brought to Dodge to account for his misdeeds. He was acquitted and promised the military that he would steal no more government horses. After serving a short sentence in Arkansas Dutch Henry moved to Old Mobeetie near Fort Elliott where he became a deputy. Later he drifted to Colorado and then to Centerville, Utah, where he became the associate of Ben Tasker, a well known outlaw of early day Utah. They became involved in a quarrel and Tasker murdered his partner near Desert Springs, on the old Spanish Abiquiu-California Trail, and burnt the body. He took two derringers from the dead man. These eventually became the possession of the late Don Maguire of Ogden, Utah."

Henry rates a biography as much as Doc Holliday, Wyatt Earp, Bat Masterson and other Dodge City alumni better known to the reader of Western folklore. This Dutch is often confused with the Dutch involved in the Kelleher murder. He claimed that he was never really the leader of rustlers on their raids but served under competent and efficient men, one of whom was Dave Rudabaugh [not true]. If this is so, it becomes another instance of the pupil emulating the teacher. Dutch Henry was not adverse to relieving wealthy cattlemen of many of their steers. Once when Charles Goodnight was taking a herd from Commission creek to Fort Elliott, he learned that Henry and eighteen of his men (proving that he was a leader after all) camped in the vicinity. Knowing that his herd was singled out for pickings, Goodnight sought a conference with the rustler. According to J. E. Haley, in his book, Charles Goodnight, the rancher said: "I am settling on the Upper Red (i.e., the North Fork of the Canadian) river and I am trying to make it a peaceful and lawful country. I much prefer to have no trouble with anyone, and I want an understanding with you. If you depredate in that country we will have to clash. I have a bunch of good men, well armed and good shots, but I dislike to be compelled to use them in that way. I would like to divide the territories with you. If you keep out of my part of the country, I will never cross the Salt Fork...." (Haley – o. c. page 287) The rustler and the cowman sealed their bargain over a bottle of fine whisky. Both sides respected the boundaries.

"Sheeney Frank is said to be at Lamy Junction making war on peaceful citizens. Hurricane Bill is hardly worth mentioning. He would like at one time to have acquired the reputation of a bad man but Mysterious Dave sat down on him and had no use for him, so he left Las Vegas over a year ago for paths unknown. It is believed by many of the fraternity that if he did not kill himself (as reported) he ought to have done so long before this. Monta Bob died at Alamosa over a year ago. Curry, the murderer of Porter, is reported killed in a street brawl in Arizona. Diaz the 'Peeler' is in the Black Hills. Billy the Kid is at large...."

Two days after the *Optic* editor printed this, Billy the Kid was killed at Fort Sumner by Pat Garrett [about midnight, July 14, 1881], There is no doubt that the boys from Dodge took over New Town. And legally. Hoodoo Brown was Justice of the Peace. His staff [city constables] was composed of Joe Carson, J. J. Webb, Mysterious Dave Mather, Dave Rudabaugh and lesser satellites. Mayhem, murder, robbery seemed to be the rule rather than the exception [a wild exaggeration]. Other towns had their man for breakfast but Vegas also enjoyed dinner, supper and the between meals snacks. It mattered little whether constables were fugitives from the law. Only three requirements were necessary for the job: a fast gun, fearlessness and a closed mouth. A whole library could be written about those days when Rudabaugh, Carson, Webb, Mather and Brown controlled the town. They were copy for the *Gazette* and the *Optic* every time they turned around. It mattered little if they had an off day. The editors of both papers graciously manufactured exploits either to keep the readers happy or to prevent their interest from flagging. Rudabaugh was as well known in New Town as he was in Dodge.

On January 20, 1880, Thomas Jefferson House, alias Tom Henry, a native of Pueblo, Colorado, who had left his native State because cowboying in Texas appealed to him, together with John Dorsey [real name Jim Dawson], James [Anthony W.] Lowe (alias James West) and William Randall entered Close & Patterson's firmly resolved to drink up every drop of rot-gut in the place or kill anyone seeking to prevent them. They went at it with all the zest of a boy with a balloon. The bilge poured in as their reason oozed out. Armed to the teeth they defied constable and customers alike. Two days and nights later they were still at it [January 22, 1880].

This was more than Constable Joe Carson could stand. He decided that Close & Patterson's, the citizens of New Town and Joe Carson had enough of their bravado. They were to give their guns to the bartender for safe keeping or quit making coyotes of themselves drinking bad whisky. This surprised them. They had convinced themselves that they had everyone mesmerized. They were bad, bad hombres and had the town cowed. So they figured, until Carson told them to stop play acting and behave themselves. They refused to give over the guns, and continued drinking. The constable told them a second time. He said they were too drunk for their own good; he was protecting both their interests and those of the citizens. Someone was bound to get hurt if they persisted. If they wanted to drink themselves to death he didn't mind at all, only they must do so naked of gunbelts and guns. This made them more bellicose, boisterous, cocky. No one was going to tell them what to do, much less a tin-horn policeman. The bartender raised his eyebrows; customers changed tables; gamblers slowed up games; cowboys lowered their voices to a whisper; body pushers stopped dancing and separated from their partners. The matron signaled them upstairs. A pall settled over the scene. Even the stale smoke from many cigars and cigarettes hung like a funeral veil as if awaiting the company of gunsmoke. A stillness over Close & Patterson's! Death hovered like a vulture and everyone in that room knew it. Fascinated, no one made any attempt to leave the saloon. Their eyes focused on Carson. He was the incarnation of determination. Alone, he decided to unarm four very drunk heavily armed men. He was going to march them all off to jail.

Jail! Arrest! Those were fighting words. "Who in the (you know what) ever heard of arresting a man because he was enjoying himself!" House wanted to know. Turning to the bartender he said: "Ridiculous." To Randall he muttered: "Did you ever hear of such a thing?" Then the fun began. No one knows who fired the first shot [primary accounts say Henry fired the first shot, hitting Carson in the left arm]. Face down on the floor behind the bar the bartender counted forty shots in all. When the smoke cleared away it was found that nine [eight] bullets hit Carson. William Randall was mortally wounded. Tom Henry was wounded but managed to escape in company with John Dorsey. Las Vegas was sympathetic. Despite his shortcomings, Joe Carson was well liked. He boasted as many friends on one side of the bridge separating the two towns as on the other. Hoodoo Brown, Dave Mather, Dave Rudabaugh, J. J. Webb, Dutchy held a conference. They vowed to avenge the death of their pal if they had to ride to hell and back. Note the difference in this affair and the Kinsley robbery. The death of Carson brings Rudabaugh's loyalty to the front as never before. From now to the date of his death this becomes the central theme in the life of this desperado, rustler, horse thief: Loyalty to friends; death to unfaithful friends.

Above Las Vegas, on the Mora road, in a hidden valley, is the timeless town of Buena Vista, still a stronghold of the Penitente Brotherhood. At this time, a native named Juan Antonio Dominguez made his home here. He had occasion to meet Henry and Dorsey out on the range and during trail driving days would come in for dinner when in the vicinity of Las Vegas or Buena Vista. It was obvious to the posse where the fugitives would head for under the circumstances. Either something they said while on the tragic binge, or because some in Close & Patterson's were aware of their Buena Vista connection, the fact remains that Rudabaugh and the others knew the pair would hole up with Dominguez. To make certain, they hired an informer to watch the Dominguez household.

Dorsey, anxious to keep moving, and suspecting that all was not well, decided that Henry's wound warranted a prolonged stay at the home of their friend who lived far enough from Las Vegas to discourage a posse; yet close enough to encourage Rudabaugh, Hoodoo Brown, Mather and Dutchy. Twenty-nine miles was nothing to men determined to avenge the death of a friend. As soon as Henry was well enough Dorsey would make tracks for the Texas Panhandle. This was not to be. The man hunters from Las Vegas surrounded the adobe hut, forced the men within to surrender, and headed back for the Meadow city [on February 6, 1880].

The editor of the *Optic*, ever on the scent for a story, nosed this one out and headed for the jail on the plaza where he hoped to interview the prisoners. They were indeed grateful that they weren't taken to the nearest tree in Buena Vista for a lynching. The reporter gave them a sardonic grin. They knew that the expected neck-tie party had not been called off; only delayed. Tom Henry admitted to the newspaper man that had he not been drinking heavily perhaps Carson would still be alive. The four would-be desperadoes had come in from Texas three weeks before to investigate the possibilities as rustlers. Whether Juan Dominguez was implicated he could not say [he was not].

There was a fertile field around Sapello, La Cueva, Guadalupita, Chacon, Buena Vista, Rociada and Mora. They had really hoped to make this area their stomping ground so as not to interfere with the activities of the larger operators around Las Vegas. It is likely that Rudabaugh, Hoodoo Brown and the others were anxious to capture Henry and his associate as much for cutting in on their territory as for the killing of Carson.

After the shooting, Henry told the reporter, he had made his way to the Olds & Llewling Livery Stable, ordered horses and guarded the entrance with a Winchester as they were being saddled, He denied any implication in the robbery of the Staburris buggy, his alibi being that he was a dinner guest at the home of Juan Antonio Dominguez at the time the robbery was reported to have taken place. This, he pointed out, would take some doing as the home where he took dinner was twenty-three miles from the scene of the robbery. During the shooting at Close & Patterson's, a bullet pierced the calf of his leg; four went through the coat he was wearing without inflicting any damage.

John Dorsey was older than the others. Thirty-three. He had no other motive for being in Las Vegas than his friendship for Randall. He was not aware of his friend's designs on the neighboring cattle herds, and insisted he was not wearing guns when Carson called on them, to turn them over to the bartender. He told the reporter that he was alone in the world; not a single living relative. Had Rudabaugh and the others arrived an hour later at the Dominguez residence they would have found the place empty for all the arrangements evacuating the place in favor of the Texas Panhandle had been completed and they were just about ready to leave.

Lowe was a real hard case. He was visited in jail by ministers representing various denominations but he told them all that they were wasting their time. He had no time for religion. Since Buena Vista was in Mora county some took to wondering how the prisoners were permitted to be taken to San Miguel county. It was later brought to light that Webb and Rudabaugh had gone to see Sheriff John Dougherty of Mora and enlisted his aid in the capture of the wanted men.

Carson, forty at the time of his death, was a native of Rome, Georgia, a city popularized by the antics of Little Abner, and known for its industrious hard working people. He had a fourteen year old daughter enrolled in a finishing school for young ladies, at Nashville, Tennessee. This and other information was fed to various groups in the cantinas, dance halls, bagnios, gaming halls, livery stables and about the streets. Voices, like the beat of a lonesome drum, called out of the night to assemble ranks of vigilantes. At two A. M. on the morning after the prisoners were lodged in jail, they marched in formation to the sheriff's office. It was closed. The nightman had either been scared off or was perhaps among the men taking the law into their hands. The mob proceeded to the sheriff's house where they found his brother who gave them the keys after they threatened to take him out and hang him if he refused to comply. [The vigilantes assembled at the jail. They broke through the entrance door and forced one of the jailers to give them the keys to the cells. The lynching was February 8, 1880, at about 3 A.M.] Tying his hands and feet, they put a gag into his mouth and cautioned him against any attempt to spread the alarm.

They went on to the jail. They broke down the outer door with little effort, and forced the jailer to surrender his guns. In a moment they were in the cell occupied by the terror-stricken men. A rope was thrown about the neck of each as they were led to the broken down windmill on the plaza. At the other end of the ropes and leading the prisoners were J. J. Webb and Dave Rudabaugh [there is no confirmation that Webb and Rudabaugh were among the lynchers, although it is likely]. Lowe [West], because of his wounds, was unable to walk. The vigilantes were kind enough to carry him to the scaffold [on a stretcher]. He pleaded with the masked men to spare his life. Tom Henry looked over to him and said:

"Jim, be quiet. Die like a man."

Shivering from the cold – January nights in Las Vegas are usually a number of degrees below zero, he managed to smile as he remarked to the man nearest him:

"Boys, you are hanging a mighty good man."

Asked which relative he wished notified of his death, he told them that his parents lived in Pueblo, Colorado.

"Boys, it's pretty tough to be hung. I wish some one will write my folks. I will stand the consequences and die like a man." Asked his age, he replied: "Twenty-nine."

The march was not executed with all the secrecy the vigilantes had wished. A small crowd had gathered about the mill in the plaza at Old Town. Two faces in that group stared more intently than the others. Dutchy and Mrs. Carson witnessed the hangings. Lowe [West] was the first one to dangle from the broken down windmill. His last words were:

"Please button up my pants."

The vigilantes had come upon them in jail in various stages of undress. The hanging of the other two did not come off as smoothly. They were cut down and shot [they were never hanged, just shot]. Some whispered that Mrs. Carson fired the first shot to avenge her husband. Others insisted that she had asked Dutchy to do it for her. Henry fell at the first shot, and crawling to the edge of the platform he yelled:

"Boys, for God's sake, shoot me again. Shoot me in the head."

They obliged.

The three were placed in separate boxes There were always a number on hand for this sort of thing but were given a common grave. That windmill which became the common hanging tree in Old Las Vegas was cut down shortly afterwards because the natives never forgot that night in January [February 8, 1880] when Webb and Rudabaugh and their friends avenged Joe Carson. They crossed themselves every time they came by the plaza, and the wind howled and scolded them for permitting such horrors to take place. It was a haunted spot. They wanted that windmill down so that they could sleep without nightmares. Was Carson worth the death of these cowboys at the hands of the mob?

Said the editor of the *Optic*, February 27, 1881: "On August 30, 1879 [correct date was August 14, 1878], the stage was robbed. The stage robbery took place on one of the mountain passes on the old stage road between Las Vegas and Tecalote [Tecolote]. The robbers halted the stage, ordered the passengers out and proceeded to rob them and the mail sacks as well as whatever money was deposited with the stage company strongbox. The robbers then unhitched the horses, mounted them and rode off. The robbers have been identified as Joe Martin, Dave Rudabaugh and Joe Carson."

The lamentable fact was that others were tried and convicted for their crime. [The falsely convicted men were William Mullen and brothers Joe and Bill Stokes They were each sentenced to one and a half years in prison. The were released when Rudabaugh confessed to the crime and named as his accomplices Joe Martin and Joe Carson.] The three bandits were part of the police force at the time. It was an easy matter to accuse others before Justice Hoodoo Brown. More than likely Brown latched on to the idea of a police station front from the notorious Henry Plummer. Just who revealed the identity of the robbers has never been revealed [it was Rudabaugh in his confession]. This is understandable. Silencing a "squealer" goes back to biblical times.

Michael Kelliher had come to New Town from Wyoming, where he had large ranching interests. Leaving his brother to take care of the ranch he came to Las Vegas in quest of blooded stock. He broadcast that he would pay above the market price for good steers. It was soon known all over town that he carried a large amount of cash for a quick sale [$2,115]. A true Westerner, he invited everyone he met to a drink. Dutchy observed his every move and held frequent conferences with Webb, Rudabaugh, Hoodoo Brown and S. Boyle. This latter was a brakeman for the Santa Fe. Boyle arranged a chance meeting with Kelliher. He was invited to Close & Patterson's for a drink. He gave his order to the bartender, gulped down his drink hurriedly and told him that Kelliher would pay. After Kelliher paid for the drinks, Boyle turned on him savagely and demanded to know why he sought to insult him before his friends. He was not a moocher, and perfectly capable of paying for his own drinks. The surprised Kelliher told him he was happy to pay for the drinks. Indeed, he was aware that Boyle was no gentleman because he expected free drinks. Boyle raised his voice; so did Kelliher. They were soon going at it like two fish-mongers. They were heard far beyond Locke & Brooks swinging doors where Dutchy and Webb were waiting. They rushed in with drawn pistols. One of them shot Kelliher. Webb caught Kelliher as he fell, removed his wallet, and hid it on his own person. Hoodoo Brown was called in as coroner and Justice of the Peace. His verdict was justifiable homicide in the line of duty. There were several versions of how it really happened but all are agreed that Webb had five hundred dollars of Kelliher's money when he was arrested [not true].

[On February 29, 1880, Kelliher and his hired hand William Brickley arrived at Las Vegas from Deadwood, South Dakota. Kelliher had $2,115 that he intended to use to buy cattle. On March 2, at sundown, the two men came into town and began visiting drinking houses. After several hours they went to Close & Patterson's saloon. Kelliher, who was belligerently drunk, was asked to disarm by Constable Webb. Kelliher refused and pulled his pistol. Webb drew faster and shot Kelliher in the chest, and then put two more slugs into him as he fell. Brickley, in his contradictory account, said that Webb fired at Kelliher without any warning after asking him to disarm.]

[Hoodoo Brown put together a coroner's jury which met over the bleeding and still-warm body, which ruled the killing justified. Kelliher had $1,950 on his body, having spent $165 in his carousing before his killing.]

[The next day Hoodoo reported to the Probate Judge that he had taken $1090 from Kelliher, which he would hold in trust. When it became known that Hoodoo was reporting the wrong amount, he and Dutchy skipped town by train with Kelliher's $1,950.]

[Hoodoo and Dutchy's fleeing lead to a preliminary examination of Webb which lead to a murder indictment for Webb for killing Kelliher. The court's belief was that Webb and Hoodoo were in a conspiracy to kill and rob Kelliher, although it was later proven that Webb got none of the money and had not conspired with Hoodoo. Nevertheless, he was later tried and convicted of murdering Webb and sentenced to death by hanging.]

New Town would have accepted the verdict and closed the case had not Dutchy and Hoodoo Brown selected that night to skip for parts unknown. Rumors began to make the rounds. Nobody bothered Boyle since his mouth was louder than his gun. The vigilantes arrested Webb [he was arrested by the sheriff after being indicted for killing Kelliher].

They then decided to go back for Boyle. He had vanished [there was no effort to arrest Boyle]. Eventually Kelliher's brother came down from Wyoming and offered a large reward for the capture of Dutchy, Brown and Boyle. Dutchy was said to have been in Chicago with Mrs. Carson but nobody took the trouble to investigate [Mrs. Carson met up with Hoodoo Brown in Parsons, Kansas, where he was arrested and then let go – she was taking he husband's body to be buried in Houston, but may have been there also to meet Hooodoo]. The vigilantes came to the jail to invite Webb to a necktie party [there was no effort to lynch Webb]. Rudabaugh and a few chosen friends promised to gun down the first to step into the jail. The crowd dispersed. "H. G. Brown," said the sage of the *Las Vegas Optic*, "vulgarly known as 'Hoodoo Brown' went East (Dodge was usually referred to as East) [he went to Parsons, Kansas, and then to Mexico] Wednesday night in company with Dutchy, against whom an indictment was returned by the Grand Jury. After the killing of Kelliher, the money in his possession, said to be $1950 instead of only $1990, fell into the hands of Neill, who was Justice of the Peace and acting coroner. Neill paid the funeral expenses and pocketed the balance departing for parts unknown." (o. c. 3-2-80)

The Governor of the Territory of New Mexico offered a reward of three hundred dollars for the "capture of Hyman G. Neil, wanted on a charge of grand larceny." Kelliher and Brown were soon forgotten and New Town went on to another killing [the killing of Kelliher was not forgotten. Webb was charged with his murder, convicted, and sentenced to hang. The governor commuted Webb's sentence to life March 4, 1881. Webb escaped jail December 3, 1881. He died of small pox April 12, 1882.] It developed later on that Hoodoo opened a store at Cripple Creek, near Meade, Kansas, after he was run out of Dodge. He married and prospered in worldly goods [not true]. He had no children. A ranchman from the Texas Panhandle, who often visited Brown at Cripple Creek, wrote: "One night when I was at his place we got into a poker game. I won his money, so he staked his cattle. I won his cattle and he staked his horses. I won his horses and he put up his store of goods. At last he said that all he had left was his wife but if I would put up one hundred dollars against her we could play her off. I balked. The next morning I tore up the paper conveying all of Brown's holdings to me but kept the money and went to Dodge where I painted the town red with my winnings." (O. Nelson, *The Cowman's Southwest*) [This story is not true.]

Brown eventually found another player and lost his store, horses and cattle. When he was killed at Caddo in the fall of the year his wife was not with him could – he had lost her also? [He was not killed at Caddo – he was in Mexico.]

The bridge below the site of Highlands University arched the gap between Old Town and New Town. In order to keep business flowing in both sectors, livery stable owners maintained a line of hacks, usually three-seated affairs, open-topped on sunny days, covered during inclement weather. Business men, booze hounds, ladies on night calls, dance hall girls, lawyers, gamblers, dentists, doctors, drummers, cowboys took advantage of the ride, paying twenty-five cents for the privilege. On April 2nd, Miguel Otero had business in Old Town as did Mrs. Adolph Mennet. Adolph Mennet, her husband, had been an adventurer and soldier of fortune. Tired of fighting for Emperor Maximilian of Mexico, and foreseeing nothing but doom for the head that wore the crown, he defected in favor of life at Hays City, Kansas, After a time he found employment with the firm of Otero, Seller & Co. as head of the wholesale and retail department. When the firm transferred to Las Vegas, he came to New Town serving in the same capacity as he did in Kansas. He married Mattie Bell, a school teacher in Hays City. She was originally from the East. The hack they were riding on this particular day belonged to J. M. Tabot who had one of the larger livery stables in the city. The driver was Carl Caldwell [Cauldwell].

The vehicle was moving along at a brisk trot when suddenly two men sprang out of the shadows and flagged it down. They proved to be Dave Rudabaugh and John Llewellyn, alias John [J.] Allen, a, mechanic and drifter who was as handy with tools as he was with painting houses. He listed his trade as mechanic and house painter. He hailed from Atlanta, Georgia, and had come West in quest of fame as the greatest gunslinger of them all. He secretly hired out to Hoodoo Brown. If he ever succeeded as a hired killer he took the secret to the grave with him. His sister in Georgia wrote to him constantly to give up the idea of becoming a six-shooter artist, and join some church which would do him more good than the career he sought. His replies to Mrs. Chapman were always the same: He had to prove himself. He made his choice. Let it stand.

Once in the hack, they bid the time of day to Mrs. Mennet, then to Miguel Otero. (The morning funeral services were being held for Miguel Otero, I thought of the opportunities I let slip by during the years I was free to interview him, never once referring to Rudabaugh and those early years in New Town. The bug hadn't bitten me as yet, and only after the passing of Otero and so many others did I realize the opportunities that were lost forever.) Otero and Mrs. Monnet got out at the Norst National Bank corner. They later remarked, in the light of events that followed, that they would have remained had they suspected what Rudabaugh and [John J.] Allen were up to. Allen had been drinking heavily. This was no cause for alarm. It was as common as sunrise or sunset during those frontier days when all sorts were moving in, out and about. The cab continued right a block, then turned left. Rudabaugh ordered Caldwell [Cauldwell] to halt. The driver was anxious to rid himself of the pair but it was not as easy as he thought. Rudabaugh's movements that evening up to the time of the tragic death of the jailer will be studied when his trial comes up.

Rudabaugh and Allen got out at the jail in Old Town. Jailer Antonio Lino Valdez was not surprised to see Rudabaugh. As brought out in the trial, he was a regular visitor, never missing an opportunity to bring Webb the things he needed. Allen tried to play the part of the desperado at the jail. As a result, Jailer Valdez was left dead, and Webb refused to take advantage of his opportunity for escape. He [Webb] later explained that his lawyer had offered encouragement and his hopes for complete exoneration in the death of Kelliher looked bright indeed. He did not wish to diminish his chances by going off with Rudabaugh and Allen. There were lots of people in Las Vegas willing to agree that Webb was a victim of circumstances and innocent of an implication in the shooting of the cattleman. Later, after Rudabaugh was lodged in jail at Santa Fe, Webb's lawyer came to visit him for testimony favorable to his client. The attorney agreed that he had never come across a man as loyal to a friend as Rudabaugh who was willing to assume the full responsibility for the crime attributed to Webb. Otero had this to say about Webb's refusal: "This act on his part counted much in his favor, in the eyes of the community, and his friends made use of it in an effort to persuade the governor of the Territory (Lew Wallace) to extend clemency. They also showed that the evidence seemed to indicate that Dutchy had done the actual killing and that Webb had been somewhat unwittingly the tool of Hoodoo Brown. After going into this case thoroughly, the governor commuted Webb's sentence to a short term in the penitentiary [it was commuted to life]. But his friends continued active in Webb's behalf, and their efforts, supplemented by those of the attorney, Judge Sidney M. Barnes, finally secured his pardon [he was never pardoned]. He left almost at once for his old home in Indiana and was never heard of again around

Las Vegas." (Otero o. c. Page 204) [He escaped jail and went to Winslow, Arkansas and died there of small pox April 12, 1882.]

For Webb's sake, we would like to think that it really happened as Otero wrote. There is more to the story than what he tells us. It was Rudabaugh who eventually liberated Webb but they came to the parting of the ways. This, not even Rudabaugh would explain. Garrett, ever on the lookout for Rudabaugh and the reward money, often visited the Grzelachowski store and home at Puerto de Luna and mentioned that he was on the lookout for Allen and Rudabaugh. In time the authors writing of these events – even Garrett and Masterson – confused the names to Webb and Rudabaugh. It was Allen and Rudabaugh who were wanted for the murder of the jailer [Valdez]. With Webb's first escape from jail, his name was added to the list. He seems to have teamed up with Davis, a notorious horse thief, and together they were looking for Rudabaugh, Greathouse and Billy the Kid. Greathouse was well known in the Anton Chico area, Las Vegas and Puerto de Luna. The process was slow, since Rudabaugh and Billy the Kid could not stay in any one place too long without arousing suspicion.

[On November 11, 1880, Webb, James Allen (not John J. Allen), George Davidson, John Murray, William Mullen, and George Davis escaped from the Las Vegas jail. Allen was in jail for killing James Morehead. Davidson was in jail for killing Charles Nelson W. Starbird. Murray was in jail awaiting trial for the murder of a railroad grader. Mullen was in jail after being convicted falsely of a crime that Rudabaugh had actually committed, a stage robbery. Davis was jail waiting trial for stealing a span of mules.]

[The posse sent after the men killed Allen and Davidson. Murray returned to Las Vegas and turned himself in. Webb and Davis were captured November 25, 1880, by Deputy Sheriff Pat Garrett at Dan Dedrick's ranch (Garrett would not become Sheriff until January 1, 1880). Murray seems to have got away.]

Meantime, Grzelachowski and others at Fort Sumner and Puerto de Luna began to wonder who the two strangers were that made repeated visits to these towns as well as Anton Chico and told Pat Garrett, who immediately placed them as Rudabaugh and Webb [a false story – Garrett knew when he captured them that he had Webb and Davis]. This is indicative of how friendly the two men were. No one seems concerned about the would-be desperado Allen; indeed, he receives scant mention all through the records and court proceedings [The *Las Vegas Daily Gazette* on February 26, 1881, reported that Allen had been killed by Rudabaugh at Martin's Well. His court case was dropped after that report and he was declared legally dead.] Suddenly, everybody is after Webb and Rudabaugh. Either Webb and Davis were easy to track down, or they were not particular about being seen. The fact remains that Pat Garrett took a posse, captured them and brought them in to Fort Sumner [They were captured November 25, 1880, at Dan Dedrick's house at Bosque Grande]. Garrett wrote to Sheriff Desiderio Romero, [deputy] sheriff of San Miguel county, and asked him to come for the two prisoners. One might also add that he probably did not omit asking about the reward money. Placing the prisoners in the custody of C. B. Hoadley, Garrett went about other business since it would be a few days before the sheriff would arrive.

The sheriff delegated Francisco Romero and four men to take an ambulance and bring back the prisoners. These were Baker, Ortiz, Sandoval and Vigil. Romero went to Puerto de Luna but did not see Pat Garrett. The men stayed overnight at Grzelachowski's. The next morning they rode on towards Fort Sumner. On the way they met Garrett, Mason, the two prisoners and the driver of the wagon taking the prisoners to Las Vegas. Romero took one look at the prisoners and recognized Webb. He told Garrett that the other man was not Rudabaugh. Rumors flew about Puerto de Luna. A small crowd assembled. Another crowd gathered about Alejandro Grzelachowski's store trying to find out what the commotion was all about. Romero brought the prisoners here, and the formal presentation of credentials took place. Romero brought Webb to the blacksmith shop in Puerto de Luna to have him fettered. While there, some shots were heard in the direction of the Grzelachowski store. Garrett and Mason had shot at Marino Leyba, of Puerto de Luna, wanted by the authorities. Wounded, Leyba, fled, but the crowd assembled as if to lynch Mason and Garrett. Romero entered the store and Mason's gun went off, the shot going wild. Whereupon the deputy placed both Mason and Garrett under arrest. The next day he took them over to the Justice of the Peace, who seemed to find a just cause for their action, and set them free.

Very few biographers mention this incident in the life of Garrett. Nearing Las Vegas with the prisoners, Romero was met by Dolores Romero, the brother of the sheriff, but no kin to the Romero deputized in this instance to bring in Webb and the man supposed to be Rudabaugh. Dolores was an actual deputy, whereas Francisco was temporary. Dolores had a companion with him. All Las Vegas was quite anxious that Rudabaugh be allowed no opportunity for escape. It was quite a disappointment to learn that Davis was not Rudabaugh. They all rode into Las Vegas and the prisoners were remanded to jail, while the search for Rudabaugh continued.

When Webb was liberated a second time, he headed for Texas [on December 3, 1881, Rudabaugh, Webb, Thomas Quillan, Frank Kearney, Edward M. "Choctaw" Kelly, William Goodman, and S. Schroeder escaped from the Las Vegas jail]. Later he was seen at Dodge, then Nebraska and finally Arkansas, where he worked as a teamster for J. D. Scott & Co. He assumed the alias of Samuel King. He contracted small-pox at Winslow, Washington county, just south of Fayetville in western Arkansas, and died there on April 22, 1882 [April 12, 1882]. He was identified by the solid gold eye tooth (left) which he had made, replacing the one he lost in the battle for the Royal George. A number of persons were arrested in Albuquerque, El Paso and Socorro who seemed to fit his description but were released because none had a gold tooth. The gold tooth prevented another from hanging in his stead. This is what the last March issue of the *Las Vegas Eureka* (1880) had to say about the killing of Valdez:

"Yesterday afternoon, about three o'clock, one of the boldest and most desperate deeds ever committed in this community, was perpetrated at the jail by Dave Rudabaugh and [John J.] Allen. The facts elicited by a *Gazette* reporter (one man owned both papers) from eye witnesses appear to be as follows: It seems the two men got into a hack in East Las Vegas and drove over to this side. The hack belonged to J. M. Talbot (among other accomplishments Talbot played the cornet as a member of the newly-formed band) and at the time was driven by Mr. Carl Caldwell [Cauldwell]. On arriving at the jail, Rudabaugh and Allen got out of the hack and asked to be admitted into the placita of the jail. They were permitted to enter and when on the inside, they asked the jailer to show them Webb's cell, The jailer showed them the cell occupied by Webb and the Stokes boys. One of the men then handed a common newspaper through the cell door to the men on the inside. They then demanded the keys of the cell from the jailer but Mr. Validez said: 'I have no right to give them to you.' Whereupon, Mr. Allen said: 'You must give them up or we will kill you.'"

"Then Valdez said: 'You may kill me, but I won't give them up.'"

"Allen then told him that it would be an easy matter to do that, and at once drew out his pistol and fired the fatal shot. The keys were then taken from the pocket of the fallen man by one of the men, who threw them down at the door of Webb's cell, and said: 'Here are the keys. I must go.' Allen and Rudabaugh then went out, got into the hack and ordered the driver to drive over to the New Town as quick as possible. They covered the driver with their revolvers and ordered him not to flinch, at his peril. They also covered everyone they met on the road until they were safely past them. On arriving in New Town they drove to Houghton's Hardware Store and one of them boldly entered the store and threw two or three rifles into the hack, ordered the driver to get out, when Rudabaugh took the lines and drove east at a rapid pace."

"The men drove east and went up on the mesa. By this time the deputy sheriff and a posse of men, who were in hot pursuit, had closed up within shooting range. Allen and Rudabaugh, in order to keep this party at bay, got out of the hack and kneeled down and fired a volley, which was returned by the pursuers. Several more were then exchanged by both parties when the sheriff's party gave back, and the two men entered the hack and drove on. The excitement in the city was intense. Crowds of men could be seen during the entire evening standing on every little eminence surveying the western slope of the Nine Mile Hill with field glasses in order to get a view of the exciting chase. The sheriff's posse was continually being increased by armed recruits from the city and at last accounts the fleeing men had been overtaken and the fighting renewed. It was reported about dark that one of the horses driven by Allen and Rudabaugh had been shot. The fighting was still going on at dark...."

In another column of the same issue, the editor enlarged on the exciting escape, using this by-line: A DICK TURPIN RIDE.

"Dave Rudabaugh and Allen made good their escape Friday night. The second party that rode after (the outlaws) made a good effort but never overtook the fugitives, or got in sight. They took the La Cinta road and after getting out two or three miles, Ignacio Sena, who was after them on horseback, caught up near enough to shoot. He fired several shots at the hack, one ball going through the upper part. The hack was stopped and one of the men got out and returned the fire. Sena, not having much ammunition, then returned for a new supply. The fugitives, after this encounter, continued their journey with increased speed. About eighteen miles out they came upon some herders with saddle horses. These they immediately appropriated to their own use, taking the pistols from the boys, and also meat and other provisions. Thus freshly mounted they outdistanced all their pursuers."

"The herders, we understand, were in the employ of Antonio Montoya. They reside at San Geronimo (a village in the hills between La Manga and Tecalote) and the name of one of them is Antonio Gonzalez. The sheriff was not in town and the deputy appeared to be totally unprepared to do anything effectually and promptly. In this emergency a number of citizens saddled their horses, hunted up their guns and started in pursuit. Among these were [Sheriff] Hilario Romero (lots of Romeros in Las Vegas), Col. Lockhart (contractor, builder, carpenter), Peter Simpson (quite a boy – later became sheriff of Socorro county, a man known to L. B. Maxwell, Tom Catron, Elkins, Otero and other New Mexico greats of the day. His life is really more exciting than Garrett's), and several other good men whose names we did not learn. They pressed forward as rapidly as possible, riding some thirty-five miles before night closed down and rendered further pursuit hopeless. Their horses by this time were tired out and the night being so dark they were farced to turn back and arrived home yesterday morning. They brought back the hack, which had been left with the herders. Allen and Rudabaugh left two of the guns in the hack, likely considering that with fresh horses they would have no use for long-range arms."

"It was a bold and desperate attempt to liberate Webb, which failed on account of the lack of nerve and courage on the part of the projectors. When they had shot the jailer and obtained the keys, they threw them in to Webb's cell, telling him that there were the keys; that they must go. How did they imagine that he should get out and escape on foot without arms? It was an ill-advised plan for their object and nervelessly executed. They made a good escape, however, and luckily for them met the mounted herders; otherwise the chances are that the Romero and Lockhart party would have overhauled them, in which case it would be a dead sure thing that they would have been captured...."

To offset the bad publicity Las Vegas was receiving at this time, the editor, using "Anonymous" as his signature, tried to tell prospective buyers, tourists and the public in general that Las Vegas wasn't as bad as pictured. This appeared in the same issue telling of Rudabaugh's daring escape:

"Under the impression that Las Vegas is a bad and dangerous place, many health and pleasure seekers who would like to come here and take advantage of the climate and the springs stay away. During my travels through Colorado during the past few months, I have noticed the feeling prevails among invalids and tourists, scores of whom I have met arid conversed with, that it is not safe to come here. I would say to such of these as may read this article, that the place has been generally misrepresented, and the accidents and crimes that have occurred here have been generally misrepresented. True, there have been several atrocious murders committed, but they have been by and upon habitués of dance halls and gambling halls and the victims, with one or two exceptions, have been toughs who are better out of the world than in it. Men of this sort always congregate in frontier towns and will continue to do so for all time, and crime must follow."

"Let any man come here and avoid low places, keep sober and mind his own business and he will be as safe on the streets of Las Vegas as any city in the United States. The majority of low characters who thronged here when the town was the railroad terminus, have taken flight. Lynching is something that they very much fear, and as that sort of thing was indulged in very extensively, they became alarmed and sought new regions wherein to ply their nefarious schemes and works of crime, and their places have been filled by a more respectable class of men. It is not to be denied that there is plenty of bad whisky in town, but where will you find a town in the West that is not more or less afflicted in the same way. The climate here is unequaled in the continent and consumptives should know it. The hot sulphur springs are, it is said, superior to those in Arkansas, and are the rheumatics' boon, but they have not yet been properly advertised. The ride to and from them, over a good road, and through a charming country, is pleasant and interesting in the extreme. The hotel and bathing house at the springs are substantial structures of stone and wood and may justly be classified among the first in the land. The tables are well supplied and the variety good and of a kind to suit the most fastidious. Invalids will do well to come here at once and here they will certainly wish to remain."

Despite placing the blame on "toughs," killings continued. Nelson V. Starbird was one of the more popular hack drivers, and had as many friends in Old Town as New Town. Shortly after Valdez was buried, Starbird was shot from ambush [on April 8, 1880, by George Davidson. Davidson was captured and jailed. He was killed by possemen two days after his jail escape on November 11, 1880]. The bullet had been intended for George Poindexter, a resident of Old Town, who came to the area shortly before the arrival of the railroad. He was employed by Romero Mercantile Company and was taking home the proceeds of the day to be deposited in the bank the following morning. Otero makes mention of the incident:

"It was generally thought that the intended victim was George Poindexter, who was being driven home to his residence in the Old Town shortly after midnight by Starbird. The murderer's bullet lodged in Starbird's back. Poindexter drove the hack to Starbird's home, but the former died before the doctor could get to him. This killing was so appalling that the vigilantes began to bestir themselves. On the night of the 8th of April a mass meeting of the law-abiding citizens of the town was held, with an attendance of virtually one hundred percent. Speeches were made by such men as my father, James A. Lockhart, Jacob Gross, Robert K. N. Cullen, Rush J. Holmes. It was decided to give warning to the lawless element. Hand bills were printed in large type, scattered over town and posted on the walls of every building. Here is how the warning read:"

"A TIMELY WARNING TO MURDERERS, CONFIDENCE MEN, THIEVES"

"The Citizens of Las Vegas have tired of robbery, murder and other crimes that have made this town a byword in every civilized community. They have resolved to put a stop to crime even if in attaining that end they may have to forget the law, and resort to a speedier justice than it will afford. All such characters are, therefore, notified that they must either leave this town or conform themselves to the requirement of law, or they will be summarily dealt with. The flow of blood MUST and SHALL be stopped in this community, and the good citizens of both Old and New Towns have determined to stop it, if they have to HANG by the strong arm of FORCE every violator of the law in this country. - VIGILANTES." (Otero o.e. pp. 205-206.)

A poster of this type, nailed to the wall of the saddle room section of an old barn that was once part of the XIT Ranch in Dalhart, and later the G. W. Tom Linnenkohl Ranch, read as fallows:

NOTICE!

TO THIEVES, THUGS, FAKIRS AND BUNKO-STEERERS,

Among Whom Are

J. J. HARLIN, alias 'Off Wheeler;' SAW DUST
CHARLIE, WM. HEDGES, BILLY THE KID,
BILLY MULLIN, LITTLE JACK, THE CUTER,
POCK-MARKED KID, and about Twenty Others:

If Found within the Limits of this City
after TEN O'CLOCK P. M., this Night,
you will be Invited to attend a GRAND
NECK-TIE PARTY.

The Expense of which will be borne by 100 Substantial Citizens.

Las Vegas March (blurred) 1882

(This poster was presented to Mrs. Oliver Jordan by Tom Linnenkohl on May 17, 1949. Jordon & Sons are bootmakers at Alamogordo, N. M. Mrs. Oliver Jordan presented the author with a photo copy. See image next page.)

The citizens of Las Vegas were not too concerned with Otero's hopes for a safer town. They were willing to tolerate more killings if only Dave Rudabaugh were brought to justice. [John J.] Allen they considered a victim of bad companions. Rudabaugh should be made an example of. Usually the citizens of Old Town were willing to forgive and forget. Rudabaugh they were willing to do neither. For him, the rope. Some months later when he was captured and taken to Santa Fe for trial, the hate was still there. He asked for a change of venue, because one of three possibilities were open: They would hang him – they would shoot him – they would poison his food.

"Rudabaugh is at the Santa Fe jail," wrote the editor of the *Santa Fe New Mexican*, March 22, 1881, "having returned from Las Vegas yesterday. He prefers Santa Fe to Las Vegas even when it comes to a change of jails. He is better provided for here both in the matter of food and as regards accommodations."

Rudabaugh confided to the reporter that the people of Old Town would not rest until they saw him in his grave. They would try every trick in the book to put him there. He was not aware that the jailer was that popular. [John J.] Allen and Rudabaugh made their way to Greathouse's freight and stage depot near Anton Chico. It was this freighter – a rustler and outlaw in his own right – who introduced Rudabaugh and Allen to Billy the Kid. [Greathouse did not introduce Billy and Rudabaugh. Rudabaugh fled to Fort Sumner after jailer Valdez was killed by John J. Allen, meeting Billy for the first time there. Allen was already dead, and was declared dead by the court April 18, 1881.]

Meantime, Webb, languishing in jail, came to the conclusion that it was tough and go all the way. The lawyers wanted more money; the authorities were anxious to see him hung; the vigilantes were ready to accommodate, but fearful of reprisals from Rudabaugh's friends forfeited the pleasure. But Rudabaugh did manage to bribe some guards and others in Old Town – Dave managed to keep in touch – and Webb managed to escape as we have seen.

The *Dodge City Times* for December 18, 1880, made note of this:

"The *Las Vegas Optic*, December 11... says: J. J. Webb, under the sentence of death for the killing of Michael Kelliher in East Vegas, and Davis, a mule thief, who separated from the other prisoners immediately after the escape from the Las Vegas jail some weeks ago, have been captured at Bosque Grande by Pat Garrett, deputy sheriff of Lincoln County, and a posse of fourteen men. It appears that the posse were not looking for Webb but were scouring the country in search of the whereabouts of Rudabaugh and his notorious gang whose depredations have been the darkest and boldest type."

"The party approached the house of Daniel Dedrick at Bosque Grande at two o'clock in the morning, where Rudabaugh was supposed to be stopping, and remained secreted near the premises until daylight broke upon the scene, when, instead of Rudabaugh, Webb and Davis came out of the house and were immediately surrounded and taken to Fort Sumner, where they are now heavily armed and closely guarded. The prisoners had very little to say. Webb remarked that he was waiting for the arrival of Rudabaugh and his men, who were to go with them to Old Mexico. There is not much danger of an attempt being made to release Webb as Rudabaugh's followers are scattered over a wide territory, and the whole country is alive with determined men, who, if necessary, will exchange an eye for an eye and a tooth for a tooth. They will either capture the outlaws and turn them over to the authorities or will kill them on the spot. Most probably the latter, if there be any resistance. The prisoners now in the hands of the officers of the law will be held under a strong guard until other criminals at large in Lincoln county are either captured or killed, when they will be brought to Las Vegas and placed in jail, from which no more breaks will be made...."

Note here how little emphasis is placed on Billy the Kid as the leader of the outlaws. Newspaper men both in Dodge and Las Vegas seemed to think that Rudabaugh took over. As time goes on Billy the Kid seems to be more and more a rustler, horse thief and braggart, who falls far short of the number of men he is supposed to have killed, and grows in stature only because of writers who are anxious to make him out to be more than he actually was. This could only mean that Billy the Kid was not known in New Mexico until the Lincoln County War, or shortly afterwards. Even though "wanted," he does not seem to be particularly singled out. Perhaps the *Police Gazette* and Pat Garrett's book had a good deal to do with his rise to popularity. Dutch Henry, Ike Stockton, Dave Mather, Doc Holliday, Luke Short, Dave Rudabaugh, were given more headlines in their day than Billy the Kid. It was only after the capture at Stinking Spring that editors began to pour it on about the buck-toothed lad. Besides, Rudabaugh was better known in Dodge and Las Vegas than Billy the Kid. It is a well known fact that Billy was never able to push Rudabaugh around the way he did O'Folliard and Bowdre. The grave markers at Fort Sumner may say PALS, but the Kid proved a heartless, selfish brute when they needed him most. At Stinking Spring it was Rudabaugh, not Billy, who made arrangements to surrender to Pat Garrett. Rudabaugh hasn't struck the public fancy like Billy the Kid, but if the Kid had objected to the surrender his career would have ended that day. Rudabaugh would have taken care of it. Before looking into Rudabaugh's life with the Kid, here is a last word about [John J.] Allen:

"A new phase is put on the killing of John [J.] Allen, who was implicated in the murder of the jailer last spring. He was taken in by Indians (at the Mescalero Reservation), as was reported, but is said to have been assassinated by Rudabaugh or the Kid, as they were afraid he might inform on them. Allen was not of a vicious disposition but whisky and evil associates changed him from a peaceful mechanic to a desperado who only commanded the respect that a pair of forty-fives give a man on the frontier. He came from a Christian family in Atlanta, Georgia, where his sister, Mrs. Chapman, now resides – and his right name was Lewelling instead of Allen. His old companions ought to have happy dreams in their lonely cells (both Billy the Kid and Rudabaugh were in the Santa Fe jail at the time) in Santa Fe when they think of their old comrade they so foully murdered and the traveler should pause when he comes to Allen's grave at Martin's Well and think on the prime causes that darken a bright life and tarnish the name of an honored family and say whether it pays to sanction gambling halls and dance halls...." (*Las Vegas Gazette*, February 26, 1881)

Martin's Well was a mile above Aleman on the Jornada del Muerto. One going from Socorro to Fort Selden could not fail to notice the solitary grave but few ever associated it with the deeds of either Rudabaugh or Billy the Kid. Nothing remains now to indicate the spot. The very name has passed on with the old-timers. Now it is part of the Elephant Butte Dam.

The *Dodge City Times* for November 20, 1880, carried this interesting item:

"Rudabaugh and his gang perfected the arrangements by which Webb and the others were delivered from the Las Vegas jail. The *Las Vegas Optic* gives the names of those delivered in the plot, being Dave Rudabaugh, Mysterious Dave Mather, Little [James] Allen, Bennett and others. These parties are not unknown in the annals of crime on this border. The *Optic* says of Rudabaugh's gang: "For some time the gang has been in New Mexico, gradually approaching Las Vegas. First Rudabaugh and twelve vassals were near San Marcial (near the ruins of old Fort Craig), afterwards at Fort Sumner, where they separated two weeks ago, and congregated again in a sequestered spot on the Pecos, thirty miles southwest of the city (La Questa present Villanueva). In this rendezvous the plan of action was perfected. Spies came into town and taking advantage of a lull in jail affairs, managed to pass tools and keys into the hands of the men in the cell from which the birds have flown. The time of the break was understood to the hour. By working quietly the prisoners were successful in gaining the open air. Skulking through the outskirts of town they went to point on the Santa Fe Trail, south of the west side (i.e., New Town) and there found horses in wait. A sharp drive brought them to the camp of the hospitable Rudabaugh, and before daybreak they were trooping over the prairies enroute to a more genial clime than any of them ever hoped to find in Montezuma (the hot springs above Las Vegas where people bathed for health."

[This entire account of Webb's jail escape, supposedly contrived by Rudabaugh and a large gang of spies and confederates, is untrue. On November 11, 1880, Webb, James Allen, George Davidson, John Murray, William Mullen, and George Davis escaped from the Las Vegas jail by picking the padlocks of their cell (there were two padlocks on each door). Because the padlocks were quite good, the Las Vegas newspapers initially argued that the escape had been engineered by outside parties and a least one jailer had been bribed. That belief was disproved when escapees Webb and Mullen, after being recaptured, confirmed they had escaped on their own by picking the padlocks with telegraph wire.]

Webb did not find Rudabaugh as suggested by the editor. Editors of frontier towns could spin yarns as fast as some gunslingers could spin a six-shooter.

The Plaza at Old Town Las Vegas about the time Rudabaugh was on the police force.

Chapter 5 | With Billy the Kid

Rudabaugh may have engineered Webb's escape, short-lived as it was, but he was too shrewd to show himself to the people of Old Town, for even Dave Mather could not prevent his being hung to the nearest tree. Of all the gunslingers and desperadoes to ever haunt the night spots in Old or New Town, Rudabaugh is the only one they are determined to kill. Word must have made the rounds that Rudabaugh was ready to drift off into Mexico. But he is not quite ready for a change of scene, nor of country. He enjoyed the hospitality of La Questa (not to be confused with the town near Costilla up near the Colorado line, once known as Rio Colorado), Anton Chico, Socorro, San Marcial, San Pedro, White Oaks, spending his time rustling, robbing stages and roaming the countryside with the mavericks that ran out of Lincoln a jump ahead of the sheriff. Here he breathed freely again, The hall of horrors for Dave Rudabaugh was Las Vegas. It was the last place in the world he wanted to be. Eyes never closed; ears were always pointed; ropes always in readiness over and against the day of his return. The vigilantes considered him more of a challenge than a risk, so they kept their masks on hand, guns primed, knives sharpened, noses to the ground – he would be back. It was written in the stars.

[The only robbery committed by Rudabaugh while on the run after Valdez was killed was the October 16, 1880, robbery of the "Star" mail and passenger line four miles north of Fort Sumner (the line was owned by Cornelius "Con" Cosgrove and managed by his brother Michael "Mike" Cosgrove). The line's mule-drawn buckboard had just left Fort Sumner and was heading for Las Vegas. (The line ran weekly both directions between Las Vegas and Las Cruces.)]

[Although historians writing about this event have asserted that Billy the Kid was one of the stage robbers, the actual robbers were Rudabaugh, Billy Wilson, and Tom Pickett, as Rudabaugh confirmed in his confession after being caught. The postal inspector investigating the crime believed that the robbery was staged by the driver and his sole passenger. The were arrested and charged with the crime, but when more information emerged, the case against them was dismissed. To avoid being identified by their clothes, Rudabaugh and Pickett robbed the stage in their undergarments.]

During those months of liberty from April to December, he came to know Billy the Kid. They played cards, changed cattle brands, took horses to Tascosa, Socorro, Lemitar, Polverdera, San Antonio (New Mexico); broke bread with solitary sheepherders; hid out in the Bosque around Anton Chico. Before he died, old Francisco Madrid told me of those days and the errands he, as a sixteen-year-old sheepherder, ran for Billy and Dave. He even brought them to his home in La Questa. There they relished the chili picoso, and tortillas, and frijoles.

During these months Billy the Kid learned it didn't pay to cross Dave Rudabaugh. The death of [John J.] Allen proved this. Jim East, who was with the posse on the ride in from Stinking Spring, had ample opportunity to study the two men. "If ever Billy the Kid was afraid of a man," he often remarked in later years, "that man was Dave Rudabaugh." The Kid once told Governor Wallace that he wore a gun for his own protection; Rudabaugh wore a gun because he enjoyed it. Rudabaugh preferred to play it alone sometimes and when he did, he used one of the abandoned buildings of Fort Bascom as a hideout. How many of the Wilson Waddingham cattle and the Watts stock in the area he ran off can hardly be estimated. Once he was nearly caught at Fort Bascom but managed to get the drop on the cowboys and made his getaway [not a true story].

The reluctance to spill blood seems to be a trait with Rudabaugh; one of the few things that made him unlike a Border Ruffian, or complemented his Border Ruffian tactics. But he did not prevent others from spilling blood, as in the case of Allen with Valdez; the fighters at the Greathouse depot with Carlyle, and in other instances, the most notable being Curly Bill vs. Wyatt Earp [this story, that Rudabaugh was in Arizona and involved in the fight against the Earps is entirely false]. In this respect, he is very much the Border Ruffian. Some soldiers at Fort Union were of the opinion that it was Dave Rudabaugh who held up the quartermaster bringing the payroll to Fort Selden [not true]. The stage had been halted near San Marcial and the money taken. Rudabaugh was also held responsible for robbing the mails at Socorro and of taking the strongbox from the stage at Canoncito [not true]. He definitely held up the stage at Puerticito near Gonzoles, about eight miles from La Questa. [That stage was robbed by Rudabaugh, Joseph Martin, and Joe Carson on August 14, 1879, while Rudabaugh was working as a Las Vegas city constable. William Mullen and brothers Joseph and William Stokes were falsely convicted of this crime and served 16 months of their two-and-half-year sentence, before they were freed by Rudabaugh's confession to the crime.] He also made an attempt on the stage at Glorieta, San Miguel del Bado, Pecos, La Manga, El Macho and Colonias [none of these charges are true]. He was in it up to his ears although given very little publicity. What he did with his ill-gotten gains he alone knew. He was forever broke. He rarely ever drank to excess but did like to gamble and was lavish with the night life ladies. Those who enjoyed his favors also kept his secrets.

George Kimball [Kimbrell] was one of the few sheriffs Billy the Kid took a liking to, even though the lawman arrested him on April 14, 1879. Kimball favored McCarthy – or Bonney – or Antrim – take your pick – all three names go with Billy the Kid – because he was on his side in drumming up votes for his election to office. McCarthy was suspicious of Garrett's motives. When Garrett arrested Webb he was actually deputy sheriff. When he defeated Kimball for office in November, he became sheriff, but did not assume office until the first of the year. This would automatically keep Kimball in office during November and December. McCarthy was not at all pleased with the election returns and voiced some choice words for the ears of the tall man from Alabama. Garrett resolved to get the Kid dead or alive. Neither the Kid nor Garrett seemed too anxious to face each other or they would have done so long before that fateful night in Pete Maxwell's bedroom. Rudabaugh did not vote. He was neither for Kimball nor Garrett. He just wanted to keep Dave Rudabaugh alive.

Dave Rudabaugh had worked for the Adams Express Company in Las Vegas [no, he was a city constable]. Jim Greathouse often went to the depot to pick up freight. The two became friends. Greathouse was from Texas. He developed a freighting business out of White Oaks, then a booming mining town and expanded his interests along the route to La Questa, Anton Chico, San Miguel, Puertocito (present Sena), La Manga, Las Vegas. His stage stop at Anton Chico is better known because of the Carlyle incident. He introduced Rudabaugh to Billy the Kid. Greathouse and a partner maintained a stage freight station and quasi-eating place on the road to the new mining location known as White Oaks, a town whose history is every bit as colorful as that of Kingston, Georgetown, Alma, Hillsboro and others that took over when "end-of-track" towns settled down to respectability.

A desperado fleeing justice decided to hide out in Albuquerque. Resting for a time in the lava country, he found gold. It held no interest for him so he traded his find for forty dollars and a pistol. Jack Winters and John Baxter made the most of it. The first mine was known as the North Homestake. Then came Old Abe, Little Mack, Confidence, Rip Van Winkle, Smuggler, Comstock. The gamblers, dance hall girls, con men, lawyers, freighters, drifters, cowboys, prospectors, drummers, cyprians, gunslingers that once frequented the "end-of-track" towns now made nuisances of themselves in the mining towns. White Oaks was on the agenda for Rudabaugh and Billy the Kid. The *Albuquerque Journal* for April 6, 1881, had this to say about White Oaks:

"White Oaks takes its name from two immense springs situated two and a half miles from the town of White Oaks, these springs being surrounded by immense growth of white oak trees. The camp was first brought to public notice by the discovery of the far-famed and world-renowned Homestake Mine. John E. Wilson, John V. Winters and other old placer miners were informed by one Baxter, a Californian of '49, who received his information from a Mexican, that there were good placer diggings in the gulch now known as Baxter Gulch, running from Baxter Mountain nearly due east to the arroyo now bounding the west side of the town of White Oaks. These men immediately proceeded to the place and commenced work, meeting with great success, although compelled to transport the water necessary to wash the dirt on the backs of mules for four miles; they established their headquarters in a cabin at the White Oaks springs and in the morning would pack to the diggings all the water they could carry, and in the evening would pack to the springs for washing all the pay dirt possible. In this way they worked nearly the whole summer, and realized handsomely as the gulch was found to be very rich, several nuggets being discovered of great value, and one pocket being found from which in one day there was taken by the men over $300. For several weeks thirty dollars was averaged by each man."

"While at work an old miner by the name of Wilson dropped in among them. He was from Arizona. After a short time he entered into partnership with John E. Wilson; they worked together for some time, the Arizona Wilson meanwhile prospecting for the lead at the head of the gulch, out of which the placer gold was supposed to have come. One day while out prospecting he sat down on a boulder to rest and eat his lunch, arid noticing on one corner of the boulder a few crystals, broke with his pick a portion of it, and exposed to view several particles of wire gold. Taking the piece with him he returned to camp and showed it to his partner. The two immediately returned to the spot, and after digging a short time exposed the vein, and located the famous Homestake."

"Upon returning to camp the Arizona Wilson offered his share for sale, and it was purchased by Winters for all the funds he could raise, viz $40 in washings, $2.00 in silver and an old pistol. (A rather different version than the generally accepted one of the fugitive outlaw escaping Texas.) Work was immediately commenced on the vein and at the depth of four feet wire gold in profusion was struck. Assays had been had from this mine showing the astounding figures of $15,000 to $40,000 to the ton. Work has been progressing continuously since that time, and an immense amount of gold has been taken out, though the ore has been worked by an arrastra. Much work has been done and is now being done on the mine. There are two tunnels – one 75 and the other 132 feet in length; three shafts one 80, one 65 and one 70 feet in depth, and the Homestake Mining Company of White Oaks, the owners of Wilson's half of the mine, are now working day and night shifts on two of the shafts and also running a tunnel on the south part, where on March 21 was struck another body of ore with gold visible to the naked eye all through the rock. When it is considered that the latest find is 900 feet from where the wire gold was first found, and where the ore has been so rich all the way down for a distance of 80 feet, some idea can be formed of the richness of the mine. An assay from a piece of ore from the last find, showing no free gold, was made on March 24th. resulting in $17,000 per ton, flour gold. Surprise to relate, the float from this vein on the side of the hill and in the bottom of the canyon near where the last gold was found, on soil being washed from it, shows free gold sticking to it on all sides, and on breaking, gold appears all through the rock, This float lies where it has been washed over repeatedly for the last three years, and yet was never discovered till a few days ago."

"On the south of the Homestake are many locations. The Ethan Allen, belonging to Mr. James Allen and others is a well defined lead, supposed to be the Homestake vein. Although no free gold has yet been found in this mine, yet the ore, free milling quartz of fine quality, runs well up, from assays that have been made of it, some going as high as $80 in gold, principally. Although on the south, on Baxter Mountain, are found the White Swan, Otis, Christopher, Discovery and others, all well refined leads, showing well in gold and silver. The Christopher, upon which considerable work has been done by Mr. A. M. Jones, the present owner, has assayed $300 to the ton. On the north is found the Little Nell, Comstock, Large Hopes, Little Mack, Omaha, Baxter Boy, Gladstone, Red Dick, Hoozier Boy, Old Abe, Starr and others. Free gold has been found in the Little Mack and Little Nell; both are well defined leads of gold bearing quartz."

"A tunnel is now being run on the Little Nell, and the vein is widening and looking better constantly. This property is owned by Messrs. [James S.] Redman, Hudgens and Sweet. The Comstock is an extension of the Homestake and yet little work has been done by the owners, James Allen, H. C. Campbell, G. W. Prichard and others. The work that has been done, however, shows it to be a well defined lead of gold bearing quartz much like the Homestake in character. The shaft on the Baxter Boy is down 40 feet. The mine is on a foothill of Baxter Mountain, known as Bald Hill. Within a few feet of the surface the ore only showed two or three dollars in silver, but at present depth shows a four foot lead of iron stained quartz, carrying ninety-seven ounces in silver and ten dollars in gold."

"The Red Dick, much like the Baxter Boy at the surface and for some distance down, only showed a few dollars in precious metals, but at thirty-seven feet, the present depth, results from assays show sixty-eight ounces silver and eighteen dollars gold. This vein is three and a half feet in width, of stained iron ore, carrying a great amount of iron and copper pyrites. The Gladstone is in the immediate neighborhood of the Baxter Boy and the Red Dick, and shows at twelve feet a good vein of iron stained quartz, about three feet in width. The Old Abe seems to be an immense deposit of gold bearing rock. The deposit is about one hundred feet in width, and from tests made with gold pan along its entire width carries gold in paying quantities. The Hoosier Boy is also in the same belt as the Red Dick and Baxter Boy. The development on this mine consists of a ten foot shaft and a seventy foot tunnel. The vein is about four feet wide, carrying gold and silver."

"On Lone Mountain, immediately north of Baxter, several good mines have been discovered and opened, such as the Captain Kidd, DuBois, Little Anne, and F. C. Kempton. The Captain Kidd and DuBois lie in the same vein. The vein crops for sixty feet in width, from wall to wall, and is composed seemingly of iron, mixed with quartz of the finest quality. The iron, however, much predominating and much of it covered with copper stain. Assays show this ore body to carry the precious metals in abundance. Ore from the shaft of the Captain Kid, only ten feet in depth, shows $30.38 and sixty-five ounces of silver, fifteen percent copper and twelve percent lead; and from DuBois at the same depth, $49.50 silver twenty percent, copper twenty-two percent. The ore body lies between porphyry and sandstone. The owners of the Kidd are Col. Watts, James Allen and Col. Pritchard; and of the DuBois, Messrs. Charles Frost, William Watson, C. Ewing Patterson of White Oaks and L. P. DuBois and Judge Otis of Atchison, Kansas."

"The Little Annie lies on the east side of the mountain and belongs to probate Judge Tomlinson. It is a large vein of carbonate ore, much of it showing a deep green color, running high in silver and copper. The L. C. Kempton lies on the southeast slope of the mountain and belongs to Messrs. Brothers, Wilson and others; it is an iron lead, cropping in width seventy-five feet. The owners have at present a seven-foot shaft on it, but expect the coming summer to tunnel across the lead from the foot of the mountain, and then to sink a fifty foot shaft from the tunnel. The ore, on testing at present depth of seven feet, shows $24 in gold."

"The Black Prince mine is on Baxter mountain, south and east of Homestake. There is at present a sixty foot shaft and 75 foot tunnel on this vein; the vein is composed of two stratas of mineral bearing ores one of a fine quality of quartz and the other apparently a carbonate. High assays had been had from this mine; 600 ounces of silver and $17 gold being one test. It is highly thought of by many experts who have examined it. The Oro Fino is another on Baxter Mountain. This mine belongs to Mr. I. E. Sligle, assayer of this place, and Professor Robinson of Las Vegas, who recently purchased one half interest. The owners are now running a hundred foot tunnel on this mine. The Monarch is also located on Baxter Mountain, belonging to Dr. Mitchell; free gold has been found in this mine, and it looks well. The vein is only four feet in width, composed of quartz mixed with some porphyry, but the porphyry is gradually disappearing, as great depth is reached and the quartz obtained with more iron. Ore from any part of this lead, crushed and worked with gold pan, shows many colors."

"The Reclusia Mine, which occupies a hill near the divide, between Baxter and Love Mountains, is claimed to be the same lode upon which the Little Mack is located. It has similar walls, and the ore is porphyritic quartz. Free gold has been found in a boulder on this claim, but all the work that has been done is the annual assessment. This mine is the property of Dr. A. G. Love. The Lottie Kirkham is situated on the level plain between Love and the White Mountains, about five miles from the town of White Oaks and one and a half miles from Baxter Mountain. The vein runs nearly north and south, as in fact do almost all the veins of this mineral belt. The crops from five to twenty feet above the plain for about 900 feet, sinking at both ends. The vein matter is fifty feet from wall to wall, the wall being granite. The developments are a forty foot shaft and an eight foot shaft. At present depth the pay streak is two feet in width, of quartz carrying considerable galena and assays sixty ounces of silver and $40 gold, and the vein, at present depth of forty feet is gradually widening. The Red Cliff Mining Company of Colorado, recently purchased of Mr. O. P. Burtt, the owner, a one half interest in this mine, and intend to push development during this spring with rapidity. This mine from its peculiar location and surroundings, has excited considerable attention. It has been examined by several mining experts, who pronounce it a very unique discovery and a valuable find. The extension, called the Nina, also belongs to Mr. Burtt, and shows the same character of ore. Other mines are The Queer of God, The Forty-Four and others."

"White Oaks is the mining and supply center of several other mining districts. Nogols, White Mountains, Pine comprising the Lincoln Mts., Malpais and Jicarillas; the first in importance being the Nogols because longer discovered, prospected and worked. The town of White Oaks is laid out in a basin formed by the Carizo and Pattis Mountains on the east, the Lone Mts. on the north and the Baxter on the west. It has a beautiful situation on a flat of about 160 acres, bounded on the east and west by deep arroyos, and has a gradual slope from the northeast to the southwest. The main street, White Oaks Ave., is about one half mile in length by one hundred feet in width, and is built up on both sides with substantial dwellings and stores for nearly the whole length."

"The permanent population is at present about eight hundred, with families coming in every day. Besides there are hundreds scattered about in the different mining districts which make White Oaks the base of their operations for their supplies. Many wells have been dug in and about the town and water is good. It is obtained at a depth of from twenty-five to sixty-feet. Mr. F. A. Blakes saw mill is running constantly. A daily mail is run to and from the town of Socorro and Fort Stanton, thirty miles away. Good and substantial buckboards are run on the line to Socorro by Messrs. Kelly & Hagarman, the mail contractors, and bring passengers from that point in sixteen to twenty hours. There is also a first class road to Las Vegas, from which point a line of hacks is run by Mr. Straumer, bringing passengers through in about three or four days...."

Two breed of men now put in appearance to baffle the sheriff, constable and people in general. They were more secretive and elusive than the gunslinger, horse thief, outlaw and bandit. To combat this new type in the annals of frontier crime, the detective was added as an integral part of law enforcement. These hidden shadows tied sheriff and posse in a knot. Cattle thieves they could track down and even enjoy a "shoot-out" now and then. But counterfeiters and confidence men puzzled them. The old days were passing. White Oaks certainly had its share of con men and counterfeiters. To cope with the situation, Pat Garrett hired big husky, pot-bellied, jovial Barney Mason to act as undercover man in ferreting out of the ring of counterfeiters said to be operating out of White Oaks. One popular scheme often resorted to was to go down to Old Mexico, buy a herd of cattle for the domestic brand of greenbacks and sell them around Socorro, Anton Chico, La Questa, Las Vegas, Sapello, Mora, Buena Vista, Santa Clara (Wagonmound), Naranjo, Fort Sumner and Santa Fe for government issue. While Rudabaugh, McCarthy, Wilson and other members of the gang refused to handle the home made money, they were not adverse to delivering cattle to isolated areas provided they were well paid. This is a rather round about way of explaining Mason's presence at White Oaks, but it set off a chain of events that ultimately led to the capture at Stinking Spring.

One day, while Mason was at Dedrick's Livery Stable, three riders came looking for feed. It must be remembered that Webb and Davis were captured at the Dedrick (seemingly a brother) place [it was Dan Dedrick's ranch at Bosque Grande], causing Mason to suspect that perhaps the brothers were implicated in some way. The three riders Mason saw approaching the stable were Billy the Kid, Dave Rudabaugh and Tom Pickett [it was Billy Wilson, not Pickett]. Big of frame as he was, Mason was aware he couldn't handle the trio by himself. He sought out [James W.] Bell and told him who the three were. He asked Bell's assistance in capturing the desperadoes. If he rode over to the little village of Roswell, he might miss a golden opportunity. He was sure Garrett would understand. Bell did not share Mason's enthusiasm for heroics. There would be gun play. Rudabaugh would refuse to agree to an arrest. Not just on general principles either. He was aware of what happened to Webb. The Kid! He might feel like Dave, Pickett? He was an unknown quantity. If he panicked there would be a hot time at West & Dedrick's. No solitary sparrow on a rooftop was Billy the Kid, who boasted he would never be taken alive. Rudabaugh would rather shoot it out and take his chances than go back to face the mob at Old Town. Bell was not a coward; nor was he foolish. Two against McCarthy and Rudabaugh! He wasn't about to make any certain little woman he knew a widow. All they knew of Pickett was that he had been on the police force in Las Vegas. He might turn out to be more dangerous than even the Kid and Rudabaugh; and these two usually hit what they aimed at. To try to trap them at the stable was both dangerous and foolhardy. Bell suggested they visit William H. Hudgens, a deputy. Jim Redmond [Redman] tells a little of the deputy's background in the *Golden Era* newspaper in the fall of 1889 (Oct. 19):

"I came to what is known as White Oaks in the fall of 1879, in company with William H. Hudgens and a bottle of whisky. We found camped there James Allen, his son, Harry, and old Livingstone. We visited the now famous Baxter Gulch and found imbedded in the side of a hill Charles Starr, George Gaines, George Gay, Tom Walters, Dick McGuiness and Jack Winters, better known as 'Old Blue Skin.' There was very little work done there at the time. In the spring of 1880, Mr. Hudgens and myself put up a saloon on the flat where White Oaks now stands. We stocked it with Dowlin & DeLaney's tanglefoot and pure Havana cigars imported from Arkansas in the same box with the late Charley Ross, and I tell you we did a rushing trade. But the town continued to grow and we concluded to build the old Pioneer Saloon. Then came James, the merchant; Jim Sweet also came and played poker with the boys, and many more too trifling to talk about. About that time we made arrangements to have the mail forwarded from Lincoln and Stanton to the Pioneer Saloon, and there, if we were sober enough, people got their mail...."

Hudgens felt that the crisis warranted his deputizing a number of men able and willing to take the outlaws, dead or alive. Redmond had sold his share in the Pioneer Saloon to John Hudgens, brother to the deputy. A number of the men deputized had been on the Murphy side in the Lincoln County War – Tom Longworth, Jim Redmond, John Hudgens to mention a few.

Meantime, totally unaware of the beehive stirring at White Oaks, Bonney, Rudabaugh and Pickett concluded their business at West & Dedrick's and rode out of town. At Coyote Spring[s], this side of the Trincheras, they halted and made camp. Here they made plans for a raid on the remuda belonging to Bell [Jason B. Bell, not James W. Bell]. The long, cold winter months lay ahead and there was need for fresh mounts. Had they known of Bell's part in the attempted capture they would not have been so half-hearted about taking fresh horses. The remuda was well guarded and they decided to try elsewhere rather than kill any of the cowboys. Many people share the illusion that winter nights in New Mexico are balmy, especially in mountainous districts. The air is cold, crisp, dry. This lack of moisture or humidity has lulled many into the belief that little clothing or blankets are necessary for sleeping in the open.

I have buried at least three frozen to death in the hills for want of proper covering. The population of White Oaks in November 1880 was three hundred. Judging from the rich strikes one would expect more and no doubt there would have been, had not hundreds of such camps mushroomed in New Mexico, Nevada, Utah, Colorado and Arizona about the same time. The big boom for White Oaks did not come until 1881. There is a story told that as Billy the Kid rode out of White Oaks he recognized Jim Redmond standing near the Pioneer Saloon. Since the miner was definitely not on the McSween side during the Lincoln county troubles, Bonney sent a shot his way to scare him. Redmond fails to mention the incident in his report to the editor of the *Golden Era*.

Deputy Hudgens and his posse were not in favor of setting out at night in pursuit of men known to be handy with a six-shooter. They decided to wait until after sunrise. The logical place to look would be Coyote Spring[s]. The Kid was known to be friendly with Greathouse and this is the path he would take if in need of supplies and horses. Warm ashes from the camp fire proved sufficient evidence that they were on the right trail. Directly ahead were two riders. Hudgens was convinced they were Bonney and Rudabaugh. The men fanned out, spurred their horses and surrounded the pair, prepared to shoot them down if necessary. Neither offered resistance. They turned out to be Mose Dedrick, brother to the owner of the livery stable, and another unidentified friend [William J. Lamper]. The deputy placed Dedrick under arrest, claiming that he had a wanted poster for him. Asked who his friend was, he replied that the man's name was

Lamper, whereupon Hudgens placed him under arrest also as wanted by the law [there were no charges against Lamper].

They now approached the old abandoned sawmill [this gunfight occurred at Coyote Springs, not at the sawmill]. Hudgens approached cautiously, fearful of being ambushed. Three shots rang out. The men rode back out of the line of fire. Using their Winchesters, they succeeded in killing Bonney's and Billy Wilson's horses [and Rudabaugh's]. It dawned on Hudgens that instead of three men the whole gang were quartered at the mill [there were only five at the springs: Billy, Rudabaugh, Wilson, Joseph "Bob" M. Edwards, and Joseph "Joe" Cook]. Firing was heavy on both sides. After a time the outlaws decided to make a run for it. Two went in one direction riding for other parts. They had enough of outlaw life. It is said that they settled clown, married and became respected citizens in the community. [The two who escaped separately were Edwards and Cook. Cook was captured and jailed by Garrett on November 25, 1880. Edwards was killed by Garrett's deputy Thomas "Kip" McKinney at Hank Harrison's ranch near Black River on May 8, 1881. Unusual for an "outlaw," Edwards was married and had four young kids when he was killed.] Bonney, Rudabaugh, Pickett and Wilson rode two to a horse and managed to escape. [Pickett was not present. Billy, Rudabaugh, and Wilson, having lost their horses, walked to White Oaks, where they obtained new mounts from West & Dedrick's livery stable.] Hudgens and his men approached the abandoned shack, rummaged about and found food, an overcoat left there by Mose Dedrick (evidently he and Lamper were riding in to town to find out the news from the livery stable owner), and a pair of gloves said to have been left there by Billy the Kid. Jimmy Carlyle, the blacksmith at White Oaks, took a fancy to the gloves and claimed them as his own.

Instead of going after the fugitives the posse returned to White Oaks where the story of their skirmish with Bonney and Rudabaugh made the rounds. Every cantina in town welcomed them, as between drinks the tale got longer and windier. Somewhere along the way Rudabaugh picked up another horse and the four [three] made it to the Greathouse stage stop without further mishap.

Fortified with liquor and spurred on by the townsmen, the posse decided to ride out again [this posse was led by Thomas "Pinto Tom" Longworth and James Carlyle]. This time not to return until they had the gang in tow, or buried. No doubt about it, they would be found at the Greathouse place. As they rode out they told each other that the Territory would be grateful to them for ridding the land of two such men as Rudabaugh and William Bonney. Carlyle in particular fulminated against Bonney, for whom he seemingly entertained a personal grudge, perhaps the result of a disparaging remark in his blacksmith shop. Redmond was anxious to even the score for the shot the Kid took at him as he left White Oaks. It seemed definitely settled. The outlaws had had their last fling.

There are many versions of what transpired at the Greathouse place. Our account sticks to the version found in the collection at Highlands University, Las Vegas. It does not agree with the story told by Joseph Steck, the cook at the stage stop, but we must remember that he wrote his version some nine years after the event, when Bonney was fast becoming a legend through the pages of the *New York Sun*, *The Police Gazette*, Pat Garrett and his ghost writer. The Steck account is found in the *Lincoln County Leader*. How much is fact or embellishment is simple conjecture. Some writers refer to Steck as Joe; others as Johnny. Whatever the name, he left the house early in the morning, axe in hand, to look for some dry log to get the fire going for the morning meal. Two of the posse, Dorsey and Baker, approached him, leveling their rifles to cover him. The action startled him for he was not aware of being wanted by the law, nor that anyone was in the vicinity. They forced him to accompany them behind some piled-up logs, where the deputy asked him if Rudabaugh, Bonney and Wilson were in the house. Steck said that he didn't know. There were some men visiting Greathouse but he didn't know their names. Hudgens described the outlaws and the cook told him that the descriptions fitted the men who were still sleeping when he came out to gather wood.

"Fine," said Hudgens. "Take up an armful of wood. Here is a note that I want you to give to Bonney." The paper read: "You are surrounded. You haven't a chance. Come out with your hands up, and without your guns." Steck was reluctant to carry the message, now that he was assured as to the identity of the men with Greathouse. Hudgens argued with him that there was no other way without a gun fight. The deputy is said to have threatened him unless he went back with the note. Caught between two fires, he gathered up some wood and went in with the message. A short time later Greathouse came out waving the same piece of paper. Under the deputy's words, Bonney scribbled three short words "Go to hell." It meant that the desperadoes would settle for nothing less than gunsmoke. Hudgens looked at his men, weighing the consequences of inexperienced miners pitted against the veterans Bonney, Rudabaugh and Wilson. For how many would it be the red badge of courage, or a shroud? If ever the need for Garrett was felt, this was it. Carlyle seemed to read his thoughts. He knew both Bonney and Rudabaugh. He would sacrifice the pleasure of killing them both if Hudgens was so intent on avoiding bloodshed and go in to convince them that they should give up without a fight. Hudgens told him it might work if Greathouse remained with the posse as hostage. "Tell the Kid," he said to the blacksmith, "that if you are not out of the house by two o'clock, it means a fight. Their friend, Greathouse, will have the benefit of the first shot. It is best for all concerned that they surrender without a fight. They are surrounded. It is useless and hopeless for them to attempt an escape. We will wait here to doomsday if necessary. They will have to come out of there some time."

Carlyle stood up so that those watching from the house could watch his every move. He held his rifle high in the air, then cast it away from him. Next he unbuckled his gunbelt, gave it to Hudgens and slowly walked toward the house. Someone from within opened the door for him. He greeted the Kid and Rudabaugh. Wilson remained at the window, watching against a surprise attack. Rudabaugh joined him as Bonney and Carlyle sat down to discuss the situation. Reaching out for a bottle and a glass, the Kid poured a drink and pushed it over to Carlyle. The blacksmith reached into his jeans for his tobacco in order to roll a cigarette. The gloves Bonney claimed were his fell out of the pocket. The Kid looked at them for a moment, as if putting them aside for Exhibit A in his mind's eye, and encouraged Carlyle to finish his drink. Rudabaugh turned from the window a second, looked at the gloves, but said nothing. He turned back to the window. Nothing stirred outside. And time ticked away. Rudabaugh, certain now that Hudgens would keep his word and not commence the attack until two o'clock, joined the two to watch the cat and mouse game. What the unarmed Carlyle hoped to accomplish was beyond him. He poured the drink and listened to the talk. After a time he went back to his station at the window. His eyes were intent on the log pile but his mind was back at the table. He wondered if the Kid would draw on Carlyle. He had been around the Kid just long enough to know his moods. From the way he was pouting, Carlyle's chances of ever getting out of the house alive were slim indeed.

"Jim, you haven't finished your drink," he heard the Kid say: "Drink up. You won't be able to later on."

"Your type (Bonney was referring to Carlyle's willingness to play in both leagues – he looked upon Carlyle as a stool pigeon) – should not be permitted the benefit of drawing even if you had a gun."

Carlyle's eyes twitched but his hand was steady as he lifted the glass to his lips, deliberately tilted it as if to venture an opinion of its quality, all the time studying his chances and wondering about the next move. Bonney took his gun from its holster, examined it a minute, and put it back. Whether the move had any particular significance Carlyle didn't bother to ask.

"So, you want me to surrender. Me, Rudabaugh, Wilson and Pickett [Pickett was not present]. To go to jail. There is a price on my head. Also Rudabaugh's. Who profits if we surrender? Certainly not us. Guess we don't surrender."

"If you don't intend to surrender, let me go out and tell the posse."

"It's not two o'clock. Time enough for that."

And the sand ran through the glass.

At two o'clock there still was no thought of surrender.

Two minutes after two, one of the posse fired a shot to indicate to the besieged that the time for games was over [this shot was an accidental misfiring by posse member John P. Eaker]. Since Hudgens had said nothing to Carlyle about a warning shot, his surmise was that the deputy had killed Greathouse. He jumped from the chair and went through the window. A bullet struck him before he landed. Wounded, he began crawling toward the posse. Both sides were now firing. Carlyle lay still. [Carlyle was shot three times, once each in the head, breast and body, front wounds suggesting he was killed by friendly fire from the posse. Rudabaugh and Wilson were indicted for Carlyle's death. Greathouse was indicted as an accomplice in Carlyle's death, even though he was outside the house without arms when Carlyle was shot. Greathouse's charges were eventually dropped.] No more bullets were wasted on the corpse. The battle began in earnest. The exchange of gunfire continued intermittently until well after dark.

Now in November the biting frost, the cold night air, the awful darkness was not all conducive to happiness. One after another of the posse voiced sentiments of a nice warm bed in White Oaks, or better still, a glass of cheer in the Hudgens saloon. About midnight there wasn't a man who didn't think "The heck with Billy the Kid, Dave Rudabaugh, Wilson and Pickett. Let Garrett worry about them. This time of the night a man should be home in bed or home in a saloon."

They brought Carlyle's body back with them. The whole town turned out for the funeral. Greathouse took advantage of the darkness to effect his escape. He guessed rightly that the posse would blame Carlyle's death on him. After the burial the men returned and set fire to the stage station.

[Following the shootout, Steck and a man named Kuch returned to Greathouse's from a nearby ranch where they had taken shelter. They found Carlyle's body "frozen stiff where he fell." They tied a blanket around him and buried him in "a hole a little toward the east from where he fell." The next day a posse led by John Hurley came to Greathouse's – they were looking for Billy, Rudabaugh, and Wilson. They dug up Carlyle and reburied him in a box in a different location. Then, taking revenge for Carlyle's death, they burned Greathouse's place to the ground. On August 5, 2022, the Billy the Kid's Historical Coalition installed a gravestone on Carlyle's previously unmarked grave.]

[From Greathouse's, Hurley's posse went to Lon Spencer's place. Interrogated, Spencer admitted that he had fed Billy, Rudabaugh, and Wilson breakfast the day after the fight. In retaliation for that act, they burned down Spencer's place.]

[When Billy and his two companions escaped the shootout at Greathouse's, they did so without horses. They walked to Spencer's place, and from there, they walked to Fort Sumner, a distance of about 90 miles.]

Greathouse was not easily discouraged. He continued to operate a freighting business. On May 9, 1881, some months after the battle, the editor of the *Optic* had this to say: "Jim Greathouse will arrive today from Anton Chico with a freighting outfit. Jim has had hard luck, and was the victim of bad associations. Last November his home on the road to White Oaks was burned, the results of a 'siege' against Billy the Kid and party. Greathouse has been hard at work at Anton Chico and has inspired a confidence in many who were inclined to believe that he has been in standing with lawless characters. He has purchased four yoke and two teams and comes here to solicit freight for White Oaks, He is regarded as an honest, faithful fellow, and any who have freight to be taken to the Oaks should make terms with him. He will run a freight train from here to the big camp."

Joel Fowler differed in this opinion. A desperado in his own right, he operated a cattle ranch in Socorro county. The *Santa Fe New Mexican*, quoting the *Socorro Sun*, December 19, 1881, has quite a story that throws some light on Fowler's background shortly before he was lynched by the vigilantes at Socorro and tells of Greathouse's activities which caused Fowler to kill him.

"For some time past Socorro has been red hot by spells from the knowledge that rustlers were operating in the country, and the arrest of the man Smith, now confined at Santa Fe, the brother of one of the Lamy Gang (an offshoot of the Ike Stockton outfit), who robbed Browne & Manzanarez's store, was the first clue to the mysterious moves of certain parties. Smith made a confession, and on that confession was booked. The trail was taken up and followed, and has led to the households of many unsuspected parties." A certain brand of cattle, C.O.D., has been disappearing. These cattle belonged to a man named (Joel) Fowler, who once lived in Santa Fe. Notice was published that any person found with cattle branded C.O.D. would be arrested for stealing, unless showing a bill of sale from the owner. Hides offered for sale bearing this brand were said to be traced to one Blackinton [Blackington], who owns a sawmill in the Gallinas and also has a large herd of cattle. He claims 15,000 head. Fowler's ranch was not many miles from Blackinton's.

"One week ago today (December 12) forty or more head of cattle were missed from Fowler's ranch grounds. A trail was found and followed up and on it was found a cow and calf, on the back track. This was over near Georgetown on the Star Road. It appears that when near the old Indian supply ranch, now deserted, Fowler and his chief herder came upon the thieves. This ranch used to be a stage station on the old Star Road to Fort Wingate from Fort Cummings. It is a fine adobe building. Here Fowler and his man met them face to face. The latter drew their guns, suspecting their pursuers, but Fowler set up a plea that he had killed a man in Socorro and was getting out of the country and wanted them to help him get his cattle out. After parleying, they consented, with the understanding that all the cattle they could get would be driven with them. There were present at this agreement Fowler and his chief herder, and three men who were thought to be employed at the Blackinton ranch or were hangers on. Their names were Jim Finley, Jim Greathouse and Jim Kay."

"Joel Fowler was often seen on the streets of Socorro with a big golden badge of a bull on his coat or vest, and was a solid set man. Greathouse was rather a tall man, with a heartless staring countenance and always wore a white hat, clown fashion. The other man was but little known. The compact was entered into and Fowler, together with his man, turned back with the gang. When they came to a place known as Point of Rocks, at the north end of the San Mateo Mts., Finley became suspicious that all was not right and opened fire. Fowler and his chief herder called the Ierio, and Fowler's double barreled shot gun, with twelve buckshot in each barrel, was best armed and brought down two of the men, and his chief herder dropped the third. It was previously known that these men had driven off the herd and must have had the money with them, but the bodies were left untouched as evidence. From the Point of Rocks Fowler and his man went directly to Blackinton's ranch and arrested Blackinton and an employee by the name of West. At the ranch Fowler found Al Burton who had just recently left the police force in Socorro and hired to Blackinton for one hundred dollars a month, to take charge of the stock ranch. Fowler told Burton that he guessed that he had better quit before he got into this thing too deep and Al thought so, too."

"Shortly afterward Blackinton and West were started toward Socorro. They came along to the Socorro canyon and Blackinton, who was loping along ahead, all of a sudden spurred his horse and wheeled from the road up into the mountain, and left them, holding the lead, as he had the best horse and it was dark, and getting away. West was brought to Socorro and put in chains. He made a confession of the whole affair. What that confession is remains in the book, but it is not yet known. Blackinton has not shown up to this hour; his whereabouts not known, West has been set free and at liberty upon the street. A posse of five men went out to hold an inquest on the bodies of the rustlers and to hunt up Blackinton. This disclosure brings into question the character of the other parties, but there is no public information that is reliable and consequently not given here. Fowler has put ten thousand dollars into cattle and his round-up did not show one-half of the stock. Greathouse was formerly one of Billy the Kid's party and kept a ranch on the White Oaks road, which was burned during the Lincoln county racket. He was known as the killer of many men. From other sources the number of the gang is given as seven. Three are dead and four are yet out. Blackinton's side of the story (he must have given himself up) is that it is a put-up job and he has sworn out a warrant for Fowler's arrest on the ground that Fowler drew deadly weapons on him and caused his servitude as a prisoner and had him criminally deprived of his liberty. He says that after his escape from Fowler he ran his horse until it dropped dead, then walked fourteen miles into town Saturday night and was out in the storm, from which exposure he was taken with lung fever. The public sentiment is that if Blackinton is guilty the move of Fowler is causing him to stand in front of those engaged in the affair, and he will bring forward his backing for protection; but if he is not guilty he is acting right...."

[Fowler met his own end twenty-five months later. On November 7, 1883, Fowler killed James E. Cale with a knife in the Grand Central Hotel in Socorro (some accounts say it happened in the street). On January 22, 1884, while awaiting trial for Cale's killing, Fowler was taken from jail by a mob of 200 men and hanged from a nearby tree.]

While Carlyle's death is attributed by many authors to Billy the Kid, no one can say with certainty that McCarthy's bullet was the deciding factor. With guns blazing on both sides, his own men might have done it. The Kid, writing later to Governor Wallace, disclaimed any responsibility for the death of the blacksmith. He argues that the men outside shot Carlyle because they thought the figure flying through the window was the Kid. None of the posse confirmed this way of thinking. Just who killed Carlyle is anybody's guess. McCarthy claims that he was in White Oaks to see Judge Leonard who was handling his case. He claims to have received a letter from the judge asking him to make the visit. Leonard's letter seems to have been lost, if it existed at all. The Kid further states that he was rude to Carlyle because the blacksmith could produce no written authority that called for his part in the arrest of the outlaws. He wanted Carlyle to remain in the house until dark, hoping to use him as a decoy when he made a break for freedom.

The threat on the part of the posse to kill Greathouse annoyed him as it did Rudabaugh who looked upon the station keeper not only as a friend but also as a victim of circumstances. He thought much more of Greathouse than he did of Roarke. He would be willing to kill Carlyle and every member of the posse if it meant saving Greathouse. Dave was made of that kind of loyalty. Border Ruffians, for all their maliciousness, knew this trait. It was part of the unwritten code of the frontier.

[There is no evidence other than hearsay that Billy wanted to kill Carlyle.]

Shortly after the fight at the Greathouse station, McCarthy, Dave Rudabaugh, Tom Pickett, Wilson and several others decided on a visit to Fort Sumner to pick up whatever newspapers were available. Possibly they wanted to find out what the Territorial papers had to say about them. No doubt they thrived on publicity. Also there was the fandango, drinks and gals, Rudabaugh said that they were anxious to secure fresh mounts as well as pleasures of the flesh. These papers were to be had at Pete Maxwell's. It is possible that the servant girl there who thought well of McCarthy, gathered them together for the day of his visit. McCarthy had a lady-love somewhere in the area. No doubt she assisted in saving papers for the gang. Maxwell himself subscribed to a number of papers. It is likely that Pete Maxwell's friendship for the Kid stemmed from these visits for reading material rather than from any personal regard. Maxwell, the rancher, was not the consort of outlaws. He might have liked his drinks, as the people of Fort Sumner knew, but he was very well liked by the respectable people because he was on the right side of the law. One of the items the Kid and Rudabaugh read in these papers came from the *Optic*:

"It is well known that there has been a gang of horse thieves along the Pecos who have run off stock from many ranches and who are believed to have committed other depredations. The headquarters of the gang are at Fort Sumner. Last week, three of the crowd, Dave Rudabaugh, Billy the Kid and Billy Wilson, went to the Oaks to dispose of some of their surplus stock and while there Sheriff Kimbrell (the spelling Kimball has also been used) of Lincoln county, who learned of their whereabouts, came with a posse expecting to corral them. They skipped out before the sheriff reached the camp and were met at Coyote Springs, seven miles away. They refused to surrender and showed resistance. A sharp fight followed. The gang seemed to have the best of the fight and drove the attacking party into the Oaks, following them up all the way. In the struggle Rudabaugh and the Kid [and Wilson] had their horses shot from under them."

It was because of the lawlessness in Lincoln and other counties of New Mexico that President Rutherford B. Hayes issued this proclamation:

"Whereas it is provided in the laws of the United States that whenever by reason of unlawful obstruction, combinations or assemblages of persons, or rebellion against the authority of the government of the United States, it shall become unpractical in the judgment of the President to enforce by the ordinary course of judicial proceedings the laws of the United States within any State or Territory, it shall be lawful for the President to call forth the militia of any or all of the States and to employ such parts of the land and naval forces of the United States to suppress such rebellion in whatever State or Territory thereof the laws of the United States may be forcibly opposed or the execution thereof obstructed: "

"And, whereas it has been made to appear to me that, by reason of unlawful combinations and assemblages of persons in arms, it has become impractical to enforce by the ordinary course of judicial proceedings the laws of the United States therein, and that the laws of the United States have been therein forcibly opposed and the execution thereof forcibly resisted. And, whereas the laws of the United States require that wherever it may be necessary, in the judgment of the President, to use the military force for the purpose of enforcing the faithful execution of the laws of the United States, he shall forth with, by proclamation, command such insurgents to disperse and retire peacefully to their respective abodes within a limited time:"

"Now, therefore, I Rutherford B. Hayes, President of the United States, do hereby admonish all good citizens of the United States, and especially of the Territory of New Mexico, against aiding, counteracting, abetting or taking part in any such unlawful proceedings; and I do hereby warn all persons engaged in, or connected with, said obstruction of the laws to disperse and retire peaceably to their respective abodes on or before noon of the 13th day of October instant." (Act of 1878)

Dave Rudabaugh and Billy the Kid hoped for peace. Bounty hunters, detectives, sheriffs, "wanted" posters, citizens in general made it difficult. Settling down to an honest living was not as advantageous financially as rustling, robbing and horse stealing. The Kid insisted that he had too many enemies to obey the injunction and demand of President Hayes. He sat down and wrote to Governor Lew Wallace (who seems to have spent his time in New Mexico chasing from place to place writing BEN HUR, judging from the number of places claiming the honor) pouring out his grievances giving his version of the battle at Greathouse's station, attributes the leadership of the posse to Carlyle. He is correct in saying that the blacksmith came in to talk him into surrendering. He said that he asked Carlyle to show him some papers as proof of his authority and right to ask anyone's surrender. Carlyle could show none.

Continued Bonney (December 12, 1880):

"I concluded it amounted to nothing more than a mob and told Carlyle that he would have to stay in the house and lead the way out that night." The Kid claimed that Carlyle was killed by his own party when he jumped through the window. He goes on to relate the vandalism in burning the stage station [Greathouse's]. He accuses Pat Garrett of taking two of his mules from the Yerby ranch, which he left with Bowdre, foreman of the place. He boldly states that he spent his time in Fort Sumner, since he left Lincoln, making a living as a gambler. He insists that he is a peaceful man, asking nothing more than to be left alone. He could not understand the persecution by [John S.] Chisum, who was actually responsible for all his troubles. He agrees that there is a tremendous amount of horse stealing taking place but denies any responsibility for this. Indeed, he recovered stolen property for Hugo Zuber, the postmaster at Puerto de Luna, as well as for Pablo Anaya. Would he have taken the trouble to aid these men if he were an outlaw?

J. S. Chism was at the bottom of all the ills of Lincoln county; not William Bonney, Dave Rudabaugh, Billy Wilson and others with him. Tom Pickett, Tom O'Folliard and Charlie Bowdre were not associated with William as long as Dave Rudabaugh, although they seem to have struck the popular fancy. Bowdre was not a bad man and sincerely hoped to sever relations with the outlaws without arousing the enmity of either the Kid or Rudabaugh. He was aware of what they did to Allen. He gave up his job as manager of the Yerby ranch in order to keep his employer from the odium brought about by Garrett's constant visits to the ranch, Yerby was in no way associated with Bonney's activities and Bowdre wanted to keep it that way.

Garrett was fortunate enough at this time to be joined by men from Texas employed to put an end to horse stealing in the Texas Panhandle. It was really the Texas Cattlemen's Association that put the pressure on Bonney and Rudabaugh. Garrett, Mason and Frank Stewart from Texas, met at Las Vegas and rode out to Anton Chico. They were joined by Charles Siringo, Jim East, Lee Hall, Lon Chambers, Cal Polk and the chuck wagon cook. Another outfit belonging to Littlefield of the LIT brand joined them. In this latter group were Tom Emory, George Williams, Lou Bausman and Bob Robinson. The two wagons from Texas went on to Anton Chico where they expected to meet Garrett and his men. It was decided that only six of the men from the outfits would be sufficient to join the posse in a move on Fort Sumner where The Kid and Rudabaugh were said to be holed up. The men from Texas had it on good authority that the outlaws made a raid into the Texas Panhandle and ran off some steers. After a rather cold night at an isolated lonely ranch, they headed for Grzelachowski's store at Puerto de Luna. A study of the life of this merchant would prove both rewarding as well as fascinating. For sheer daring and adventure it tops both Garrett's and The Kid's.

Puerto de Luna is as euphonious and fascinating a name as any in the Land of Enchantment. The community [founded in 1862] had a checkered and varied career, even attaining the dignity of county seat before Santa Rosa snatched away the courthouse by sheer force of numbers. At the time that Garrett and the men from Texas stayed there it was a popular resort well known to freighters from White Oaks, Las Vegas, Anton Chico and Villanueva. Since it was in San Miguel county, it belonged to the jurisdiction of the sheriff of San Miguel county, not Lincoln county. Capturing Rudabaugh and The Kid was an obsession with Garrett, one of the promises of his campaign for office. Could there have been the ulterior motive of reward money?

An important thing to remember in following the movements of these men is not to follow modern maps which will only confuse you. Too many new counties have been created since Rudabaugh rode the outlaw trail for any of the more recent maps to be of service. The map of Fort Sumner in 1879 shows it to be in the center of the Navajo and Apache Reservation, consequently under federal jurisdiction. Fort Sumner, now in the southeastern part of Guadalupe county, was then so isolated from the world that it was difficult to say which sheriff had jurisdiction. In 1880 and 1881 it was still part of the reservation (See Bancroft *History of Arizona and New Mexico*), even though many cattlemen lived there.

Perhaps the Rutherford proclamation gave any sheriff the right to ride to Fort Sumner for Billy the Kid. It would be interesting after all these years to come up with something that questioned Garrett's authority in Fort Sumner. Rudabaugh was wanted for robbing the U.S. Mails. Was it the job of a U. S. Marshal, a Deputy U. S. Marshal or a sheriff-elect to hunt down Dave Rudabaugh, or even Billy the Kid? Was Garrett one jump ahead of himself? Kimbrell was still sheriff and would continue to be until the new year. Remember the days when a president was elected in November but did not take office until March 4th? The former president ran the country until that date. A question arises, did Garrett usurp the right of Sheriff Kimbrell? Please don't get in a stew about it. Just thinking out loud. After all these years, who cares? [Kimbrell specifically appointed Garrett his deputy so he could go after Billy.]

Alexander Grzelachowski's store and home at Puerto de Luna became landmarks from the day they were built in 1877. The Nally Rand map for 1879 lists two towns

Rudabaugh (back of driver) and Billy the Kid being brought in by Stewart and Garrett – Las Vegas, December 27, 1880. Courtesy Mercaldo Archives.

of this name one on each side of the Pecos. The first settlement was made by colonists from the Rio Bonito region. Melquíades Ramirez, Sisto Ramirez, Mercedes Carbajal, Pablito Bacheco, Miguel Chavez, Fabian Brito and several others came here during the early years of the Civil War [1862] mostly to get away from the attacks of wandering Mescaleros. The original settlement was on the west side of the river where lawyer Melquíades Ramirez built his grist mill.

When Jose Luna, a. member of one of the most prominent families in the history of New Mexico, built his home in the pass between the mountains or puerto, as the natives called it, the place became known as Puerto de Luna [little port or little gateway of the moon]. Cypriano Flores is the present owner of the big adobe place built by Grzelachowski. It is said that the original owner once gave orders to his clerks to let Bonney have anything in the store he wanted. Here one could view the passing parade: Garrett, Bonney, Rudabaugh, Greathouse, Gerhardt, Keyes, Labadie, Abreu, Pete Maxwell, Browne, Manzanares, Blanchard, Giddings, Otero, Ortega, Nieto, Padilla and countless others known all over New Mexico.

Grzelachowski was a cheerful individual and the soul of hospitality. [He had come to the U.S. from Poland as a catholic priest. He left the priesthood to become a shopkeeper.] The man who fed Rudabaugh and Bonney also gave a night's lodging to Garrett and his men out to take Rudabaugh and The Kid dead or alive. After a good breakfast cooked by the host, the posse decided to spend the rest of the day at Puerto de Luna and stretcher their visit to last through the night and the following day. Grzelachowski was gracious throughout.

During the second evening a spy reported that The Kid and Rudabaugh were seen at Fort Sumner. Juan Roybal and two Anglo men joined the posse [Charles Frederick Rudolph and George Wilson]. Garrett went to Pablo Beaubien's place to find out if he knew anything. Beaubien could give him no help. He rode on to Gerhardt's where he decided to rest the horses. At midnight the posse continued south. Garrett was too late. The outlaws left a cold trail. Undaunted, the sheriff-elect doubled his efforts. After supper at the Wilcox ranch The Kid, Rudabaugh, Pickett, Wilson, Bowdre, O'Folliard and one other rode into the night. Christmas would soon be upon them and their thoughts were heavy as report after report reached them of Garrett's determination. They were in the land of manana. Tomorrow and tomorrow they would move into Old Mexico. Snowflakes, soft and whirling, skipped and settled. Horses protested the cold. Only the men braved the elements.

Near the outskirts of the little settlement of Fort Sumner, the Kid rode to the rear. Why! Premonition? A sixth sense? Cowardice? Suspicion? Garrett's men opened fire. They had aimed at Pickett who had taken Bonney's place, but missed (blame it on the night, the snow, the cold or the nervous anxiety of each man to say he brought down the Kid they were all marksmen or so they claimed) and hit (by chance) Tom O'Folliard, who would never live to see his twenty-first birthday just a few months away. Rudabaugh's horse had been hit. He kept riding it until it fell. He jumped up behind Pickett and the little mare took the added weight without complaint.

Thus they rode safely to the [Thomas] Wilcox & [Manuel Silvestre] Brazil ranch house. Brazil gave them something to eat, made an excuse about having to leave them for a time and rode into Fort Sumner where he reported to Garrett. The hunter and the hunted took to the road again the fast trackless expanse, the awful silence from White Oaks to Puerto de Luna. Garrett and his men never gave up. In the next engagement Bowdre was killed. This story is too well known to be repeated here. One wishes that Bowdre could have completed his wish before he died.

It was Rudabaugh who arranged the terms of surrender with Pat Garrett. Bonney did nothing to prevent him. If he had, it probably would have been Rudabaugh, not Garrett who ended the Kid's days on earth [Both Rudabaugh and Billy were insistent that they would not surrender unless Garrett agreed to jail then in Santa Fe, not Las Vegas. They were afraid that they would be lynched in Las Vegas. Garrett readily agreed to these terms]. Christmas evening they were at Grzelachowski's where he gave them a feed which would be long remembered. They never had another to equal it. It was the only satisfying occurrence since the chase began and the only ray of joy in keeping with the season. On the following day they made a triumphal entry into Las Vegas. Of the whole group the saddest face was that of Dave Rudabaugh. Las Vegas was the last place in the world he wanted to be but Garrett assured him that no harm would come to him.

The *Las Vegas Optic* for December 27, 1880, had a ball:

"Posses of men have been in hot pursuit of them for weeks. However, the right boys started out well mounted and heavily armed, and were successful in bagging their game. Yesterday (Sunday) afternoon .the town was thrown into a fever of excitement by the announcement that the Kid and other members of his gang of outlaws had been captured and were nearing the city. The rumor was soon verified by the appearance in town of a squad of men led by Pat Garrett, deputy sheriff of Lincoln county, and Frank Stewart of the Panhandle country, having in custody the Kid, Dave Rudabaugh, Billy Wilson and Tom Pickett. They were taken at once to the jail and locked up and arrangements made to guard the jail. Feeling was particularly strong against Dave Rudabaugh, who was an accessory to the murder of a (New) Mexican jailer in an attempt to liberate Webb some months ago."

"It will be remembered that Frank Stewart, with a party of picked men, left Las Vegas on December 14, to join Pat Garrett and his squad who were waiting at Fort Sumner. (No two accounts are ever alike, are they?) The boys made a quick try of it, arriving at the designated place of meeting on the night of the 17th. instant. Nothing unusual transpired until the following night, when the Kid's party approached the place for the purpose of cleaning out Garrett's squad, not knowing that reinforcements had come. Precaution had been taken to place a squad on the outside of the house, and upon hearing the clatter of horses hoofs in a distance, he warned his companions of the danger and they at once prepared to give the outlaws a warm reception. The night was very dark and foggy and even moving objects could be seen only at a very short distance. The first rider who came in range of the trusty Winchesters was Tom O'Folliard, who fell dead from his horse under the unerring aim of half a dozen frontiersmen. Torn Pickett was following immediately behind but after the first volley he turned his horse and fled for his life."

"Pursuit was out of the question owing to the intense darkness that prevailed and the additional fact that a heavy snowstorm had set in. Dave Rudabaugh's horse was shot but succeeded in carrying his rider a distance of twelve miles before dropping dead. The party of plucky pursuers now laid over two days starting forward on the evening of the third day – the 23rd. Promptly at the hour of twelve, they mounted their horses and rode twelve miles to Wilcox's ranch. Here it was obtained that the Kid and his followers had taken supper there the night before and were at their rendezvous, a vacant stone house about three miles further on. After a few moments halt, the brave pursuers, for such they proved themselves to be, put spurs to their horses and rode quietly to the house designated as the hiding place of the Kid's men. Upon approaching the premises at two o'clock in the morning, three horses were seen hitched to the front door ready to be mounted at a second's notice."

"Garrett and Stewart at once surrounded the house, giving their men instructions to lay in the snow and await further developments. Just at daybreak, on the morning of the 24th., a man supposed to be the Kid, but afterwards proving to be Charles Bowdre, appeared at the door. His body was pierced by two balls almost in an instant. The signal for shooting was given almost immediately upon the appearance of Bowdre, as the Kid, who is a sure shot, had often boasted he would never to taken alive. The only way to capture him was to shoot him on sight."

"The shooting of Bowdre alarmed those inside the house and they endeavored to ascertain what party was in pursuit of them. Their calling however, elicited no response. Two of the three horses standing near the door were shot down in their tracks and the third shot in the doorway while the Kid was in the act of getting the animal inside, out of reach of the deadly bullets. The carcass of the dead horse across the threshold prevented the Kid from leaping upon his horse, which was in the room with him, and attempting to escape. About four P. M. the surrounded party displayed a flag, and Rudabaugh walked out boldly and said they were willing to surrender provided they were guaranteed protection. This was promised them, and in turn the Kid, Billy Wilson and Tom Pickett (who evidently didn't get far in his flight due to the storm) joined Rudabaugh upon the outside and gave themselves up to their captors, who put their prisoners on horses, doubling up as the occasion required, and rode back to the Wilcox ranch, from which place a wagon was sent back after the young arsenal left at the robbers' rendezvous. The captors and their prisoners remained at the ranch all night, starting for Las Vegas Christmas morning and arriving here before supper last night, riding very rapidly."

"The party of men who risked their lives in an attempt to rid the country of a bloodthirsty gang of murderers are deserving of unbounded praise and should be rewarded handsomely for their services. They will undoubtedly obtain the reward of $500 offered by the governor for the capture of the Kid and it remains for interested citizens to raise a purse of money and present it to these sixteen men as they have paid out money and endured hardships in an endeavor to hunt down and bring to justice one of the most desperate gangs of outlaws that ever terrorized the Southwest."

"Billy the Kid is about twenty-four years of age, and has a bold, pleasant countenance. When interviewed between the bars at the jail this morning, he was in a talkative mood and said that anything he might say would not be believed by the people. He laughed heartily when told that the newspapers of the Territory had built him up a reputation second only to that of Victorio. The Kid claims never to have a large number of men with him and that the few who were with him when captured were employed on a ranch. This is his statement and is given for what it is worth."

"Dave Rudabaugh looks and dresses about the same as when in Las Vegas, apparently not having made a raid upon clothing stores. His face is weather-beaten from long exposure. This is the only noticeable difference. Rudabaugh inquired somewhat anxiously in regard to the feeling in the community and was told that it was very strongly against him. He remarked that the papers had all published exaggerated reports of the depredations of the Kid's party in the lower country. It was not half as bad as had been reported."

"Tom Pickett, who was once a policeman in West Las Vegas, greeted everybody with a hearty grip of the hand and seemed reasonably anxious to undergo an examination. Pickett is well connected. (He was from a good family. His father lived in Decatur, Texas and had served as a member of the legislature. All the home property was once mortgaged to keep the would-be outlaw out of trouble, but he skipped the country much to the sorrow of his mother who was confident that he would mend his ways given another chance.)"

"Billy Wilson, the other occupant of the cell, reclined leisurely on some blankets in some corner of the apartment, and his meditations were not disturbed by our Faber pusher. There remains no doubt of the fact that James Greathouse was a member of the Kid's marauding party. Letters written by him to the talented rascal were intercepted in the mails. (The *Optic* is no longer going to bat for Greathouse.) At one time he furnished horses for the Kid and his followers to escape from his ranch [not true], and while in Las Vegas wrote the Kid warning him to leave the country or he would be captured. While in town, he dispatched a courier to Dell's ranch for a horse which he undoubtedly obtained and rode on."

"The Kid, Wilson, Rudabaugh, under the escort of Garrett, Frank Stewart, M. Cosgrove and one or two others, were taken to Santa Fe this afternoon. As the train was ready to leave the depot an unsuccessful attempt was made by Sheriff [Hilario] Romero to secure Rudabaugh and return him to the county jail. (None of the men who captured Rudabaugh were federal men hence Romero felt that he had prior right to Rudabaugh. Garrett, just a deputy sheriff officially until the New Year [he was a U. S. Marshal, which gave him the authority to arrest Billy and his companions outside of Lincoln County], claimed that Rudabaugh was wanted by the government for robbing the mails. Romero insisted that a U. S. Marshal handle Rudabaugh or that he be detained in Las Vegas. Garrett was not sheriff or deputy in San Miguel county; hence out of his jurisdiction. He contended that once Rudabaugh left Lincoln county and entered San Miguel county Garrett's authority over him ceased. Romero was in charge in San Miguel county. Had Romero and his men been shooting men rather than talkers, the subsequent history of many or all of these men would have been differently written.) The engineer of the outgoing train was covered by guns and told not to move his engine. If the sheriff had been as plucky as some of the citizens who had urged him forward, the matter would have been settled without any excitement whatsoever. The prisoner, Rudabaugh, the only one wanted, was in the hands of United States authorities and having been arrested by deputy U. S. Marshals, they were in duty bound to deliver him to the authorities in Santa Fe. (Romero contended that the men were not U. S. Marshals. Half were employed by the Texas Cattlemen's Association; the other half Lincoln county lawmen. I have found no documentary proof in support of the contention. It would make an interesting study for someone anxious to go deeper into the subject. Even the editor is not sure. He repeatedly refers to Garrett as sheriff not deputy marshal.) The sheriff and a few picked trusty men might have gone over to Santa Fe with the party, and after Rudabaugh's delivery (into the hands of the authorities there) could have brought him back to Las Vegas where he is badly wanted, not only by the (New) Mexicans but all Americans who desire to see the law vindicated...."

The editor is speaking for himself. Rudabaugh had many friends who were interested in snatching him from the hands of the law. Rustling and robbing just wasn't the same without him. A few of the "Old Guard" loyal to the end, despite the disappearance of leader Hoodoo Brown, and a number of boys formerly of Dodge, contributed a purse as a retainer for the services of attorney Edgar Caypless. The lawyer was just one month younger than Rudabaugh. He must have been a capable man for it took the influence of Wilson Waddingham, Elkins, Otero, Morley, Springer, Catron to talk him into leaving his home base to come out to the Maxwell Land Grant headquarters at Cimarron, to hang out his shingle. A short stay convinced him that Cimarron would never be a metropolis so he moved to Santa Fe as a free lance lawyer. He knew, as well as every one else in Santa Fe, that Rudabaugh didn't stand a chance. The outlaw faced the Federal Court on two charges of robbing the U.S. mail from a train; robbing the U.S. mail from a stage. Convicted, he was condemned to serve twenty years for the train robbery and twenty years for the stage robbery [his actual sentence was life in prison at hard labor]. The prison guards ignored both Rudabaugh and Bonney, often treating them with meanness and contempt.

The *Santa Fe New Mexican* for December 30th makes comment on the treatment of the prisoners:

"The Kid, Wilson, Rudabaugh were jailed in Santa Fe about 7:30 Monday evening. Tuesday morning, about eleven o'clock, when Garrett and his men went to see them, it was discovered that they had not had a mouthful to eat since they were put in jail. Whereupon one of the posse went to the keeper of the restaurant who had a contract for feeding the U. S. prisoners and asked why he had not sent down meals to the three. The man said that he had done so and after a little examination it was discovered that Jailer Silba [Jesus Silva], or some of his henchmen, had eaten the grub themselves. It's pretty rough on prisoners when their jailers eat the meals sent to them." Perhaps it was such treatment that caused Rudabaugh to attempt mayhem on George Parker, a prison guard, when he was being returned to his cell following his trial on February 16, 1881 [Rudabaugh's trial was February 26, 1881]. "Although heavily shackled and handcuffed, on leaving the courtroom Rudabaugh managed to strike George Parker a severe blow in the face in payment of an old grudge." (*Santa Fe New Mexican*)

"The examination of Dave Rudabaugh was held in Santa Fe on Tuesday and he pleaded guilty to the robbery of the stage at Puertocito (present Sena) and the train here at Las Vegas. He stoutly refused to disclose the names of any of the men engaged with him in the robberies [Not true. He named himself, Joseph Martin, and Joe Carson as the robbers] Sentence was deferred but it is said that the judge promised to give him all that the law allows, which is eighteen to twenty years." (*Las Vegas Optic*, February 17, 1881)

Both crimes were committed in San Miguel county. Puertocito is a thriving village between the little hamlets of Pueblo and Gonzolez on the San Miguel-Villanueva road. Because it is off the beaten track, few tourists or artists have discovered its Nineteenth century adobe church, homes and way of life. The Penitente Brotherhood is still active here despite the modern school and farming methods. At the junction of the Pecos river and Gonzolez creek, it is one of the most fertile spots of New Mexico. About anything planted there grows, although alfalfa and chili seem to be the main crops. In the days Rudabaugh pillaged from San Miguel to La Questa (Villanueva), the village boasted a mercantile store that also served as a stage stop and post office. Rudabaugh, Dutch Henry, Joe Carson considered it an ideal spot for a holdup [the third robber was Joseph Martin, not Dutch Henry; the hold up was August 14, 1879]. The nearest village of any consequence was San Miguel del Bado, made famous by Salazar and the prisoners of the ill-fated Texas-Santa Fe Expedition.

Eight miles to the south was La Questa. The railroad by-passed San Miguel del Bado, but built a depot at Ribera about two miles further west. The mail was dropped off here and taken by stage to San Geronimo, El Cerrito, Tecalote, Puertocito, La Laguna, Bernal, and other mountain villages by pony express and stage. Las Vegas, controlled by Dave Mather, Rudabaugh, Cardon, Hoodoo Brown, Dutch Henry and the Dodge City gang, received no news of the hold-up nor did the robbery receive any publicity in the Territorial papers. Miguel Otero, an authority on Las Vegas history, fails to mention it, possibly because he was using the *Optic* years later as a guide.

This is about as good a place as any to go into the trial at Santa Fe. These aspects of the case are seeing print for the first time. It must be understood from the beginning that Rudabaugh was tried as an accomplice and under the same penalty as if he, not [John J.] Allen, pulled the trigger on the jailer. The *Las Vegas Acorn* makes this clear:

"Today Sheriff Hilaro Romero returned from Santa Fe in charge of desperado Dave Rudabaugh, whose name is legend under every western roof. It is well remembered that the bad Rudabaugh was captured last December in company with the young killer Billy the Kid, brought to Las Vegas and taken to Santa Fe. Dave is back to stand trial for complicity in the murder of Antonio Lino Valdez of this city last April, in which Little Allen figured as chief actor. Rudabaugh was brought up in irons and showed a restless, uneasy condition of mind when he was taken from the cars. He retained a stolid, hang-dog demeanor and showed no disposition to recognize any of his old acquaintances. He is poor of flesh, and does not weigh by twenty pounds as much as he did a year ago, while prancing up and down the streets of Las Vegas. What a change a year has brought forth! Then the free man, now the chained culprit, doomed to the decree of justice or possibly Judge Lynch's mandate, for we hear the grumblings of men who have revenge in their hearts...."

The New Mexico law called for any two or more with a killer at the time of the action to be held equally guilty and to receive the same punishment [there was no such law]. Thus the fact remains that Rudabaugh was with Allen when Jailer Valdez was shot. When asked to sign a paper showing he could not afford to pay for his trial he signed his name David Radebaugh, the spelling he used all his life. Only eminent writers of western folklore used the spelling Rudabaugh (when the author used Radebaugh elsewhere, several wrote that he should learn how to spell the name Rudabaugh); the Territory in filing the case used the spelling Rodebaugh; the Untouchables of Western Americana use

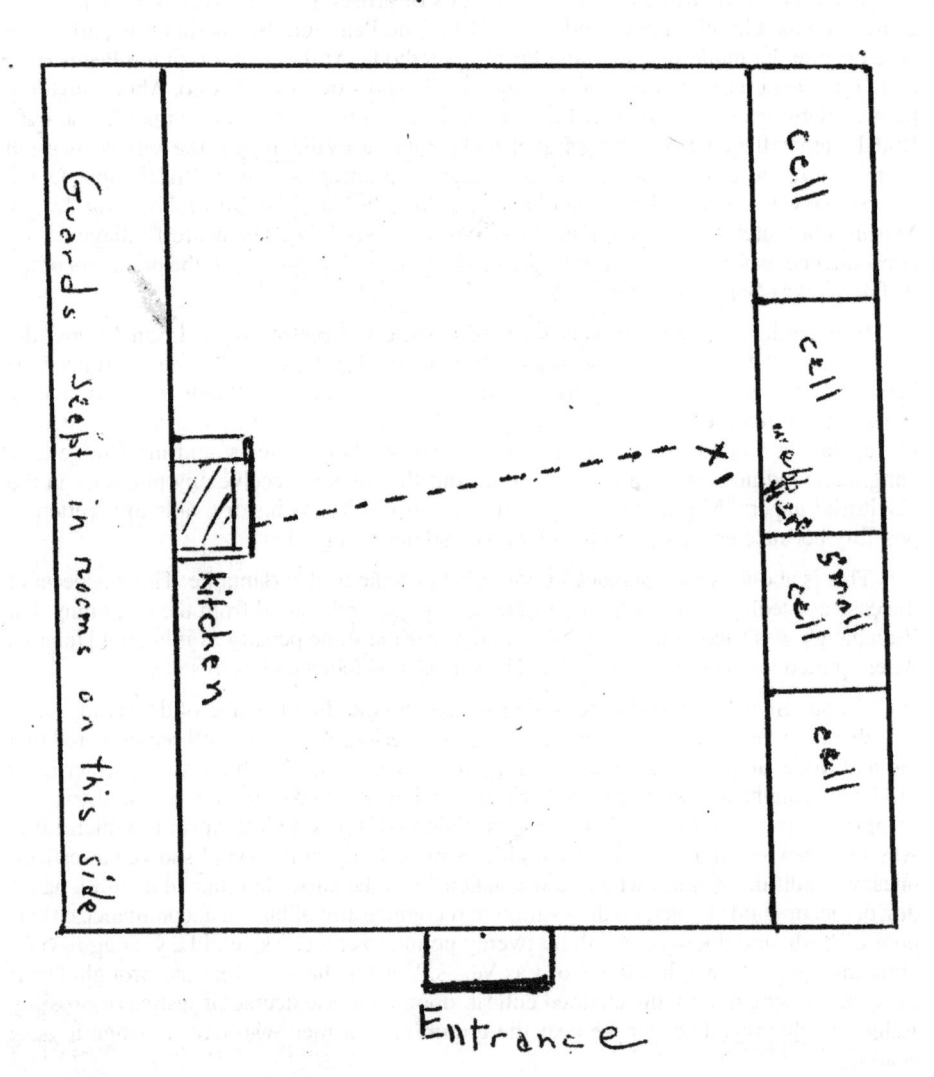

X1 - The spot where the jailer was shot. Valdez was carried by the Stokes brothers to the jail kitchen. He died that night.

X2 - Where Hilario Romero was standing in front of his house when the shot was fired.

Diagram drawn by Hilario Romero, a witness in the trial of Dave Rudabaugh.

Rudabaugh, forcing others to conform for the sake of uniformity whether the spelling is correct or not.

When Rudabaugh went on trial, the following were sent a summons to appear: Joseph Stoker of Socorro; William Mullin; Jose Ramirez; Tomas Suaso; Martin Koslowski; J. Murray; J. Maria Tafoya. By April 21st, it was ascertained that Rudabaugh had no money or means to pay costs. The jailer was killed on April 5, 1880, [the correct date is April 2, 1880] a year and two weeks previously. Foreman of the jury was Demetrio Perez; F. W. Clancy was court clerk; and the case was filed on August 18, 1880. Since the trial did not take place until some time later, the following witnesses appeared: Benedicto Duran; J. Maria Tafoya and William H. H. Allison. [The witnesses for the prosecution at Rudabaugh's trial were Sheriff Hilario Romero, County Clerk Jesus Maria Tafoya, and jailer José Ramirez.] Foreman of the jury was H. L. Swope, who found Rudabaugh guilty of murder in the first degree as charged April 19, 1881. The other jurymen were Walter V. Hoyt, Vicente Garcia, Simon Filger, Manuel Sandoval, A. M. Dettelback, P. A. Peinold, Benito Pacheco, Juan Luis Gallegos, R. M. Stephen, J. Torres and Facundo Duran. The lawyers pro and con were William Whiletan [Whitelaw], E. Cayhless [Caypless], M. A. Breeden and Gordon Posey. [The prosecuting attorney was William Breeden. Attorneys Whitelaw and Caypless were sick, so Rudabaugh was defended by George G. Posey and Marshal A. Breeden. Marshal Breeden was the brother of prosecutor William Breeden.]

The first witness brought to the stand was Hilario Romero. He was known to both Valdez and Rudabaugh. His house was the one next to the jail [it was part of the courthouse complex and was a free benefit of being sheriff], and he was standing in front of it when the shot was fired. He heard the shot and saw Allen and Rudabaugh running. He later saw the wounded man. Valdez was shot about 2 P. M. and lingered until 10 P. M. He could tell Rudabaugh apart from Allen because Rudabaugh was taller than Allen. This latter was about five feet, five inches tall considered extremely short in that part of the country; hence, the name Little Allen. The hack driver (whose name appears as J. C. Cauldewell in the written manuscript of the case on the files in the courthouse) was on hand to give his story [the trial records and newspapers give his surname as Cauldwell]:

"I was rather suspicious of the way Allen was acting. When they got out of the cab and told me to wait for them, I didn't want to. I moved the cab a little farther west but soon they were out running for my hack. They got in the back seat and Allen took out his gun and began to play with it. I turned around and he said 'You s-o-b, if you make a move I'll blow your brains out.'"

"Rudabaugh said to Allen: 'Don't make a fool of yourself, I will drive.' He saw that I was nervous and he felt that Allen would not dare shoot if Rudabaugh were driving. He took the lines and drove to the hardware store. When they came out of the store Rudabaugh sat in the seat behind the driver and Allen sat in the seat behind Rudabaugh...."

J. Maria Tafoya said that he had helped to carry Valdez from where he fell to the kitchen, where he died. He remembered that the coroner said that the "pistol was fired on the breast, belly and body of said Antonio Lino Valdez with malice and forethought." [He was shot in the chest.] The bullet had penetrated six inches.

William Mullen, who moved to Socorro, lived in Las Vegas at the time of the shooting. [Mullen was a defense witness, not a prosecution witness.] He saw the shooting because he was serving time for some offense [he was in jail because he had been falsely convicted to the stage robbery committed by Rudabaugh]. He had nothing more to add than already told by other witnesses. He did remember that Rudabaugh came to see Webb three times a week and brought him tobacco and newspapers. Valdez and Rudabaugh were well known to each other. Webb introduced Rudabaugh to Mullen. Allen was to the left of Rudabaugh when the shot was fired. They came in the jail and Rudabaugh greeted both Webb and Mullen with a handshake through the bars. Rudabaugh asked Webb: "How do you feel? Do you need anything?"

At this point, Allen turned to the jailer and said "You s-o-b (he always seemed to use those words in his talk) give me the keys." They were in the jail about a minute when the shot was fired. Asked why he was in jail, Mullen said that he had been associated with a train [stage] robbery, and had served nine months from the time he first entered to the day of the murder. He knew Rudabaugh for four months of that time.

The Stokes brothers were also in jail for the same offense as Mullen. Their story substantiated everything Mullen said [the Stokes brothers did not testify at the trial]. They did add that when Tafoya needed help to carry Valdez from where he fell to the kitchen table where he was laid out, the Stokes boys opened the cell and assisted in carrying him. They made no attempt to escape. No doubt this explains why Mullen and the Stokes Brothers were released after the Valdez funeral [they were released after Rudabaugh confessed to the crime they were convicted of].

Rudabaugh was called to the stand. Among other things he said: "I was a police officer prior to the time of the killing and I was a personal friend of J. Webb. Valdez never refused me admittance when I went to see Webb. The jailer and I were good friends."

Asked to account for his actions of the day, he said: "I went earlier to the Summer House (saloon) in West Las Vegas. On the way I met Allen, who asked to go along with me. I did not refuse him and we went in together. I went there to see a man who owed me money. His name was Tom Pickett. I was told that he was home sick in bed. I went to the place where he lived and talked to him for about twenty minutes. He decided to get up and go to town. I waited for him to dress and we went to town together. We stopped at the Summer House and Allen had some drinks. He had been drinking some before we met on the street. Pickett decided to stay in town while Allen and I went to the jail to see Webb. While I was asking Webb how he felt, I heard a shot. I saw the jailer fall. I said to Little Allen: 'What did you do that for?'"

"The jailer drew a pistol on me and I jumped out of range. There was a knocking on the front door. I opened it and ran out. The hack had left the front door. I ran down the street and overtook it at the plaza. I asked the driver why he didn't wait. By the time I got back into the hack Allen was there. He got in back. He was a bit drunk. He took out his pistol and tried to load it. He couldn't. He asked me to. We drove down the street to Goodlett's saloon, where Allen had left a double-barreled shotgun. We then drove to the hardware store. Allen told me later that he was acquainted with the Stokes brothers and had tried to get in to see them but was not admitted. He knew of my visits to Webb and came looking for me. That is how we got together that day. He was slightly acquainted with Webb...."

The *Las Vegas Gazette* for December 27, 1880, gave a slightly different account of the capture of Dave Rudabaugh than the *Optic*:

"Our readers are familiar with the depredations committed in the lower country by a gang of desperadoes under the leadership of Billy the Kid, and the repeated and unsuccessful attempts to capture them. They have roamed over the country at will, placing no value upon human life, and appropriating the property of ranchmen and travelers without stint. Posses of men have been in hot pursuit of them for weeks, but they succeeded in eluding their pursuers every time. However, the right boys started out, well mounted and heavily armed, and were successful in bagging their game."

"Yesterday (Sunday, December 26) afternoon the town was thrown into a fever of excitement by the announcement that the Kid and other members of his gang of outlaws had been captured, and were nearing the city. The rumor was soon verified by the appearance in town of a squad of men led by Pat Garrett, deputy sheriff of Lincoln county, and Frank Stewart of the Panhandle country, having in custody the Kid, Dave Rudabaugh, Billy Wilson and Tom Pickett, They were taken at once to the jail, and locked up, and arrangements made to guard the jail against any attempt to take the prisoners out and hang them. Feeling was particularly strong against Rudabaugh (spelt Radabaugh) who was an accessory to the murder of the Mexican jailer in an attempt to release Webb some months ago."

"It will be remembered that Frank Stewart, with a party of picked men, left Las Vegas on December 14, to join Pat Garrett and his squad, who were in waiting at Fort Sumner. The boys made a quick trip of it, arriving at the designated place of meeting on the night of the 17th inst. Nothing unusual transpired until the following night, when the Kid's party approached the place for the purpose of cleaning out Garrett's squad, not knowing that reinforcements had come. Precaution had been taken to place a guard on the outside of the house, and upon hearing the clatter of horses' hoofs in the distance, he warned his companions of the danger and they at once prepared to give the outlaws a warm reception. The night was very dark and foggy and even moving objects could be seen only at a very short distance. The first rider who came in the range of the trusty Winchesters was Tom O'Folliard, who fell dead from his horse under the unerring aim of a half-dozen frontiersmen. Tom Pickett was following immediately behind, but after the first volley he turned his horse and fled for his life. Pursuit was out of the question, owing to the intense darkness that prevailed and the additional fact that a heavy snowstorm set in."

"Dave Rudabaugh's horse was shot but he succeeded in carrying his rider a distance of twelve miles before dropping dead. The party of plucky pursuers now laid over two days, starting forward on the evening of the third day, the 23rd. Promptly at the hour of 12, they mounted their horses and rode twelve miles to Wilcox's ranch. Here it was ascertained that the Kid and his followers had taken supper the night before and were at their rendezvous, a vacant storehouse about three miles further on. After a few moments' halt, the brave pursuers, for such they proved themselves to be, put spurs to their horses and rode quietly to the house designated as the hiding place of the Kid's men. Upon approaching the premises, at 2 a. m., three horses were seen hitched to the front door ready to be mounted at a second's notice. Garrett and Stewart at once surrounded the house, giving their men instructions to lay flat in the snow and await further developments."

"Just at daybreak, on the morning of the 24th, a man supposed to be the Kid, but afterwards proving to be Charles Bowdre, appeared at the door. His body was pierced by two balls almost in an instant. The signal for shooting was given immediately upon the appearance of Bowdre, as the Kid, who is a sure shot, had often boasted he would never be taken alive. The only way to capture him was to shoot him down on sight. The killing of Bowdre alarmed those on the inside of the house and they endeavored to ascertain what party was in pursuit of them; however, their calling elicited no response. Two of the three horses standing at the door were shot down in their tracks, and a third one was shot in the doorway while the Kid was in the act of getting the animal upon the inside out of reach of the deadly bullets. The carcass of the dead horse across the threshold prevented the Kid from leaping upon his horse which was in the room with him, and attempting to escape."

"About 4 P. M. the surrounded party displayed a flag and Rudabaugh walked out boldly and said they were willing to surrender, provided they were guaranteed protection. This was promised them, and in turn, the Kid, Wilson and Pickett joined Rudabaugh upon the outside and gave themselves up to their captors, who put their prisoners on horses and rode back to Wilcox's ranch, from which place a wagon was sent back after the young arsenal left at the robbers' rendezvous. The captors and their prisoners remained out at the ranch all night, starting for Las Vegas Christmas morning and arriving here before supper, last night – very rapid riding. The party of men who risked their lives in the attempt to rid the country of this bloodthirsty gang of robbers and murderers are deserving of unbounded praise and should be rewarded handsomely for their services. They will undoubtedly obtain the reward of $500 offered by the governor for the capture of the Kid, and it remains for interested citizens to raise a purse of money and present it to the sixteen men, as they paid out money and endured hardships in the endeavor to hunt down and bring to justice one of the most desperate gangs of outlaws that ever terrorized the Southwest."

"Billy the Kid is about twenty-four years of age, and has a bold yet pleasant cast of countenance. When interviewed between the bars at the jail this morning, he was in a talkative mood, but said that anything he might say might not be believed by the people. He laughed heartily when informed that the papers of the Territory had built him up a reputation second only to that of Victorio. The Kid never claimed to have had a large number of men with him, and that the few who were with him when captured were employed on a ranch."

"Dave Rudabaugh looks and dresses about the same as when in Las Vegas, apparently not having made any raids on clothing stores. His face is weather-beaten from long exposure. This is the only noticeable difference. Rudabaugh inquired somewhat anxiously in regard to the feeling in the community, and was told that it was very strong against him. He remarked that the papers had all published exaggerated reports of the depredations of the Kid's party in the lower country. It was not half as bad as reported...."

Despite leg irons and handcuffs, the prisoners made plans to escape. Dave Rudabaugh was more than anxious for his freedom since he learned that Judge Prince had reconsidered his case and decreed that Las Vegas had the prior right over the outlaw. Sheriff Romero never ceased pulling strings, nor crying aloud over Garrett's right to take the prisoners to Santa Fe. Was he right? Why did the judge reverse the decision of the Federal court which had already passed sentence and remanded Rudabaugh back to Las Vegas?

"The boys have no hankering after prison houses, and the action of Judge Prince in setting aside the life (!) imprisonment sentence of Rudabaugh in order that he may be brought to this city to be tried for murder, has made them more desperate. [Judge Prince did not set aside the Federal sentence. He stayed it so that Rudabaugh could be tried for the killing of Valdez.] These men are game and will have to be closely guarded if they are kept. Yesterday afternoon it was discovered that the Kid and his gang had concocted, and were stealthily carrying out a plan, by which they hoped to gain their freedom and escape the fate that awaits them. And fortunate it was that the discovery was made just when it was, for a night or two more would have sufficed for completion of the well laid scheme."

It appears that Sheriff Romulo Martinez, fearing that the four desperate men Bonney, Rudabaugh, Wilson and Kelly would ere long make a desperate effort to get out, had promised to pay one of the prisoners if he would assist the guard in keeping watch, and yesterday that fellow informed him that the men were trying to dig out. Sheriff Martinez, accompanied by Deputy Marshal Neis, at once proceeded to the jail and examined the room and found that the bed ticking was filled with stones and earth and removing the mattress discovered a deep hole (tunneled through the floor and under the wall covered by the mattress the prisoners had no beds). Further investigation showed that the men had dug themselves nearly out and by concealing the loose earth in the bed covering had almost reached the street without awakening the suspicions of the guard. Last night they were closely guarded and heavily ironed and today further precautions will be taken." (*Las Vegas Gazette*, March 4, 1881.)

"Chief Justice Prince has decided to return Rudabaugh to the Las Vegas jail as ordered. Previous to his decision in the matter, a considerable pressure was brought to bear upon him to prevent the order. It was argued that the people here were greatly incensed against him (i.e., Rudabaugh), and that he would surely be lynched if returned to this county. Judge Prince took a more sober and hopeful view of the matter and relying upon the love of good order and the law-abiding character of the people of Las Vegas, decided that this was the proper place for Rudabaugh, and that there was no reasonable or well-grounded fear that he would be dealt with illegally."

"Judge Prince, we are of the opinion, has taken the right view of the question. We express the general sentiment of Las Vegas in saying that Rudabaugh will not be lynched when brought here. The people of this city are strongly inclined to frown down and prevent mob law. We have reached a condition of society wherein the laws of the land can be enforced with due regularity, and, we apprehend, successfully. Besides that we have a sheriff and deputies who will neither permit prisoners to escape nor allow a mob to take them out and butcher them. We have confidence in our officers that prisoners will be protected both ways. They will neither escape from justice nor be mobbed. We should hate to form one of the party to take Rudabaugh or any one else out of the Las Vegas jail unless the prime requisite for a requiem was a desirable object. The jail is well guarded by capable men who will defend the law. There is no feeling on the community against Rudabaugh which would have sufficient strength to overcome ordinary means of protection. Let the laws be strictly enforced with even handed justice and with certainty and crime will decrease and mob law disappear. Judge Prince is right in his estimate of the good character of the people of Las Vegas." (*Optic* ibid.)

"Dave Rudabaugh, the criminal who is to be turned over to the authorities at Las Vegas, will probably not leave for that place for a day or two. The sheriff of San Miguel will, it is expected, send after him. In case the U. S. Marshal is obliged to take him over, a guard of several reliable men will be sent with him and Sherman (the marshal whose privileges and rights the sheriff of San Miguel county contended Garrett violated) will go himself." (Ibid, March 8, 1881.)

"Dave Rudabaugh and Kelly, who killed Reardon at Carbonateville, were taken yesterday to Las Vegas to await trial.... Rudabaugh goes to be tried of the (murder of the) jailer at the Las Vegas jail, the judge of the U. S. Court having suspended his sentence of imprisonment for life for robbing the U. S. mails. The prisoners were accompanied by the sheriff of San Miguel county, to whom U. S. Marshal John Sherman delivered Rudabaugh in accordance with the instructions of the court, and by Sheriff R. Martinez. Rudabaugh was very uneasy lest the people of Las Vegas would lynch him as soon as he reached the depot of that town, and many people believed that his fears would be verified. Persons who have an opportunity of knowing were of the opinion that there would be no evidence produced against him." (Ibid.)

"The entire time of the District Court was taken up yesterday in the case of the Territory vs. Dave Rudabaugh, indicted for murder. The crime for which the prisoner was tried was committed in Las Vegas, and was the killing of the jailer of the place. Major A. Breeden and Col. Wm. Breeden for the prosecution [the prosecuting attorney was Major Marshal A. Breeden. Col William Breeden was an attorney for the defense]. The hearing of the evidence took up the time of the court until about six o'clock P. M., when the court counsel was heard, and the case was given to the jury about half after eight o'clock, After about an absence of one hour and a half the jury brought in a verdict of murder in the first degree, Rudabaugh appeared perfectly calm. Throughout the trial, giving no evidence of excitement or agitation of any kind. His manner was serious and impressed with the fact that he fully realized his situation, but had no occasion to resort to an assumption of that stolid indifference behind which prisoners frequently strive to hide their feelings in such cases."

"When put upon the stand, Rudabaugh told a very probable story of the murder, and the parts which he and Allen took in it. He said that the two went to the jail together to see Webb and were admitted by the jailer. He was standing with his hands resting upon the timber above the cell door, when he heard a shot and turned around to find that Allen had killed the man who let them in. He turned to run, and saw a man running out of the kitchen with a revolver in his hand. The prisoner stepped out of range by going into the doorway and from there made his way into the street. He ran and overtook a hack and he and Allen, who preceded him, got in and drove off. The story was very consistent with the facts as they appeared in evidence, except that it threw the blame on Allen. All the statements made by witnesses except as to the actual killing and who fired the fatal shot, were dovetailed in very cleverly and if the account had come from a man of better character than Rudabaugh's, and under different circumstances, it would possibly have carried conviction with it. As it was, however, it had no good effect and Rudabaugh stands a good chance of swinging. The appeal to the Superior Court will carry the matter over until next winter so that the prisoner will have time to look after his opportunities to escape...."

"M. G. Gordon Posey, who was appointed by the court to defend Dave Rudabaugh yesterday, did so very ably, notwithstanding that he had no time whatever to prepare for the trial...." (Ibid.)

Rudabaugh was brought back to Santa Fe after the trial. He did not feel safe in Vegas and the U. S. Court in Santa Fe thought that as long as there was strong feeling against him in the Meadow City he could be serving time for robbing the mails to be deducted from the first of the two twenty-year sentences he would have to obey until Las Vegas made up its mind about him. That he would be lynched was a fixation. He was uncomfortable in Vegas.

"He filed an affidavit to that effect in the court yesterday and asked that he be allowed to remain in Santa Fe until his appeal can be tried. His petition was overruled and he will be taken (back) to Las Vegas at such time as the sheriffs of the two counties may designate. The court does not seem to think that there is any reason to fear mob violence at Vegas, and did not when he was sent up before. That chance to lynch the prisoner having passed it is not probable that he will be molested now that he is under sentence." (Ibid.)

It was customary in those days to give a long-winded talk in sentencing a prisoner. Really loquacious were Judges Benedict, Long, Waldo, Breeden, Catron and others of equal note, but Judge Prince had less to say to Dave Rudabaugh than the prisoner expected to hear. Still the few remarks seem to sum up the desperado's life:

"David Rudabaugh, you are indicted by the Grand Jury of San Miguel county at the term of August, 1880, for the highest crime known to man, that of willful murder of a fellow being. In this case, the crime as alleged is made, if possible, even more grave by the person killed being a public officer engaged in the performance of his duties. A change of venue was taken on your application to the county in order that an absolutely impartial jury might be impaneled to try your case. And such a jury was obtained, all its members being acceptable to your counsel. Although the counsel originally assigned for the defense were prevented by sickness from attending, yet others of marked zeal and intelligence conducted the defense, and labored with ability and earnestness to secure for you every right and privilege which the law provides."

"The jury, in the performance of their duty as judges of the facts, have found you guilty of murder in the first degree, the punishment for which is the penalty of death. Nothing which I can say or do could add to the solemnity of this verdict or of the criminal circumstances which now surround you as its subject. Certainly I am far from desiring to add a single word which would increase the profound sense of sorrow which now must fill your heart. For some years your life seems to have been one of lawlessness. By your own admission in open court you were a prominent actor in two outrages against society and the laws, in the stage robberies between Las Vegas and this city which attracted so much attention a year or two since, and after the commission of this murder you were found in the company of notorious breakers of the law in the southeast part of this Territory."

"Let us all hope that this awful example of the result of such a course of life is one whose natural abilities might have led him to success and honor; this evidence that the law is strong to punish as well as protect, and that in the long run it is sure to overtake even those who are most successful in avoiding its power and penalties. This will be the means of restraining others from a similar course of violence and crime, which might lead to the same fate. And let me here admonish you to use well and profitably the time which the laws of the Territory still remain to you in this life, so that you will be prepared as fully as possible for the other life in another world so soon to come."

"It now only remains for me to perform the sad and impressive rite of pronouncing the dread sentence which the law imposes in your case, which is, that you be conveyed hence to the county of San Miguel and delivered to the custody of the sheriff of that county and there kept safely until Friday, the 20th day of May, 1881, and on that same day you be taken by the sheriff of that county to some suitable place within said county of San Miguel, and there between the hours of ten A. M. and twelve P. M. be hung by the neck until you are dead. May God have mercy on your soul!"

"The above sentence, however, will not be carried into effect, at least on the day mentioned, as the counsel for the prisoner have taken an appeal to the higher court; all motion for a new trial having been overruled, and, as is well known, such an appeal stays sentence. David Rudabaugh, therefore, has until next winter to await execution as his appeal cannot be heard until that time." (*Santa Fe New Mexican*, April 22, 1881.)

Chapter 6 | The End of the Line

Dave Rudabaugh's day were numbered, dated, sealed and doomed by decree of judge and jury. The judge fixed the time and the moment. The place was of no importance save to the hangman and Dave Rudabaugh. This was a fitting and proper way for a Border Ruffian to die. It was a violent way, never cherished but always expected. It was the way for a transgressor. Redlegs, guerillas, skirmishers, aggressors, barn burners, squatters, marauders, horse thieves, land grabbers, gamblers, Cyprians, rustlers, desperadoes – at what time in his life had he not identified himself with them? They were his heritage, his bloodstream, compulsions. Judge Prince recognized in him some latent talent; possibilities and capabilities pulled out of focus by the high winds of violence that hurled him like dry tumbleweed into the ranks of the lame and the halt that outlawed themselves from society. He faced the gallows as lonely and isolated as a solitary sparrow on the housetop, in the driving rain. This was the price for his loyalty to Webb. His thoughts, like his countenance, were inscrutable as he permitted himself to be taken back to the Las Vegas jail. Dangerously had he lived, but he loved life too well to be convinced, as the jury was, that he was guilty of death. He was not afraid to die. He merely wanted to live longer. The fact that he had killed [James] Allen failed to compensate now for the ordeal he had to face.

On February 27, 1881 [April 22, 1881], the door of the cell in the Las Vegas jail closed on Dave Rudabaugh. One friend was there to greet him: J. J. Webb. What they had to say to each other was of no concern to the jailer. The reporter from the *Optic* sought an interview but Rudabaugh turned his back on him. The disgruntled newspaper man reiterated what was said before: "The prisoner retained a stolid hang-dog look and is not disposed to recognize anyone." His lawyers fought for a stay of execution and for a new trial. [Rudabaugh's lawyers filed an appeal on the same day Rudabaugh was convicted of Valdez's killing. The Supreme Court accepted the appeal and stayed Rudabaugh's execution until after his appeal could be hear.] The date set for the hanging came and went. Rudabaugh waited and hoped. Friends smuggled in a case knife and a handleless pick. Secretly, noiselessly, he started to dig his way out. It would take a long time.

Once an opportunity for escape had presented itself and an attempt was made. "Yesterday at three A. M.," wrote the editor of the *Las Vegas Gazette* for Tuesday, September 20, 1881 (as you can see Rudabaugh had been in jail for some time) "in the guardroom of the county jail, occurred one of the most terrible hand-to-hand encounters we have ever been called upon to chronicle. Four desperate and daring criminals confined in the middle cell of the county jail, having secured a pistol from the outside and freed themselves by picking the lock of their cell, made a rush upon the three Mexican guards, who were asleep at the time in the guardroom and whose names are Florencio Mares, Guadalupe Hildago and Herculano Chavez. David Rudabaugh, the leader of the gang, fired two shots at old man Mares, one just grazing his temple. Mares sprang to his feet and catching hold of the weapon with both hands, succeeded finally in wresting it from his grasp. Another of the prisoners, Thomas Duffy, immediately closed with Mares, and in the struggle that ensued Mares threw Duffy to the floor and called upon Chavez to shoot him, which he did in good style, the ball striking a little to the left of the center of the forehead and lodging in the brain. A fierce and determined hand-to-hand contest for the mastery then began, and finally ended by the prisoners being forced back into the cell and secured."

"The prisoners confined in the cell were Dave Rudabaugh, Thomas Duffy, J. J. Webb, held for murder, and H. S. Wilson and A. Murphy, held for robbery. Rudabaugh is under sentence of death for the murder of Deputy Sheriff A. L. Valdez on April 3, 1880 [April 2], in an attempt by him and Jack [James] Allen to rescue Webb from jail. Rudabaugh escaped at the time and was captured with Billy the Kid. He has been confined in this jail except when taken to Santa Fe for trial. Thomas Duffy was arrested a month ago for the unprovoked and brutal murder of Thomas Bishop, a clerk in Gillerman's store at Liberty. Rudabaugh seemed willing to talk and was very apprehensive of his personal safety. When we suggested to him that it would have been an easy matter for him to have made his escape after opening the door of the cell without attacking the guards, he declared that he had no intention of harming them and that owing to his weakness from long confinement he was unable to climb the wall. His manner during the interview indicated great nervousness and apprehension that he might be lynched. The man who shot Duffy is scarcely twenty-one and he seemed to take the whole matter coolly and very much as a matter of course." [Duffy died the next day.]

The next attempt proved successful. By this time, Webb, aware of the hopelessness of his own case, aided in using the handleless pick still in Rudabaugh's possession. Other prisoners, not chained to the wall, aided in hitting at the mortar, making sure that the debris fell soundlessly on the mattresses. Never once during the slow process of tunneling out the escape hatch did any of the four guards across the hall ever suspect what was taking place. So skillfully did Rudabaugh engineer the whole affair that the prisoners were not missed until breakfast time of the morning of Dec. 3rd., at 7 A. M. The sheriff marveled that the men could wiggle through the small opening seven by nineteen inches. Poor prison fare all those months may have helped.

All of Las Vegas was convinced that the jail could hold Dave. It was found out afterwards that the fugitives had crawled through the small opening stripped of all clothing. First they bundled the clothes, placed them outside the hole, and then followed through. This the sheriff learned from the four prisoners refusing to escape. Their names were Griffin, Rogers (who was to become a terror in Colfax county and eventually lost his life in a gun battle in front of the Springer courthouse), Fogerty, alias Cutter, and Jack McManus, "Texas" Quinlan, a desperado from Texas, with a price on his head. Pat Garrett and Deputy Franklin, who decided to track down Rudabaugh and the escaped prisoners, found Quinlan in Santa Fe enjoying himself at a gaming table. He was taken back to Texas and Garrett split the thousand dollars reward with Franklin.

The other prisoners were Goodman, Kelley, Schroeder, Webb, Kearney and Rudabaugh. Quinlan, Webb and Rudabaugh went to the St. Nicholas Hotel where they were given a joyous welcome by Mrs. Quinlan who was suspected in playing a major role in the affair. It was not easy for Rudabaugh who had to drag along his chains. A little food, a six-shooter and off he was along the railroad tracks. The night watchman for the Blanchard Mercantile Company heard the clanking of the chains against the ties and went to investigate. Rudabaugh spotted him and raised his pistol. The man froze in his tracks. Rudabaugh motioned him away. A shot at this moment would spoil everything and surely bring about a lynching. The watchman out of sight, Rudabaugh labored along until he arrived at the little hamlet of Naranjo some six miles out of Las Vegas. There he found a friend willing to cut his chains. Rudabaugh must have had some redeeming qualities for people were always willing to help him, which cannot be said for his contemporary, Billy the Kid. If Rudabaugh had a word of regret for the outlaw when he learned that Pat Garrett had shot him, the newspapers of the day do not tell us. Since Rudabaugh languished in jail at the time reporters from the *Gazette* and the *Optic* could have visited him for his reaction to the death of the Kid had they chosen to do so but they felt that Rudabaugh was no more copy until the day of his hanging. Rudabaugh's escape was sensational enough to make copy for quite some time.

Here are a few of the comments:

"The people of Santa Fe are provoked beyond measure by the news of the escape of Dave Rudabaugh and his compadre Webb from the Las Vegas jail. The news reached this city by means of a dispatch from the sheriff of San Miguel county to Sheriff Martinez of this (Santa Fe) county which was simply as follows: 'Jail delivery here last night. Look out for Rudabaugh and Webb.' The announcement was even more unwelcome than such news really is, on account of the desperate character of the criminals who are once more at large. They were both companions in crime of Billy the Kid – both desperadoes in all that the word implies and both are men whom reasonable citizens have reason to fear. They are at enmity with all friends of law and order and are sworn to kill all various officers and citizens, Dave Rudabaugh's frank admission of his various crimes in open court in this city was proof enough of the recklessness of the man and that he was absolutely careless of the consequences. He is cool and fearless and a thoroughly dangerous man."

"Webb is on the same order and should the two make good their escape the people have reason to fear a renewal of those outrages which the Kid indulged in after he had become aware that there was nothing else he could do which would make him more amenable to the law than he already was. This is the case with Rudabaugh and Webb and they are likely to make things hot unless, indeed, they adopt the wiser plan of leaving the country, which they were about to do when they were captured before. This is not the first time the prisoners escaped from the Las Vegas jail, and the jail deliveries from that town have been too frequent to indicate the belief that the jailers are absolutely reliable. The frequent occurrence of such escapes is productive of the double evil of discouraging officers from arresting desperate men and thereby rendering themselves liable to be murdered after the latter have regained liberty, and of superinducing crime by holding out chances of escape. The Las Vegas officers should be closely investigated with a view to punishing whosoever is guilty." (*Santa Fe New Mexican*, October 4, 1881)

"News reached this city last night by telegram that the prisoners in the Las Vegas jail had broken out. There were six of them, among whom was Dave Rudabaugh, one of the most notorious outlaws in the Western country, and Webb, a condemned murderer, No particulars of the escape could be learned, This delivery turns loose upon the community a band of the most desperate robbers and cut throats that ever infested the Western country." (The *Albuquerque Journal*, October 4, 1881)

"Governor Sheldon, recognizing the importance of the re-arrest of Dave Rudabaugh and his companion desperado John Webb, who with a number of others escaped from the Las Vegas jail on Friday (Oct. 2) night, has deemed it proper to offer a reward for their apprehension, and yesterday Secretary Ritch was furnished a proclamation of which this is a copy: 'Whereas David Rudabaugh and John J. Webb, convicted and confined in the county jail of the county of San Miguel, have escaped from custody and are now at large: Now, therefore, I, Governor Lionel A. Sheldon, Governor of the Territory of New Mexico, under, and by the authority of the power in me vested by the laws of the Territory of New Mexico, do offer and proclaim in the name of the said Territory, a reward of $500 for the said Dave Rudabaugh and $500 for John Webb to be paid out of the treasury of the said Territory upon satisfactory proof of the capture and delivery of the aforesaid.

December 5, 1881. This should induce the officers of the law to exert their utmost to try to capture Rudabaugh and Webb." (*Santa Fe New Mexican*, December, 1881)

"A man reported to the officers yesterday (Friday Dec. 8) that Webb and Rudabaugh came into Santa Fe a few days ago. He says that he saw them walk into town. This is not very probable, but it may be true. Everybody in Santa Fe knows Rudabaugh and it is not very likely that he would have escaped falling into the hands of the officers had he appeared here. He has no friends here as far as it is known and almost any man would have taken pleasure in giving him away to the authorities. This is one place Rudabaugh has reason to avoid, and he doubtless knows as much." (Ibid., Dec. 9, 1881)

"Dave Rudabaugh has a pair of U. S. Marshals shackles, which he might return if politely inclined as they are of no further use to him. Doubtless Dave will not care to return them in person." (Ibid., Dec. 21, 1881)

By December 27, 1881, authorities gave up looking for Dave Rudabaugh, believing that by this time he certainly took advantage of his escape and made tracks for Mexico. (See: *Santa Fe New Mexican* for December 27) Las Vegas did not forget Rudabaugh so quickly. When repairs were made on the jail two years after these events, the editor of the *Optic* took a dig at the mason presenting the bill to the city: Webb and Rudabaugh knocked a hole in the jail and didn't charge a cent. Now comes William R. Williams, the stone mason, and asks ten dollars for doing a similar job. It is an outrage. (*Las Vegas Optic*, November 29, 1883)

Meantime Billy the Kid was fast becoming a controversial figure as well as a legend. He was still warm in his grave when the *New York Sun* (July 22, 1881) exploited the possibility that the Kid was a New York hoodlum named McCarthy: "There is a general belief in the Fourth Ward that notwithstanding statements to the contrary, 'Billy the Kid' who on Saturday last was shot dead by Sheriff Garrett was born and brought up in that ward. The dispatch announcing his death reported that his real name was McCarthy, and that he was a New Yorker by birth. The Fourth Warder's name was McCarthy. He is described as answering in personal appearance to the description of the Kid, and it is said that he fled to the West in 1876 after committing a murder in this city."

"'I'm convinced that the Kid and McCarthy are one and the same person,' said Policeman Thomas Dwyer of the Oak Street Station last evening. 'McCarthy was of same height as the Kid, had hair and eyes of the same color, and the same projecting teeth. I remember McCarthy well, and the murder committed was the most brutal that ever came under my notice. It happened on the night of September 9, 1876. He had been on bad terms with Tom Moore, a brush maker, living at 9 Vandewater Street. Moore worked in a factory in Fulton Street, and was the only support of his mother. He was not twenty years old and was a fine, broad-shouldered fellow. On the night of the 9th, he went to the grocery store of Matthew Dwyer at the corner of Pearl and Hague Streets. There McCarthy met him, and they quarreled. McCarthy ran into the grocery store, and picking up a beer glass with one hand and a large knife, such as is used to slice ham with, in the other, came out. He threw the glass at Moore, who dodged it, and attempted to clinch with him. McCarthy met him with the knife, sending it through Moore's chin, cutting into his throat, and burying the blade ten inches into his breast. One of Moore's thumbs was cut off as he attempted to ward off the blow."

"McCarthy ran down Hague Street and through a passage to 84 Frankfort Street, where he threw away the knife. Moore staggered to 357 Pearl Street, and fell dead into the arms of a friend. McCarthy was traced to Brooklyn, where he was lost sight of. His father kept a fruit stand at the corner of Nassau and John Streets, and was thought to have money. Shortly after his son's disappearance he left the city, and was gone for several months. It was said at the time that he had taken McCarthy to Ireland. When he returned, I know that his son was with him, and I afterward learned that his son went West. In 1878, the old man died, and 'Dad' McCarthy, his other son, and Mrs. McCarthy died a few months later. There are two girls of the family still living."

"McCarthy was bad from a child, and had some Western experience before he fled West in 1876. When thirteen or fourteen years old he was sent to the House of Refuge, and through the Children's Aid Society, I think it was bound out to a Western farmer. He stayed a year or so, and then he escaped and came back to this city. He was born in Vandewater Street, and went to the Vandewater Street School. His given name was Michael, but I heard that he changed it after the murder. He was little past seventeen when he murdered Moore, and looked younger. His teeth were strong and white, but the two front upper teeth were longer than the rest and projected. He was then about five feet five inches tall, but may not then have got his growth. He had blue eyes and brown hair. His face was somewhat tanned. He learned to ride, I know, while on the farm out West. 'As soon as I read the account of Billy the Kid's death, and saw that his real name was McCarthy,' said the man into whose arms Moore had fallen after being stabbed, 'it occurred to me at once that he was Moore's murderer. The descriptions tallied and McCarthy was just the man to turn out a desperado.'"

"A *Sun* reporter talked last night with twenty Fourth Warders, all of whom had known McCarthy. They were all of the opinion that he and Billy the Kid were identical. 'There is one way to make sure of it,' said one young man employed in a grocery store in Pearl Street, near Hague, 'McCarthy, when ten years old, was badly burned with acid, and treated at the Chambers Street Hospital; I think he must have a scar on the upper part of one of his legs and on his body.'"

In many respects Rudabaugh was more fortunate in his escape than Billy the Kid. Of great advantage was his freedom of choice. Not tied down with affairs of the heart in Fort Sumner like Bonney (most authors agree that a love affair kept the Kid in Fort Sumner), nor anywhere else for that matter, Rudabaugh had long since given up calling Kansas home – once loosed from his chains he shook the dust of New Mexico forever. What he did until he arrived in Arizona, how he got there and who helped him are secrets he carried to the grave.

Changes took place during those long months in prison. And he was quick to note them. Railroads took care of more and more freighting, mail, hauling, passengers. Polly express, the stage coach, gaming tables, dance hall girls, variety shows in saloons, horse stealing, cattle rustling and so many other things were bowing out, not completely, for rustling goes on to this day, but with a change of pace, tactics, profit. Sidearms were less in evidence even in smaller towns. Brains were becoming increasingly more important than guns. Issues were settled in court rather than on the street. Gunslingers were heading for the last round-up. Dodge, Raton, Vegas, flirted with civilization and courted law and order. The Old Guard sought refuge in raw mining camps and the last frontier in Tombstone. The Border Ruffian could not change his ways any more than he could amend or even atone them. He simply had to go on as before. It was the only way of life he knew. He must rustle cattle, steal horses, hold up stages. Tombstone held the excitement he craved. Besides, the Earp Brothers were there. He would give it a try.

Webb and Rudabaugh had agreed to go their separate ways. It was harder for the law to track down a lone wolf than a traveling pack. Wyatt and Warren Earp are authorities for Rudabaugh's trek to Arizona. "Wyatt and Warren Earp arrived here (Dodge City) some days ago and will remain awhile. Wyatt is more robust than when a resident of Dodge, but in other aspects is unchanged. His story of the long contest with the cowboys of Arizona is of absorbing interest. Of the five brothers four yet live, and in return for the assassination of Morgan Earp they have handed seven cowboys 'over to the majority.' Of the six who participated in the assassination they have killed three – among them Curly Bill, whom Wyatt believes killed Mike Mayer at Caldwell (Kansas) last summer. Stillwell, Curly Bill and party ambuscaded the Earp party and poured a deadly fire into them. Wyatt receiving a charge of buckshot through his overcoat on each side of his body, and having the horn of his saddle shot off. Wyatt says after the first shock he could distinguish David Rudabaugh and Curly Bill, the latter's body showing well among the bushes. Wyatt lost no time in bringing him in and will receive the reward of one thousand dollars offered." [In spite of this newspaper report, Rudabaugh did not go to Arizona after his escape. He went directly to Mexico.]

"From what I (E. F. Calborn, the editor) could learn, the Earps have killed all of the leaders of the cowboys, who number nearly one hundred and fifty, and the troubles in Arizona will, so far as they are concerned, be over. Wyatt expects to become a candidate for sheriff of Cochise county this fall, and as he stands very near to the governor and all the good citizens of Tombstone and other camps in Cochise county, he will without doubt be elected. The office is said to be worth twenty-five thousand and will not be bad to take...." (*Ford County Globe*, May 23, 1882)

While Earp may have failed to tell S. Lake that Rudabaugh was the man at the side of Curly Bill the day the Arizona outlaw was shot, it does not mean that he fabricated when he spoke to Editor Calborn. One must remember Lake did not take down his notes until a number of years had passed. Also, Earp was concentrating on Wyatt Earp vs. Curly Bill or just plain Wyatt Earp, as he was wont to do – Lake to the contrary notwithstanding to the exclusion of Dave Rudabaugh. At the time Calborn was writing, the incident was still fresh in his mind. Earp knew Rudabaugh as well as Curly Bill. He had to look to the man at Curly Bills' side if only as a defense reaction to see if that man was ready to gun him down. Rudabaugh was not that interested. Had it been J. J. Webb instead of Curly Bill that Earp shot, Rudabaugh would have finished him off then and there.

There is some dispute that challenges Earp's word. Judge Hancock, Jim Hughes, Jones and others say that Curly Bill left Tombstone long before October 26, 1881. This may be true. But Earp never professed to have killed Curley Bill at Tombstone but in the hills some distance away. Since Curly Bill was a rustler he did not necessarily have to be on his New Mexico ranch after Wallace shot him in the cheek. He may have been there the day Jones came by but that does not mean that he stayed home. No doubt he went to New Mexico and remained long enough to recuperate from the wound; then went back to rustling, a more profitable business than ranching at the time at least for him and the men who followed him. Cattle barons from England and Scotland were taking over the ranges. The day of the big spreads the Matador, Spur, Anvil, Laurel Leaf, Rocking Chair, Turkey Track and hundreds of other vast ranches were changing the scene, but tempting the rustler nevertheless with tremendous herds. This was the time of the rustler. The Hash Knife in Arizona, where Rudabaugh, Wilson and Pickett all worked for a time may very well have kept Curly Bill in Arizona Territory. No one disputes that Curly Bill left Tombstone, but did he leave Arizona?

Curly Bill was a free-booter, land pirate, rustler, horse thief, bandit, outlaw, and a handy man with a gun. Large of body bordering on the rotund, rather than stocky, he was jovial by nature, vain about fine clothing, and had qualities of leadership. The number of men taking orders from him varied according to the type and importance of the raid. At times he had twenty, forty, even a hundred terrorizing Arizona and Northern Mexico.

He was a man of intense likes and violent dislikes. He had very little use for lawmen in general and Marshal Frederick White and Deputy Wyatt Earp in particular. Not because they introduced him to Tombstone's jail but because he was innocent of the charge. Fresh from Texas, William Brocius (or William Graham according to some authors) was not informed of the law prohibiting the use of firearms in Tombstone. Some of his cowboy friends decided to "Hurrah" the town, firing pistol shots at random and riding out of town before the law could take any action. Curly Bill was in a saloon on Allen Street at the time, enjoying some hard liquor. About midnight he decided he had enough and left for his hotel room. He encountered Marshal White on the street and was surprised when the lawman blocked his way demanding his gun.

"Why me," Curley wanted to know. "Do you think I did all that shooting?"

The marshal repeated: "Give me your gun."

Just as Curly Bill was in the act of taking it out of the holster to turn it over to the marshal Wyatt Earp came up behind him, threw his arms about him, grabbed for the gun causing it to discharge and wounding White. Earp went into his favorite act of buffaloing Brocius and dragging the unconscious man to jail. Earp was known for these tactics in Dodge. How he loved to play the hero! A study of the memoirs he dictated to Lake bears this out. He claims to be modest throughout but he gives very little credit to the supporting cast. One might excuse his action in this instance with the explanation that perhaps Curly Bill intended to use his gun on White, but White should have been aware of this and asked for the gunbelt rather than the pistol. Even the process of unbuckling the belt would not have deterred Earp since he was behind the outlaw and couldn't see what Brocius was doing with his hands. Earp's role as a lawman has been overrated.

White lingered a few hours and died. When it was learned that the marshal was dead a mob gathered about the jail intent on lynching Curly Bill. It is to Earp's credit that he stood them off and sent then home. Brocius never thanked him and held him accountable for the whole affair. He blamed White's death on the deputy. Hatred for Earp became an obsession with him. Others who shared his dislike were Ike Clanton, Finn Clanton, Bill Clanton, Old Man Clanton, Tom McLowery, Frank McLowery, Johnny Ringo, Pete Spence, Frank Stillwell.

Tombstone's first marshal died on the night of October 27, 1880. Curly Bill was known never to forget a kindness nor forgive an injury. What that kindness was that caused him to accept Dave Rudabaugh is not recorded. No doubt the two met during rustling days in the Texas Panhandle. Curly Bill holed up at Galeyville and sometimes at Charlestown, but this latter place was too close to Tombstone, the Earps and Doc Holliday, so he spent most of his time at Galeyville, a village of three hundred. Curly Bill's seventy-five thousand dollar robbery of the Don Miguel Garcia mule train, in Skeleton Canyon, took place before Rudabaugh joined him at Galeyville. Of all the marauders in Western history from the Border Ruffians to Butch Cassidy, none spilt as much blood (with the exception of Quantrill's attack on Lawrence, Kansas) than Curly Bill the day he captured the smuggler's train, July 1881, the month Bonney was killed at Fort Sumner.

U. S. Deputy Marshal Virgil Earp was killed on Wednesday night, December 28, 1881, three weeks after Rudabaugh's escape from the Las Vegas jail, and ample time to work his way to Arizona. While he is not associated with the actual killing since the feud which led to the killing took place prior to his arrival, he was against Wyatt Earp because of the track down to Fort Griffin, and the lawman's efforts to collect a reward on him. This meant that he could no longer be Doc Holliday's friend. Any enemy of Wyatt Earp automatically became the enemy of Doc Holliday. Witnesses to the murder speak of an unidentified man at the scene of the crime. This could have been Dave Rudabaugh. [Rudabaugh was not there or even in Arizona.]

Just before midnight Virgil Earp left the Oriental cantina and crossed Fifth Street. Against the pale light, his figure assumed grotesque proportions, silhouetted in shadows to narrow down as he went by the lighted window of the Eagle Brewery saloon. Across the street, lost in darkness, was a half-constructed building, the hiding place of five killers bent on ridding Tombstone of all the Earps. They poured buckshot into the moving target. Or thought they did. Some missed. A hole in the left side; left arm shattered at the elbow showed that some of the shot went astray. The men left. Three took one direction; two another. Witnesses testified that the three were Ike Clanton, Frank Stilwell and Hank Swilling. Of the other two, a miner said one was Johnny Ringo, but his companion was a stranger in Tombstone.

Since Wyatt Earp told the editor of the Dodge paper that Dave Rudabaugh was with Curly Bill, this stranger very probably was the wanted fugitive. Everybody watching the five ride away could identify four. All agreed that the fifth was new around the mining camp. Wyatt Earp knew Dave Rudabaugh although he did not suspect him as the fifth man until he saw him with Curly Bill. He had no way of knowing that Rudabaugh would choose Arizona in preference to Old Mexico after his escape. Wyatt Earp sought justice for his wounded brother but the sheriff refused to act. Instead he added fuel to the fire by deputizing one hundred cowboys and rustlers known to be sympathizers to the cause of Curly Bill and Ike Clanton, if not actual followers. We are of the opinion that David Rudabaugh was in this group. Sheriff Behan said that the only reason he deputized the cowboys was to keep order at the polls on election day, Tuesday, January 3, 1882. The Earps thought differently. For every armed deputy the opposition supplied two armed vigilantes. Behan lost. He billed the county for two thousand dollars which he claimed covered the cost of the hundred deputies.

Meantime a group, spurred on by John P. Clum, known more for his work with the Apaches on the San Carlos Reservation than for his activities with the vigilantes at Tombstone, formed a Safety Committee and swore out warrants for the arrest of Ike Clanton, Frank Stilwell and Hank Swilling for the attempt on the life of Virgil Earp. Clum was anxious to bring these men to justice not only because of his friendship for Wyatt Earp, but to avenge the attempt made on his own life. The *Tombstone Daily Citizen* for December 16, 1881, relates the attack on Clum:

"Honorable John P. Clum arrived in town last evening, looking none the worse for the attempt made on his life while traveling on the stage from Tombstone last Wednesday night. As to the motive which led to this attack, Mr. Clum says it could have been prompted only by the animosity felt towards him for having always opposed robbers, lawlessness and murder. During the last few weeks threats have been made against the lives of the mayor and other citizens of Tombstone who had assisted and had been active in bringing these outlaws to justice."

"In regard to the statement made that the rustlers were out for the purpose of robbing the stage, knowledge of the facts attending this portion of the story shows the lack of truth it contains. The stage carrying Wells, Fargo & Co. treasure, bullion and registered mail left Tombstone at 10 A. M. Wednesday, under the charge of two 'shotgun messengers' and had that been the object of the rustlers, they could readily have posted themselves as to the time it left town and the matter it was carrying."

"The stage on which Mr. Clum left Tombstone did not start until eight o'clock in the evening, with no treasure whatever and but a light load of passengers, and hence robbery could not have been the motive of the bandits, as it is a well known fact that none are better posted as to when treasure is placed upon a coach than those persons who rob them."

"It is further evident that they had no murderous designs on any other passengers, as the attacking party were within ten feet of the coach when the shooting began, and although upwards of twenty-five shots were fired, not even one struck the coach. From this it is quite clear that it was the purpose of the attacking party to stop the stage and making sure of killing the person they were after, perhaps robbing the passengers as a blind to cover up their real designs."

"The order to halt and the commencement of the firing were simultaneous. To the command 'Hold-up' the driver responded 'All right' but the shots frightened the horses and they broke into a run. After running about a mile one of the horses fell back and the coach stopped. Upon examination it was found that the horse was fatally shot. While this horse was being cut out of the traces, Mr. Clum stepped to one side of the road to listen as a second approach of the assailants was feared. Believing that the purpose of the attack was to kill him, and that the others in the party were in no danger, Mr. Clum decided to leave the coach and take his chances on foot as he realized that he had no show of making a fight in the coach. He walked to the Grand Central Mill about seven miles distant, where he was kindly provided for. After a sleep of about two hours he started on horseback for Benson, arriving there without any further trouble."

"It may be mentioned as a singular premonition that before leaving Tombstone Mr. Clum had remarked to a couple of his friends that what he most feared on his journey was that the cowboys would get up a sham stage robbery, during the process of which they would make it convenient to create a vacancy in the mayoralty of Tombstone. Mr. Clum will leave for the East in a few days to spend the holidays and on his return will again take up his residence in Tombstone. To use his own language, Mr. Clum said: 'I have lived in New Mexico and Arizona for the last ten years and circumstances have always thrown me amongst the very worst classes of Americans and Indians, I have never murdered or robbed anyone or intentionally caused anyone a serious injury, and things have come to a pretty pass when a good citizen cannot travel three miles from home without danger of assassination; and now that people realize that such is the fact, I believe that they will speedily provide a remedy which will insure protection to good citizens, and swift and retributive justice to outlaws....'"

That Wyatt Earp remembered Dave Rudabaugh while visiting Dodge but not in 1928 shortly before his death (which occurred on January 13, 1929) is a good argument in favor of checking contemporary newspapers, court house records, diaries, periodicals. More and more of this is being done now that Westerners clubs are forcing writers for more data and less description; more fact and less imagination; more research and less copying.

There hasn't been a Western writer who didn't refer to Dave Rudabaugh as a "Killer of Jailers" just because someone who began the legend took it for granted. It is surprising, isn't it, that he never killed a jailer in his life! No two accounts agree as to the events that culminated in the killing of Curly Bill by Wyatt Earp. Those in favor of Earp say he acted in the line of duty as marshal; those who question his authority as marshal say he was bent on murder, vowing to kill everyone and anyone implicated in the death of Morgan Earp. Wyatt justified the killing years later, insisting that he was under orders from the right side of the law, but the motive of revenge was of primary consideration. Lawman or not he would have hunted down the men. And he alone was judge and jury. There was only one sentence – no reprieve, no extenuating circumstances, no 'buffaloing' and carting off to jail to await the district term of court. The sentence was inexorable death by any kind of gun on hand when he caught up with the murderers.

Earp never sought out or tracked down any outlaw with the consistency and insistency that he went after those implicated in his brother's death. It is strange that for one eternal moment Rudabaugh and Earp were face to face when Curly Bill was killed. Why didn't one kill the other? Only the two men knew the answer. It went to the grave with them. Tombstone was fed up with the Earps, T.V. movies and hero worship to the contrary notwithstanding. The same goes for Doc Holliday, Johnny Behan, Johnny Ringo, Curly Bill and Dave Rudabaugh, The miners would have rejoiced if someone came along and rid the town of all of them and their bullying, six-shooter tactics. Rogue or great lawman, an avenging angel or marshal, he did have a proclamation from Mayor John Carr dated January 24, 1882, authorizing him to rid Tombstone of outlaws.

But Curly Bill was not in Tombstone when he was killed. Earp sought him out much like a rancher tracks down a mountain lion who has killed one of his cattle. Perhaps Curly Bill needed killing, without benefit of trial by jury.

"TO THE CITIZENS OF THE CITY OF TOMBSTONE"

"I am informed by His Honor, William H. Stillwell, Judge of the District Court of the First Judicial District, that Wyatt Earp, who left this city yesterday with a posse, was entrusted with warrants for the arrest (not killing) of divers persons charged with criminal offenses. I request the public to abstain from any interference with the execution of said warrants. – Mayor John Carr."

Wyatt Earp was never a U. S. Marshal neither at Dodge nor at Tombstone. He may have been a deputy. Nothing in the proclamation gave Earp the right to kill Frank Stilwell and Indian Charley any more than Curly Bill. The order asked that warrants be served. Nothing more. Earp killed Stilwell because he was involved in the death of Morgan Earp. The death of Stilwell was the opening Behan awaited. He had every right now to arrest Wyatt Earp. He swore in eight deputies and proceeded down Allen Street. Wyatt and Doc Holliday had returned to Tombstone reasonably certain that neither Behan nor Curly Bill would further molest Virgil. It is inconsistent that Wyatt should tell some friends that he was tired of Tombstone yet inform the editor of the Dodge paper that he proposed to return and run for sheriff of Cochise county. Earp never fully intended to leave Tombstone. He just wanted Behan to think so. By catching him off guard he might be able to collect evidence to convince the public that the sheriff was not fit to hold office. He sold his holdings and prepared to leave. Warren, his brother, decided to go with him, as did the ever faithful Doc Holliday, Sherman McMasters, Texas Jack Vermillion, Jack Johnson. They repaired to the Oriental for one last toast to Tombstone. Wyatt took the opportunity to blow his own horn. He would be remembered when the O.K. Corral, Behan, the Clantons, Curly Bill, even Tombstone itself became dim shadows of the past. And this is the man authors said was reluctant to talk of himself!

Behan walked into the Oriental, squared his shoulders, assumed an air of transcendent authority, reached into his pocket, pulling out the warrant and solemnly declaring for all to hear:

"I have here warrants duly sworn out in Tucson charging one Wyatt Earp and one J. H. Holliday with the murder of Frank Stilwell. It is my duty to arrest these men."

Falling snow could not be more silent than the hush that followed. All eyes focused on Wyatt Earp. Slowly, deliberately, he set his glass down on the bar. Then he made one of the longest speeches of his life ending with:

"I'll see you in Hades before I consent to be arrested by you." Behan noted the six-shooters and rifles. Holliday and the others would use them on his deputies if he insisted on arresting Earp. He stood there as the defiant Earp and his men left the cantina. Aware of the drama taking place, crowds lined the sidewalks, silent as the group took its last ride along Allen Street. Among them were many who hated Earp enough to attempt a shot now that they believed he and Holliday were being railroaded out of town. There were others who hated to see him go because he was their only hope against Behan and his henchmen. Those who wanted Earp dead kept their thoughts to themselves as did those who hoped he would remain. The only noise on Allen Street was made by the horses. Doc Holliday noted that hostile looks outnumbered the regretful. He kept his six-shooter in readiness. It was more like a funeral procession on its way to the graveyard.

But Earp had other plans. There would be a funeral, but not his. They found Indian Charlie chopping wood at Pete Spence's ranch on the western slopes of the Dragoons. Four bullets, and he chopped no more. Earp merely said: "Another one for Morgan." Indian Charley had mentioned a stranger as participating in the assassination of Morgan Earp. Rudabaugh had been in the area several weeks. Until records come up with another name we can only assume he was the man.

South of the old Fort Bowie-Tubac road, practically on the midway mark, was the Valle de San Pedro and the oasis known as Ojo de San Pedro. Later these names were changed to Iron Springs (still later to Mescal Springs) and the Valley of San Pedro at the foot of the Whetstone Mountains. Here Curly Bill, Dave Rudabaugh and others rested as they pondered their assignment as deputies, according to some old timers, wondering just how to go about bringing in Wyatt Earp for the murder of their pal Frank Stilwell. That Behan knew Curly Bill was in the Babocomari area at all is surprising since it is at least twenty-five miles northwest of Tombstone. Wyatt Earp seems to have been as well informed as Sheriff Behan. Not all authors agree that Curly Bill and his men had been deputized by the sheriff, but knowing Behan's methods the scale is in their favor.

Earp and his men rode to Iron Springs. He was strangely equipped for a man who later insisted that he wasn't expecting trouble: a shotgun, Winchester, two six-shooters. Less than seventeen yards from the Springs, he halted his mount and got down. Cautiously, shotgun in hand, he walked forward. An enemy could be hidden in the Bosque that curtained the water from view. As he appeared over the rise, he saw Curly Bill and Dave Rudabaugh lying-in wait. McMasters, still mounted, spotted them at the same time. He turned his horse and fled out of range. Earp thought only of his brother Morgan.

Rudabaugh had one fleeting glance and decided to let Curly Bill and Earp fight it out. He broke for the trees. Better to fight Indian style than to be a target in plain view. Curly Bill sent a double charge in Earp's direction without taking aim. Some of the shot went through Earp's coat; most missed. Earp raised his gun, pressed both triggers. Curly Bill screamed once, then lay still. Earp then ducked behind his horse and the battle was on. Years later when telling of the fight Earp mentioned Pony Deal, John Barnes, Ed Lyle, Johnny Lyle, Milt Hicks, Rattlesnake Bill Johnson, Bill Hicks, Frank Patterson, claiming he had warrants for their arrest. What about Rudabaugh? Since he was always referred to as the "stranger" he could not be named in the mayor is proclamation. Since

Earp was wanted for questioning he was hardly in the position to serve warrants. Yet, to have forgotten Rudabaugh, wanted in Las Vegas as a fugitive from justice, seems strange indeed. Rudabaugh topped Curly Bill in notoriety. Milt Hicks was wounded in the arm. Johnny Barnes was wounded in the shoulder. Rudabaugh was not hurt. The outlaws forced Earp and his men to leave. They were still at Iron Springs when the Epitaph published an account of the fight. The Cattlemen's Organization offered one thousand dollars for Curly Bill, dead or alive. Earp used it to buy fresh mounts and provisions for his men.

The gang broke up after the death of Curly Bill – mostly because cattlemen were making it uncomfortable for rustlers to operate. They offered rewards too tempting to resist. Some went to New Mexico; most went to Old Mexico. Rudabaugh went to Old Mexico for a time, returning to Arizona in 1883 to work for the Aztec Land and Cattle Company better known as the Hash Knife outfit [after his escape, Rudabaugh went directly to Mexico and stayed there until his death in 1886]. Two of his former associates, Billy Wilson and Tom Pickett worked here under foreman John Jones. According to old timers and accounts in the current Arizona newspapers Rudabaugh lost no time holding up stages and rustling cattle. He was forced to flee across the border and ranchmen hoped he would stay there.

Luis Terrasas had been a poor man but he had a patriot's love of his country. When a revolution threatened he aroused his fellow citizens to fight for their country. As a reward the president of Mexico told him that wherever he drove a stake on the open range, that land would be his. In time he acquired many cattle and looked about for an experienced foreman to handle his stock. As a further reward for his services he was named governor of Chihuahua. Rudabaugh was placed in charge of one of his ranches. It was brought to the notice of the governor that Rudabaugh helped himself to a number of the cattle. He was promptly discharged. Bitter at this turn of events he went to Parral, [Mexico], entered a cantina and began abusing the patrons. In the gunfight that followed, he killed two and wounded another before he was killed. This was on the night of February 18, 1886. Word was sent to the Arizona and New Mexico newspapers. The *Las Vegas Optic* printed this story, February 23rd:

"Dave Rudabaugh, who was recently killed at Parral, in the State of Chihuahua, Mexico, was what might be called an 'all-around desperado.' He was equally proficient in holding up a railroad train or a stage coach, or, as occasion offered, robbed a bank, 'shooting up' a frontier settlement, or running off stock. He indulged in these little peculiarities for a year or two in Arizona, and inasmuch as many of our old timers doubtless remember him, some of them to their cost, the following sketch of the antecedents of Rudabaugh, communicated to the *Tombstone Democrat*, Arizona, by one who knows, will prove of interest."

"Ten years ago, just after the Santa Fe railroad had invaded western Kansas, a train was held up near Kinsley, and robbed of everything (!) of value that it contained [the robbers got nothing in the robbery]. Detective Hugens [it was Bat Masterson] got after the gang and soon had them all in the Leavenworth penitentiary, with the exception of Dave Rudabaugh, who turned state's evidence. After that David became a desperado and was finally outlawed at Las Vegas for numerous other crimes. In 1880, he became a member of the famous Billy the Kid gang which eventually got him into jail. He escaped the jail at Las Vegas and fled to Arizona where he rustled with varying success for nearly two years when he was driven out of the Apache country and struck for Old Mexico, where he became manager of the cattle interests in Chihuahua of the governor thereof. David continued to be a desperado, however, and became engaged in his final difficulty

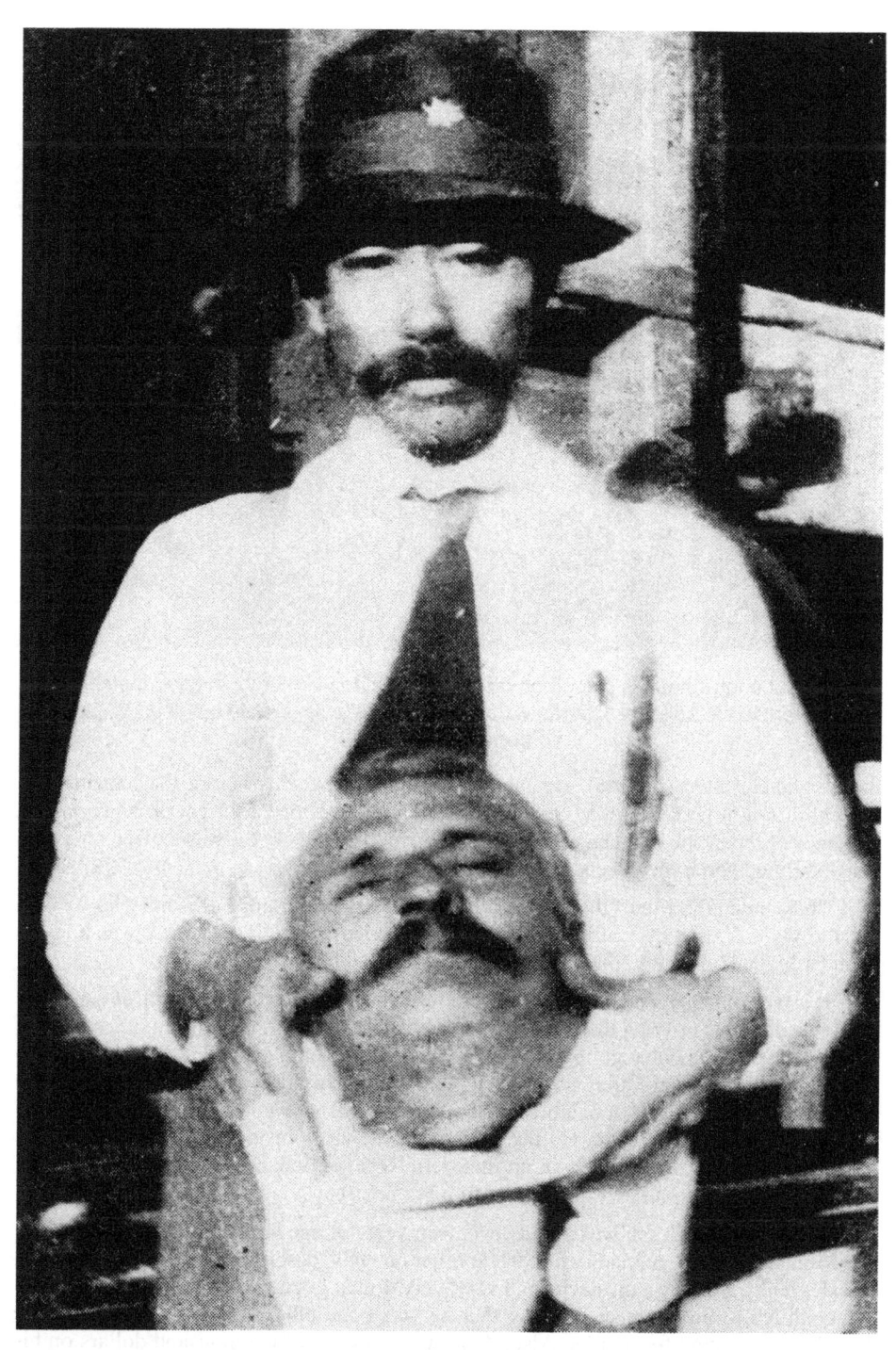

Dave Rudabaugh, Headless in Parral. Courtesy, Jo and Fred Mazzula. [Photo by Albert W. Lohn, February 18, 1886.]

114 ~ Chapter 6

Rudabaugh's head is placed on a pike in Parral to warn othrs to keep their six-shooters in the holsters. Courtesy, Jo and Fred Mazzula. [Photo by Albert W. Lohn, February 18, 1886.].

in the ancient town of Parral. He fatally shot up two persons before the buzzing ball caught him in it fatal shot that ended his life. The natives of Parral got up a procession in honor of the event, and Dave's head was severed from his body, was carried on a pole and exhibited about the streets...."

Thus ended the life of the man about whom East and Frank Collison (who worked for the Wyle & Coggins outfit in eastern New Mexico) said: "if ever there was a living man Billy the Kid feared, that man was Dave Rudabaugh."

It is part of the legend of many of the mould of Billy the Kid, Curly Bill, Jesse James to have adherents proving that they were not killed but living incognito in other parts of the world. Dave Rudabaugh is no exception. Schuyler Colfax Small, a former cowboy, treasurer and sheriff of Valley county, Montana, as well as a member of the State prison staff at Deer Lodge, is responsible for the story that it was not Dave Rudabaugh who was killed in Parral. Schuyler Colfax, named for the vice president of the United States (1869-73) as was Colfax county in northeastern New Mexico, became chief clerk for the Montana State Railroad before retiring from public life.

In 1889, when Small was about seventeen years of age he worked as a cowboy for the Montana Cattle Company. In 1892, another cowboy, described as of medium height, slender build, wearing a mustache and very, very drunk, got into a discussion with Small. He confided to the younger cowboy that he was none other than the notorious Dave Rudabaugh, wanted for murder. Also, there was a reward of ten thousand dollars on his head. Fantastic! The next day in a more sober frame of mind he asked Small to keep his identity a secret. Small promised to do so and soon forgot the incident.

Thirty-five years later, when he was superintendent of the motor vehicle license plate factory at Deer Lodge, another member of the prison staff, George Ayers, father of the governor of Montana, called him up one night saying that there was a man out on his ranch who wanted to talk to him. It was the man claiming to be Dave Rudabaugh. He had married, raised a family of three daughters and lived happily until his wife died. He took to drink; lost his home and self respect. Small told Ayers that the derelict was Dave Rudabaugh only on the strength of the drunken conversation so many years before. Ayers bought him a new suit and a ticket to Spokane, Washington. Some time later Small received a letter from Oregon. On the surface it was a thank you note. Actually the writer asked for twenty-five dollars. Small said he refused, knowing that the man would drink it up. He said that he learned that the man died a year or so after that [this is a tall tale; the "other cowboy" was not Rudabaugh].

As a public figure in Montana, Small was in the news, a singled out victim of a con man. No doubt the man was acquainted with Rudabaugh in some way but hardly the outlaw. There is no record anywhere of a ten thousand dollar reward being offered for Rudabaugh. Neither Earp nor Garrett nor any bounty hunter in the country would have left the opportunity for such rich reward slip by without an effort of tracking him down even if it meant going to Mexico. (See the Small account in the *New Mexico Historical Review*, April, 1948, pp 146-151.) With the passage of time Rudabaugh will become more and more of a controversial figure simply because the public had about enough of Billy the Kid, Butch Cassidy, Doc Holliday, Black Jack Ketchum and will look to lesser known desperadoes for fresh excitement in this field of daring deeds of frontier days.

Westerners' Posses all over the country have already tapped the surface. Some one will come up with a paper before the group entitled – Was The Man Small Worked With In Montana Really Dave Rudabaugh? – and the discussion begins. Nobody solves anything but all agree that it was a lively meeting.

Dave Rudabaugh lies buried in unconsecrated ground in a forgotten corner of the old graveyard in Parral. People who have gone there to photograph the grave of Pancho Villa have looked in vain for his grave. Natives have long since forgotten it since Rudabaugh meant no more to them than a burro, a mad dog. Such graves are not remembered.

[On February 18, 1886, Rudabaugh was killed by a Winchester rifle shot to the chest in Parral, Mexico, by a grocery man named José. Following his killing, Rudabaugh was decapitated by José. His head was placed on a pole and paraded around the Parral plaza. Present at Rudabaugh's beheading was Albert W. Lohn, a nineteen-year-old photographer.]

[Lohn took four photographs of Rudabaugh's decapitated head. The two negatives he printed were confiscated by Mexican authorities. The other two negatives remained in Lohn's files, entirely forgotten by him.]

[In 1943, Fred W. Mazzulla, an avid collector of Western memorabilia, met Lohn in Nogales, Arizona, where Lohn was operating a photography studio. The two became good friends. During one of their conversations, Lohn mentioned that he had been present in Parral when Rudabaugh was decapitated and he had taken photos of the event. Prompted by Mazzulla's collector's interest, Lohn located the two negatives he had put away 57 years earlier and gave them to Mazzulla. See Appendix C.]

[The photos shown on pages 113-114 are prints of the two negatives acquired by Mazzulla.]

Bibliography

1. COURTHOUSE RECORDS AND CRIMINAL DOCKET RECORDS

   Colfax County Records, Raton, New Mexico
   Socorro County Records, Socorro, New Mexico
   Santa Fe County Records, Santa Fe, New Mexico
   Bernalillo County Records, Albuquerque, New Mexico
   Hemphill County Records, Canadian, Texas
   Wheeler County Records, Wheeler, Texas
   Census Records, Topeka, Kansas
   Kinsley County Records, Kinsley, Kansas

2. INTERVIEWS

   Relatives of Gov. L. Terrasas, for whom Rudabaugh worked in Chihuahua, Mexico
   Oldtimers

3. COLLECTIONS

   The Ritch Collection, Huntington Library
   The Bush Collection, Amarillo, Texas
   The Fordyce Papers, Santa Fe
   Kansas Historical Collection, Topeka
   New Mexico Historical Collection, Santa Fe
   Coronado Room Collection, University of New Mexico
   School of Mines Collection, Socorro, New Mexico
   Bishop FitzSimon Collection, Amarillo, Texas
   Highlands University Collection, Las Vegas, New Mexico
   Springfield, Illinois, Burial Records Civil War Veterans
   Border Ruffian Letters 1858-60, Author Unknown

4. BOOKS

   American Guide Series all the Southwestern States, Kansas, Colorado and California
   O'Connor, Richard, "Pat Garrett," Doubleday & Co., N. Y., 1960
   Waters, Frank, "The Earp Brothers of Tombstone," C. N. Potter, N. Y., 1960
   Hamlin, William Lee, "The True Story of Billy the Kid," Caldwell, Idaho, 1959
   Spring, "The Prelude to the War with Kansas," Riverside Press, Cambridge, Mass., 1885
   Howes, Charles C., "The Place Called Kansas," University of Oklahoma Press, Norman, Oklahoma, 1952
   Doran, Thomas, "Kansas Sixty Years Ago," Kansas State Historical Collection, Vol. XV, 1919-1922
   Buel, J. W., "The Border Outlaws," St. Louis, Mo., 1882
   Forrest, Earle R., "Arizona's Dark and Bloody Ground," Caxton Printers, Caldwell, Idaho, 1952
   Gardner, Theodore, "The Last Battle of the Border War," Kansas Historical Collection, Vol. XV, 1919-1922
   Nevins, Allan, "Ordeal of the Union," 2 Vols., Chas. Scribners Sons, N. Y., 1947
   Haley, J. E., "Charles Goodnight," University Press, Norman, Oklahoma, 1949

Haley, J. E., "Jeff Milton, A Good Man with a Gun," University Press, Norman, Oklahoma, 1948
Adams, R., "A Fitting Death for Billy the Kid," University Press, Norman, Oklahoma, 1960
Poe, Sophie, "Buckboard Days," Caxton Printers, Idaho, 1936
Harris, Frank, "My Reminiscences as a Cowboy," Chas. Boni, N. Y., 1930
Horan & Sann, "Pictorial History of the Wild West," Crown Pub. N. Y., 1954
Beebe & Clegg, "Hear the Train Blow," Dutton & Co., N. Y., 1952
Brown & Schmidt, "Trail Driving Days," Chas. Scribners Sons, N. Y., 1952
Bradley, G. D., "The Story of the Santa Fe," The Goram Press, N. Y., 1920
Marshall, M., "Santa Fe, The Railroad That Built An Empire"
Waters, L. L., "Steel Rails to Santa Fe," University of Kansas Press, Lawrence, Kansas, 1950
Cleaveland, A. M., "No Life for a Lady," Houghton-Mifflin Co., Boston, 1941
Keleher, William A., "The Fabulous Frontier," Rydal Press, Santa Fe, N. M., 1942
Hening, H. B. (Ed.), "George Curry, 1861-1947," University Press, Albuquerque, N. M., 1958
Burns, Walter N., "he Saga of Billy the Kid," Grosset & Dunlap, N. Y., 1926
Roberts, W. Y. (Lt. Gov. of Kansas), "The Border Ruffian Code of Kansas," Greeley & McElrath, The Tribune Office, N. Y., 1856
Horan, James D., "The Wild Bunch," New American Library, N. Y., 1958
Kelley, Charles, "The Outlaw Trail," Devin-Adair Co., N. Y., 1959
Hunt, Frazier, "The Tragic Days of Billy the Kid," Hastings House, N. Y., 1956
Hendricks, George, "The Badman of the West," Naylor Co., San Antonio, 1942
Dykes, J. C., "Billy the Kid Bibliography of a Legend," University Press, Albuquerque, N. M.,. 1952
Garrett, Pat, "Authentic Story of Billy the Kid," Atomic Books, N. Y., 1946
Myers, John Myers, "Doc Holliday," Little Brown & Co., Boston, 1955
Jahns, Pat, "The Frontier World of Doc Holliday," Hastings House, N. Y., 1957
Burns, W. N., "Tombstone," New American Library, N. Y., 1955
Lake, Stuart N., "Wyatt Earp, Frontier Marshal," HoughtonMifflin Co., Boston, 1931
O'Connor, Richard, "Bat Masterson," Doubleday & Co., Garden City, N. Y., 1957
Raine, Wm. M., "Famous Sheriffs and Western Outlaws," Permabooks, N. Y., 1929
Hendron, J. W., "The Story of Billy the Kid," Rydal Press, Santa Fe, 1948
Scanland, John M., "Life of Pat Garrett," C. Hodge Press, El Paso, 1952
Debo, A., "The Cowman's Southwest, Reminiscences of Oliver Nelson," Arthur Clark Co., Glendale, Calif., 1953
Kelliher, Wm., "Violence in Lincoln County," University Press, Albuquerque, N. M., 1957
Otero, Miguel, "My Life on the Frontier 1864-1882," Vol. I, Press of the Pioneers, N. Y., 1935

S. WESTERN CLUBS

Denver Posse Brand Book -- All Issues
New York Posse Brand Book -- All Issues
Los Angeles Brand Book -- All Issues

6. NEWSPAPERS

Edwards County Kansas Leader, Feb. 7, 1878
Ford County Globe, Jan. 28, 1878

Ford County Globe, Feb. 5, 1878
Ford County Globe, July 2, 1878
Ford County Globe, Dec. 21, 1880
Ford County Globe, April 6, 1880
Dodge City Times, Feb. 2, 1878
Dodge City Times, June 22, 1878
Dodge City Times, May 23, 1882
Dodge City Times, July 12, 1881
Dodge City Times, Nov. 20, 1880
Dodge City Times, Dec. 18, 1880
Live Stock Journal, August 5,. 1884
The Valley Republican, Feb. 9, 1878
The Valley Republican, Feb. 2, 1878
The Valley Republican, Feb. 18, 1878
Dodge City Times, Jan. 4, 1879
Ford County Globe, Nov. 16, 1878
Ford County Globe, Oct. 2, 1883
Kinsley Graphic, June 22, 1878
Eureka Real Estate Pilot, Feb., 1871
Las Vegas Gazette, Feb. 26, 1881
Las Vegas Daily Gazette, March 4, 1881
Albuquerque Journal, April 6, 1881
The Golden Era, October 19, 1889
Las Vegas Optic, All Issues 1879, 1880, 1881, 1882, 1886
Santa Fe New Mexican, All Issues 1879, 1880,. 1881, 1882, 1886
New York Sun, July 22, 1881
Tombstone Daily Citizen, Dec. 16, 1881
The Ritch Scrap books, 16 volumes of newspaper clippings, possession of Huntington Library
New Mexico Newspaper Collection, Museum Building, Topeka, Kansas
New Mexico Collection, Bancroft Library, Berkeley, Calif.

7. MAGAZINES

TRUE WEST, Austin, Texas, All Issues
FRONTIER TIMES, Austin, Texas, All Issues
REAL WEST, Derby, Conn., All Issues
NEW MEXICO MAGAZINE, Santa Fe, N. M., All Issues
NEW MEXICO HISTORICAL REVIEW, Santa Fe, N. M., All Issues
NEW MEXICO STOCKMAN, Albuquerque, N. M., All Issues
SUN TRAILS, Albuquerque, N. M., All Issues

Appendix A | Rudabaugh's Confession

Here is Rudabaugh's confession to the Kinsley train robbery, which he gave to the court after pleading guilty and turning state's evidence. This is an extraordinary statement. It shows that Rudabaugh possessed a superb memory. He gives moment-by-moment details: locations, distances between locations, times of events, what each robber was wearing, the colors of their horses, what weapons each man carried, which person did what, compass directions, remembered dialog, intentions, and even self-admitted mistakes. This exhaustive, straightforward chronicle suggests that Rudabaugh was unreservedly truthful. – *Editor*

"My name is David Rodebaugh; age 23; born in July [14], 1854; my home is in Greenwood County, near Eureka, Kansas."

"I met Roark [Roarke] and Thomas Gott in August last, and Dement about the first of October. I was acquainted with Roark and Dement about one year previous to this."

"I met J. D. Green in January, about the first, and West about the same time."

"About Wednesday January 16, 1878, we were all together on Wolf creek – Roark, Dan Dement, Ed. West, Thomas Gott and J. D. Green and myself. I think that Roark and Dement were the two that first broached the subject of attacking the train at Kinsley. It was agreed that the party should consist of the six named. This was the second attempt. The first attempt was to attack the train at Dodge City. This was to have been on or about the first of January, but failed on account of a snow storm. Green was not with us at that time. All the rest were. The first was planned on Beaver creek, about forty-five miles north of Wolf creek. This was planned about the time it was to have been carried into execution. The day after it was planned we started for Dodge. It would take us two days to get there, as it was sixty-five miles from where we planned the attack to Dodge City."

"Roark went west and Gott went to Dodge. I and Dement only went 25 miles. On account of a heavy snow storm, Dement and I went back. Roark and West went into Dodge, but did not stay, as they came right back."

"After this failure we returned and moved over to Wolf creek. We stayed at or near there till the second attempt, which was made on the morning of January 27, 1878. About five days before the attack we started. Mike Roark was leader. He rode an iron gray horse. Dan Dement rode a black horse, Gott rode a sorrel horse, Green rode a roan horse, West rode a bay horse and I rode a sorrel horse. West, Gott and I had rubber shoes. West got his shoes at Jones and Phimmer's ranch. Gott and myself got ours at Dodge City. Roark got Gott's rubber shoes at Dodge, I think at Rath's. These shoes were got a month before the attack, except West's, which were got at Jones and Phimmers' just before we started. Roark got his gun, a (45) Sharp's, at Rath's sometime before. He got the pistol the time the first robbery was planned of Green; he had only one. Dan Dement had one gun, a Sharp's rifle, and one six-shooter, a Colt's 45. Don't know where he got them. Thomas Gott had a 44 Sharp's and no revolvers. He bought his gun from Roark. Green was armed with one 45 U.S. Springfield patent gun; he had two 45 Colt's pistol's [sic]; he bought one of the pistols at Zimmerman's in Dodge City, between the time of the first plan and before the second robbery; he and I went to Dodge together at this time."

"Ed. West was armed with one United States Springfield gun and one six shooter, Cole's [sic] 45; don't know where he got it. I was armed with one of Sharp's 40 calibre guns and had two Smith and Wesson pistols. We always had a wagon with us and left it on the Beaver and started in the evening. This is about eighty miles from Dodge City. We rode that night about twenty-five miles and camped again on Beaver. The camp is twenty miles about the trail where it crosses the Beaver. The next morning we went across the Cimarron, and that night camped at the head of Sand creek. The next day we went over to Buffalo creek on the Camp Supply road."

"The next day we left at noon. We met the Reynolds stage about five miles north of Bluff creek. We stopped that night on Mulberry, about five miles south of Pat Ryan's ranche. This was Friday, January 25, 1877 [1878]. The next day we went within ten miles of Kinsley. Got there just about dusk. It was in the sand hills, the other side of the river. We carried our food with us. We stayed there about four hours, crossed the river and went over to Kinsley; got to Kinsley about two hours before the western bound train was due. We went to a house near the railroad track and about half way between Kinsley and the water tank. Ed. West asked how far it was to Kinsley, and was told it was abut a mile and a half. We were all close together when the question was asked. He then asked how far it was to the tank, and was answered about the same distance. Two of the party got lost, Dement and West; I think Green fired a pistol when West was lost, and West fired his pistol when Dement was lost. After we left the house we went about half a mile up the railroad. We left the horses at the trestle, half a mile from the tank. Thomas Gott held the horses for the party."

"Ten miles from Kinsley we intended to take the eastbound train, but a snow storm came up and we changed the plan, and decided to take the westbound train, on account of not being able to get to Kinsley in time to take the eastbound train. We just got to the track as the eastbound train passed, and could not have stopped it if we wanted to. After the eastbound train passed we waited about an hour. Gott took charge of the horses and walked down a [on] foot to Kinsley. Roark gave the orders, assigning each man his position. Roark, Dement and I went inside the depot and talked to [Andrew] Kincaid. Roark and I went behind the railing. Dement stayed outside, and I don't think anybody was with him. Green and West was on the platform outside. Roark talked with Kincaid and I talked with him. Roark took Kincaid's pistol away from him and gave it to me and I gave it to Gott. Kincaid intended to shoot me with it. Roark says, 'I'll take that,' and Kincaid gave it to him. When Roark went in he asked Kincaid if he had any money. Kincaid told him he was too late; that the money was all sent on the other train, that had just passed, and pulled open the drawer that was in the counter and showed him there was none there. He offered us a lot of post cards which we did not take. Roark told him to unlock the safe. Kincaid said that Gardner had the key and he was over to the hotel. We all left the office together as the train was approaching. As we stepped outside a man came on the platform and Kincaid told him to go back. Says he, 'Blanchard, go back. These men have all got pistols.' Blanchard not understanding it came to where Kincaid was. By that time the train had got to us."

"West and Dement got on the engine. Roark, Green and me was to get into the express car. When the engine got opposite to us, Kincaid made a sudden jump landing in front of the cowcatcher, barely missing it, and got on the other side of the engine. Then

West and Dement started for the engine, and Roark started for the express car. Green and Roark went to the door of the car, and I went to the rear of the baggage car at the front of the coach."

"Roark then tried to get into the express car and the shooting commenced. I took the conductor as he stepped off the coach. There were several men on the platform. I told him and the rest of them to go back. I knew it was the conductor from his lantern and the badge of his hat. The first shot was fired by the express messenger."

"I was to have got into the express car, with the rest. The train running beyond the platform upset our plan completely, as the height from the ground to the car door was so great. Roark could not get in. Roark and Green both ran to the car door to get in quick. Roark spoke to the messenger; don't know what he said. The first shot fired by the messenger came within three inches of hitting Green in the head. I was still on the platform of the depot. I fired four shots, at no one, but merely to keep any one from coming out of the cars. The train then started. Dement told me that he told the engineer to start the train. The object was to rob the train while in motion, and by the time we got to our horses. The signal, in case we got into the express car, was to be two shots. Instead of two there was about a dozen, which scared the men on the engine and let them know there was something wrong. After the train had run past, I walked up the track and overtook Dement and Roark. Green was ahead of us abut half way to the horses. West came in the last. We got to our horses and started for camp."

"We blacked our faces when we stopped ten miles from Kinsley to get supper. We used gunpowder and wet it, as it was easy to wash off. We were all blacked but Gott. We washed it off the next day, twenty miles from Kinsley, south of the river. We crossed the river and was in the Sand Hills by daylight. A party fired at us near where we got our horses, and as we rode off. Sunday night we camped on the prairie near a little lake on the flat. Gott's horse gave out Sunday morning. We left the horse, and hid the saddle in deep grass off of the trail about five miles from the river, in the Sand Hills, about fifty yards to the left of the trail we made. The next day we went to Bluff creek; staid there all night and the next morning separated. Roark and Dement, Green and Gott went towards camp on the Beaver. I have not seen any of the rest except West since. Tuesday night West and I staid at the head of Sand creek. Wednesday night we stopped at Lovell's camp and were arrested."

"Mike Roark is a man about six feet tall, sandy complection [sic], blue eyes, thirty years of age, sandy hair; wears a mostache [sic] and imperial; wore an old black, soft felt hat; wore a canvas overcoat, like mine, and canvas overalls; he wore rubbers; I think would weight about 190 pounds."

"Dan Dement is a man about five feet eight inches high, thirty years of age, weight abut 150 pounds, black hair and eyes; wears a black mustache, very heavy; thin face; dressed in canvas overalls and a coat like mine; he wore a black soft hat. He and Mike Roark have been buffalo hunters for the last two years. (Then follows a description of West, Green and Gott [not given])."

"(Signed:) David Rodebaugh"

"Emporia, Kansas, February 26, 1878"

Appendix B | Trial Testimony – Territory vs David Rudabaugh, Murder

Rudabaugh's trial for killing jailer Antonio Lino Valdez opened April 19, 1881, in the First District Court in Santa Fe, Judge L. Bradford Prince presiding. The charge was murder in the first degree, the penalty death by hanging.

Rudabaugh's defense attorneys were Marshal A. Breeden and George G. Posey (the lawyers that had handled his change of venue motion were sick). The attorney for the Territory (the prosecution) was William Breeden. Rather oddly, especially for a criminal trial, Prosecutor William Breeden was the older brother of Defense Attorney Marshal Breeden.

The jurors were: H. F. Swape, Walter N. Hoyh, Manuel Sandoval, A. M. Dettelbach, Benito Bacheco, R. M. Stephens, Jesus Torres, Viscente Garcia, G. Felgard, R. A. Biersuth, Juan Luis Gallegos, and Fasmundo Duran. -- *Editor*

Testimony

Be it remembered that upon the trial of the above entitled cause at the April AD Term of the District Court for the County of Santa Fe, the following proceedings were had, to wit:

The following evidence which was all of the evidence given in the case was given upon the trial of the cause.

Prosecution Witness – San Miguel County Sheriff Hilario Romero

Hilario Romero Sworn:

Direct Examination by Col. Wm. Breeden

> ***Wm. Breeden:*** *Do you know the defendant?*
> ***Romero:*** *Yes sir.*
>
> ***Wm. Breeden:*** *Did you know Antonio Lino Valdez?*
> ***Romero:*** *I did.*
>
> ***Wm. Breeden:*** *Do you know where he is?*
> ***Romero:*** *He is dead.*
>
> ***Wm. Breeden:*** *Where did he die?*
> ***Romero:*** *In Las Vegas.*
>
> ***Wm. Breeden:*** *What time?*
> ***Romero:*** *On the second day of April 1880.*
>
> ***Wm. Breeden:*** *Do you know what occupation he pursued when he died?*
> ***Romero:*** *He was a jailer.*
>
> ***Wm. Breeden:*** *In the San Miguel County jail?*
> ***Romero:*** *Yes sir.*
>
> ***Wm. Breeden:*** *Where is the jail in San Miguel County?*
> ***Romero:*** *In Las Vegas.*
>
> ***Wm. Breeden:*** *Did he die at the jail?*

Romero: I suppose so.

Wm. Breeden: Do you know how he came to his death?
Romero: I do.

Wm. Breeden: State how.
Romero: From a shot.

Wm. Breeden: In what part of the person?
Romero: I think it was either in the right or the left side.

Wm. Breeden: Do you know who fired the shot?
Romero: No sir.

Wm. Breeden: Where was it you saw the deceased after his death?
Romero: I saw him before his death.

Wm. Breeden: Where was it you saw him after he was shot?
Romero: I saw him in one of the guard rooms of the jail.

Wm. Breeden: Do you know how long after he received the shot that you saw him the first time?
Romero: From five to ten minutes.

Wm. Breeden: Had he been moved from the place where he received the shot?
Romero: Yes sir. They had either moved him or he had gone himself into a room.

Wm. Breeden: What time was it?
Romero: About one o'clock in the afternoon.

Wm. Breeden: Did you see the defendant that day?
Romero: I did.

Wm. Breeden: Where was it you saw him?
Romero: I saw him running from the hall of the Court House to the corner, as he turned around.

Wm. Breeden: Was he running.
Romero: Yes sir.

Wm. Breeden: Any one with him?
Romero: Yes sir.

Wm. Breeden: Who was with him?
Romero: Another man whose name I did not know at the time.

Wm. Breeden: Did he have anything with him?
Romero: They had pistols in their hands.

Wm. Breeden: Did the defendant have pistols?
Romero: Yes sir.

Wm. Breeden: You saw them running out of the hall of the Court House?
Romero: I saw them running until they turned the corner.

Wm. Breeden: *How far was this hallway from the place where deceased was shot?*

Romero: *The hall was about six or eight yards inside the enclosure [placita].*

Wm. Breeden: *Did this hallway lead from the enclosure where the deceased was shot.*

Romero: *Yes sir.*

Wm. Breeden: *Had you at the time shortly before seeing the defendant, or had you seen or heard anything that attracted your attention?*

Romero: *Yes sir.*

Wm. Breeden: *What?*
Romero: *I heard a shot.*

Wm. Breeden: *Where did the sound of the shot come from?*
Romero: *From inside the enclosure.*

Wm. Breeden: *The enclosure where the man was shot?*
Romero: *Yes sir.*

Wm. Breeden: *How long after you heard the shot did the defendant run out?*

Romero: *About six or seven minutes.*

Wm. Breeden: *Do you know what defendant did then?*
Romero: *I know what I was told. I did not see.*

Wm. Breeden: *What County did this occur in?*
Romero: *San Miguel County, Territory of New Mexico.*

Wm. Breeden: *You say you saw Antonio Lino Valdez afterward?*
Romero: *I saw him wounded and saw him dead.*

Wm. Breeden: *How long after he was wounded did he die?*
Romero: *I was not there.*

Wm. Breeden: *How long after was it you saw him dead?*
Romero: *I saw him dead the next day. I was not in town that night* [he was leading the posse that went after Rudabaugh and John J. Allen]. *When I returned he was dead.*

Wm. Breeden: *Did you know him before?*
Romero: *Yes sir.*

Wm. Breeden: *When did you see him last?*
Romero: *We had been at our store about 12 minutes before.*

Wm. Breeden: *What was his condition as to health?*
Romero: *Good condition.*

Wm. Breeden: *Was he a jailer?*
Romero: *Yes sir.*

Wm. Breeden: *How long after you saw the defendant run out did you go into the jail?*
Romero: *As soon as he turned the corner.*

Wm. Breeden: *How far were you from it?*
Romero: *I was about eight yards.*

Wm. Breeden: *You immediately went in where the wounded man was?*
Romero: *Yes sir.*

Wm. Breeden: *In what condition was the wounded man?*
Romero: *He was lying down on a bed. He attempted to speak and shake hands with me but could not. It appears he wanted to talk to me but could not.*

Cross examination by Mr. Posey

Posey: *Where were you Mr. Romero when you heard the shot fired?*
Romero: *I was in front of my house.*

Posey: *How far is your house from the jail?*
Romero: *The south wall of my house is the north wall of the jail.*

Posey: *What portion of your house were you in?*
Romero: *I was in front in the street. [Marked H on the map on page 80.]*

Posey: *Is the jail in front or on the side of your house?*
Romero: *On one side of my house. On the South side.*

Posey: *How far was the place where you found the deceased from where you were standing?*
Romero: *About twenty yards, twenty yards in a direct line.*

Posey: *How many walls are between your house and the jail?*
Romero: *One.*

Posey: *I mean from the spot where you found the deceased?*
Romero: *If you go around, there are several walls. If you go straight through there is one.*

Posey: *How many shots did you hear?*
Romero: *One.*

Posey: *Do you know how long he had been shot where you found him?*
Romero: *I did not have a watch in my hand at the time but from six to seven minutes.*

Posey: *What door did the defendant come out of?*
Romero: *He came out of the door of the hall.*

Posey: *How is that door situated with reference to your house?*
Romero: *The door is on the south side and my house is on the north.*

Posey: *How far is the door from your house?*
Romero: *Going around it is about fifty yards.*

Posey: *The first place you saw the defendant he was coming out of the door?*

Romero: When they came out of the hall I saw them for the first time.

Posey: Where did they go?
Romero: They went inside the Plaza.

Posey: How did they go?
Romero: They were running.

Posey: How long did you see them after they left the hall?
Romero: Just about the time it took them to run twenty four or thirty yards.

Posey: Is the Plaza in front of your house?
Romero: It is South.

Posey: Can you see the Plaza?
Romero: From in front I can.

Posey: That is the extent of the Plaza?
Romero: I don't know.

Posey: Is it as large as this Plaza [meaning Santa Fe]?
Romero: I think it is a little larger.

Posey: You can see all the way across that Plaza?
Romero: No you can't see the whole but a part from the alley which communicated with the street on the East side.

Posey: Did you make any effort to arrest these men at that time?
Romero: No sir.

Defense Witness – County Clerk Jesus Maria Tafoya

Jesus Maria Tafoya Sworn

Direct Examination by Col. Breeden

Wm. Breeden: Do you know this defendant?
Tafoya: I do.

Wm. Breeden: Did you know him last April?
Tafoya: I did.

Wm. Breeden: Did you know Antonio Lino Valdez?
Tafoya: Also.

Wm. Breeden: Do you know he is dead?
Tafoya: He is dead.

Wm. Breeden: Where did he die?
Tafoya: In the jail of San Miguel County.

Wm. Breeden: When?
Tafoya: On or about April 5 1880.

Wm. Breeden: Do you know how he came to his death?
Tafoya: I don't know any more but what he told me before he died.

Wm. Breeden: Did he make a statement before he died?
Tafoya: Yes sir.

Wm. Breeden: *What was his condition?*
Tafoya: *He could understand everything I asked him.*

Wm. Breeden: *What condition was he in regard to heath?*
Tafoya: *He was badly wounded.*

Wm. Breeden: *How was he wounded?*
Tafoya: *By means of a shot.*

Wm. Breeden: *Did he understand his condition?*
Tafoya: *Yes sir.*

Wm. Breeden: *You say he was badly wounded. In what part of the person?*
Tafoya: *On the breast. Somewhere on the breast.*

Wm. Breeden: *Did he say anything about his condition?*
Tafoya: *Yes sir.*

Wm. Breeden: *What did he say as to his condition?*
Tafoya: *He said he was very ill or sick.*

Wm. Breeden: *Did he say anything more?*
Tafoya: *He answered to the questions I asked him.*

Wm. Breeden: *Do you know how he felt or whether he knew he was very ill or not?*
Tafoya: *He told me he expected to die.*

Wm. Breeden: *How long after did he die?*
Tafoya: *He died about nine or ten o'clock at night of the same day.*

Wm. Breeden: *When did he make the statement as to how he received the wounds?*
Tafoya: *About two o'clock in the afternoon.*

Wm. Breeden: *What statement did he make?*
Tafoya: *I believe I am going to die. I am very sick.*

Answer and question objected to.

Wm. Breeden: *What did he say about it?*
Tafoya: *When I saw him he was wounded. I asked him who gave him that shot and the said that it was the smallest man of the two, who went inside the jail. He fired the shot at me, and the other man took the keys which I had tied at my belt and threw them into Webb's cell. That is all he told me.*

Wm. Breeden: *Did you see the defendant about there that day?*
Tafoya: *Yes sir.*

Wm. Breeden: *State where and under what circumstances you saw him.*
Tafoya: *I was at that time at the office of the Probate Court. One of the jailers, Benito Duran, was with me. A few moments after he had been there we heard a shot. I heard that the shot thundered very much. I told the jailer I thought that shot was inside the jail and he went out and I heard a noise at the door of the hallway to the jail. He rapped it for the second time. When I heard him rap the door the second time I came out and looked towards the door. Then*

I went towards the door myself. I stood there until he turned around. He told me the prisoners were going out on the other side. Few minutes after I rapped two times and no one responded. I heard the grunts or complaints of someone inside the jail, I did not know who. A few minutes afterwards Rudabaugh opened the door with his left hand. He opened the door and with his right he had a pistol which he pointed at me and said "Look out Jesus." Then I turned to one side of the door and he kept pointed the pistol at me and Allen came out of the hallway and went under his arm and then they went away together. After they went away, I went inside the jail. There I met Ramirez, one of the witnesses in this case, with a sharp shooter in his hand. I went on further in and saw the pool of blood where the deceased first fell. I tracked the blood or spots of blood to the kitchen where he was lying down. I found him lying down on a bed there.

Wm. Breeden: *Can you make a map of the premises there?*

Witness draws a map of the premises which is attached to his testimony and marked Exhibit A [shown on page 106].

Wm. Breeden: *This main entrance is the south side?*
Tafoya: *Yes sir.*

Wm. Breeden: *What is the open space?*
Tafoya: *It is the placita.*

Wm. Breeden: *The cells of the jail open onto the placita?*
Tafoya: *Yes sir.*

Wm. Breeden: *What sized man was Allen?*
Tafoya: *He was smaller than Rudabaugh.*

Wm. Breeden: *Did you see the prisoner again after you went inside?*
Tafoya: *No sir.*

Wm. Breeden: *How long before you saw the deceased wounded had you seen him before?*
Tafoya: *I had seen him in the morning.*

Wm. Breeden: *What was his condition?*
Tafoya: *He was in good health.*

Wm. Breeden: *What kind of a pistol did the defendant have?*
Tafoya: *From what I could see they were new pistols, 44 Cal.*

Wm. Breeden: *He said when he pointed the pistol at you, he said, "Look out Jesus." Did he say anything more?*
Tafoya: *No sir.*

Wm. Breeden: *This all occurred in Las Vegas, San Miguel County, New Mexico?*
Tafoya: *Yes sir.*

Cross Examination by Mr. Posey

Posey: *When you went into the jail who was there?*
Tafoya: *The first man I saw was Ramirez after they went out.*

Posey: Where was Ramirez?
Tafoya: He was coming out of the kitchen to the hallway.

Posey: The kitchen is the place where you found the deceased?
Tafoya: Yes sir.

Posey: Ramirez was there with him?
Tafoya: I suppose so.

Posey: Was there anybody else there?
Tafoya: Yes sir.

Posey: Who?
Tafoya: I saw Martin Kozlowski and somebody I did not know.

Posey: Where were they?
Tafoya: Kozlowski was standing at the kitchen door.

Posey: Anybody else there?
Tafoya: Yes sir.

Posey: Who else?
Tafoya: I don't know the names of the other persons.

Posey: How far was the pool of blood from the [jail cell] door?
Tafoya: Five or six feet at the most.

Posey: Were there any persons in the cells?
Tafoya: Yes sir.

Posey: Could a person standing at the door of the cells see the spot where you saw this pool of blood?
Tafoya: Yes sir.

Posey: Could he see all over the placita?
Tafoya: No sir.

Posey: What was the condition of the deceased when he spoke to you, was he weak?
Tafoya: He did not appear to be weak.

Posey: Could he breathe freely?
Tafoya: Yes sir.

Posey: No blood came out of his mouth?
Tafoya: No sir.

Posey: Have any trouble talking?
Tafoya: The pain only.

Posey: What effect did the pain have on his mind?
Tafoya: The blood spurted out of the wound when he spoke.

Posey: Did he seem much excited?
Tafoya: Yes sir.

Posey: He told you the man who shot him was the little fellow?

Tafoya: Yes sir.

Posey: Allen was much smaller than Rudabaugh?
Tafoya: Not much but some smaller.

Posey: Where is the house of Mr. Romero situated?
Tafoya: On the North side of the jail.

Witness located the house on the map

Posey: Tell me which way Romero's house fronts.
Tafoya: It fronts East.

Posey: Could a man stand at Romero's front door and see a man come out of the door?
Tafoya: No sir.

Posey: When these men came out of the jail where did they go?
Tafoya: They went down the street East to the street which is in front of the jail and then to the Plaza.

Posey: How long did you see them?
Tafoya: I saw them until they turned the corner.

Posey: How did they go there?
Tafoya: They were trotting.

Posey: You did not see any of the shooting yourself?
Tafoya: No sir.

Posey: How long was it after the shot was fired that you went into the jail?
Tafoya: About fifteen minutes.

Posey: Did you go into the jail immediately after these men came out?
Tafoya: I entered inside. I did not stay only long enough to ask Ramirez what was the matter.

Posey: This was bout fifteen minutes after the shot was fired?
Tafoya: Yes sir.

Prosecution Witness - Jailer José Ramirez

José Ramirez Sworn

Direct Examination by William Breeden

Wm. Breeden: Do you know the defendant?
Ramirez: Yes.

Wm. Breeden: Do you know Antonio Lino Valdez?
Ramirez: I did.

Wm. Breeden: Do you remember the day Antonio Lino Valdez was shot?
Ramirez: Yes.

Wm. Breeden: Where were you at that time?
Ramirez: I was a jailer in Las Vegas.

Wm. Breeden: *Were abouts in Las Vegas were you at the time of that occurrence?*
Ramirez: *I was in a room inside the jail.*

Wm. Breeden: *State what you heard and saw then?*
Ramirez: *I heard a shot and then I saw the defendant and another one running out of the jail.*

Wm. Breeden: *Immediately after hearing the shot?*
Ramirez: *Yes.*

Wm. Breeden: *What were they doing?*
Ramirez: *When I heard the shot, I stepped out of the door of the kitchen and went out. I saw two men, they had pistols.*

Wm. Breeden: *Did this man have a pistol? (indicating defendant)*
Ramirez: *Yes sir.*

Wm. Breeden: *How did he have it?*
Ramirez: *In his hand.*

Wm. Breeden: *Do you know where Antonio Lino Valdez was?*
Ramirez: *He was at the door of a cell.*

Wm. Breeden: *Well what did you do then?*
Ramirez: *I followed them to see where they were going.*

Wm. Breeden: *Where did they go?*
Ramirez: *They went out and went to the new town [East Las Vegas].*

Wm. Breeden: *What did you do then?*
Ramirez: *I followed them.*

Wm. Breeden: *Where did you again see Antonio Lino Valdez?*
Ramirez: *In the night.*

Wm. Breeden: *Is that all you know about it?*
Ramirez: *Yes sir.*

Wm. Breeden: *What jail did you say this was?*
Ramirez: *The Las Vegas jail.*

Wm. Breeden: *About what time did this occur?*
Ramirez: *In April.*

Wm. Breeden: *What year?*
Ramirez: *1880.*

Wm. Breeden: *Last year?*
Ramirez: *Yes sir.*

Cross Examination by Mr. Posey

Posey: *When you came out of the room after you heard the shot, what did you do?*
Ramirez: *I stood at the door.*

Posey: Did you pull your pistol?
Ramirez: No.

Posey: Didn't you have a pistol?
Ramirez: I did not.

Posey: Was you a jailer there?
Ramirez: I was.

Posey: You say the deceased was standing in front of a cell when you came out?
Ramirez: He had fallen down in front of a cell.

Posey: Who was in the cell?
Ramirez: There were several persons there. I don't remember their names.

Posey: Was Mullen there?
Ramirez: Yes sir.

Posey: Could he see the man that was shot?
Ramirez: Yes sir.

Posey: Did these men say anything to you?
Ramirez: No sir.

Posey: I mean the men who went out?
Ramirez: No sir.

Posey: Did they offer to do anything to you?'
Ramirez: No sir, they just passed out of the door.

Posey: Was this man who was shot able to talk?
Ramirez: Yes sir.

Posey: Did he say anything to you?
Ramirez: No sir.

Posey: What was his appearance. Did he look as if he was frightened and excited?
Ramirez: When I saw him the first time he said nothing to me.

Posey: You saw him fall?
Ramirez: I saw him falling.

Posey: How long after the shot was fired did you see him falling?
Ramirez: Just as I stepped to the door, I saw him falling?

Posey: How long was that after the shot was fired?
Ramirez: About a minute.

Posey: Just about the time it took you to step out of the door?
Ramirez: Yes sir.

Posey: Were you standing near the door?
Ramirez: I was laying down asleep.

Posey: Which was the larger of these two men?

Ramirez: This man. (indicating defendant)

Posey: Allen was smaller?
Ramirez: Yes sir.

Prosecution Witness - Hack Driver J. C. Cauldwell

J. C. Cauldwell Sworn

Direct Examination by William Breeden

Wm. Breeden: Where do you live?
Cauldwell: In Las Vegas

Wm. Breeden: Do you know this defendant?
Cauldwell: Yes sir.

Wm. Breeden: Where were you in the early part of April 1880?
Cauldwell: In Vegas.

Wm. Breeden: Do you know this man here? (indicating defendant)
Cauldwell: Yes sir.

Wm. Breeden: Do you remember the time a jailer was killed Las Vegas?
Cauldwell: Yes sir.

Wm. Breeden: Were you in Las Vegas at the time?
Cauldwell: Yes sir.

Wm. Breeden: What was your occupation?
Cauldwell: I was a hack driver.

Wm. Breeden: Did you see the defendant that day?
Cauldwell: Yes sir.

Wm. Breeden: Now state all you know about the circumstances connected with this case that you know of.

Cauldwell: I don't know as I can call the day of the month. Somewhere between the third and the fifth. I have been driving a hack ever since Las Vegas had a new town. I was driving a hack at that time. It was between one and two o'clock. It was might have been after two in the afternoon that I saw this man Rudabaugh and John Allen. I came from the new town with a load of passengers and drove them to the Sumner House. Rudabaugh and Allen told me to wait. And they would go to the new town. And I waited and they told me to drive around by the jail, as they wanted to see Webb. After they got in, I drove around to the jail and stopped and Allen spoke to Rudabaugh and said something to Rudabaugh about he is not here and told me to drive up on the hill to the house of Tom Pickett. And I drove up there and they got down out of the hack and went in and had a conversation for half an hour. And then Rudabaugh and Allen and Pickett and another man, I never learned his name, came out of Pickett's house and got into the hack. They then told me to go on and I came down the back street to Mendenhall's and from there I intended to drive into the stable but they said "hold on we want to see Webb."

Then Pickett and the other man got out of the hack and went out into the Plaza and I went down to the jail with Rudabaugh and Allen. Then they got out of the hack and told me to wait. They went and rapped on the jail door and the man who was killed let them in. In a few minutes I heard a pistol shot and got a little frightened, and as I had an idea that something was the matter, I drove my team around to the Plaza. I did not know whether they had done anything, and I was kind of anxious to find out, so I stopped my team as soon as I got in the plaza. I thought I would tie my team and go back on foot and see what they had done. Just as I was in the act of getting out of the hack they came running around the corner and jumped into my hack and Allen said "drive to the new town." And I drove them over to the new town.

Wm. Breeden: *What kind of pistol were they?*
Cauldwell: *Large pistols.*

Wm. Breeden: *Six shooters?*
Cauldwell: *Yes.*

Wm. Breeden: *Did they have arms when they went through the jail?*
Cauldwell: *They had revolvers in their belts and before we got to the jail, I saw Allen's revolver.*

Wm. Breeden: *You drove them to the new town?*
Cauldwell: *Yes sir.*

Wm. Breeden: *Any thing occur on the road?*
Cauldwell: *They each held their pistol in their hands from the old to the new town. Where we crossed the creek, Allen was pointing his revolver at me and I turned around to push it away. As I turned around Rudabaugh is the man who loaded his revolver at that time.*

Wm. Breeden: *Was it a cartridge pistol or what?*
Cauldwell: *Yes sir.*

Wm. Breeden: *How many loads did he put in?*
Cauldwell: *One load.*

Wm. Breeden: *Did he remove anything?*
Cauldwell: *He took out a shell.*

Wm. Breeden: *You saw him remove a shell from the pistol and afterwards put in a new cartridge?*
Cauldwell: *Yes sir.*

Wm. Breeden: *You afterwards found an empty shell in the carriage?*
Cauldwell: *Yes sir.*

Wm. Breeden: *What was done with the cartridge?*
Cauldwell: *He put into the pistol.*

Wm. Breeden: *Well?*
Cauldwell: *When we got to the new town Rudabaugh jumped out and went into Goodlett's and I wanted Allen to get out and let me go. He wouldn't do that and then I wanted him to take the hack and let me go. Then Rudabaugh came*

out with a double barrel shot gun and laid it in the back and I started to get out. Allen said, "you son of a bitch, if you make a move I will blow your brains out." Then I said to Rudabaugh, you can take the team and go as far as you please, and he did not make any reply. So I jumped out of the hack and Allen was going to shoot and Rudabaugh said, "don't make a fool of yourself, I will drive." Then Rudabaugh took the lines and drove across to Houghton's Hardware store. They went in and Rudabaugh got some guns, I don't know how many, and put them in the hack and drove off.

Wm. Breeden: Who was Webb?
Cauldwell: Webb was a prisoner then and is now.

Wm. Breeden: In the Las Vegas jail?
Cauldwell: Yes sir.

Wm. Breeden: When they rode in the hack after leaving the jail and between there and the new town, did they say what they had done?
Cauldwell: I asked Allen what he had done and he said, "that Greaser wouldn't give us the keys and we killed the son of a bitch."

Cross Examination by Mr. Posey

Posey: Allen said that?
Cauldwell: Yes sir.

Posey: Where did Rudabaugh sit?
Cauldwell: He sat in the back seat.

Posey: Did he hear what Allen said?
Cauldwell: He could have heard it. Allen was in the middle seat and Rudabaugh in the back seat and I in front.

Posey: Did Rudabaugh say anything?
Cauldwell: Not that I heard.

Posey: Did he say anything about what had happened during the ride?
Cauldwell: No sir.

Posey: Is that all that was said at that time?
Cauldwell: Yes sir.

Posey: How did you go back from the old town to the new town?
Cauldwell: We went about as fast as the horses would take us.

Posey: What kind of a road is it?
Cauldwell: Very good road, except rocky at the creek.

Posey: What is the character of the road generally between the towns?
Cauldwell: Good.

Posey: Where did this conversation between you and Allen about killing the son of a bitch occur?
Cauldwell: While crossing the creek.

Posey: That was in the rocky part of the road?
Cauldwell: I had just crossed the rocky part.

Posey: You were going pretty fast?
Cauldwell: Yes sir.

Posey: How did you happen to see Rudabaugh loading the pistol?
Cauldwell: He might have put all of the loads in at that time.

Posey: He might have had his pistol empty for all you know?
Cauldwell: Yes sir.

Posey: Allen was the man who made all these hostile moves?
Cauldwell: Yes sir.

Posey: Rudabaugh made no threats to you?
Cauldwell: He made no threats but only spoke to me about driving faster.

Posey: How long was it after you heard that shot until these men came up and wanted you to take them to the new town?
Cauldwell: I should judge about three or four minutes.

Posey: You say Rudabaugh made no reply when Allen said, we have killed this man?
Cauldwell: I did not hear him.

Posey: What became of these other men you spoke of?
Cauldwell: They went out in the Plaza. I saw Pickett the same evening and talked to him.

Posey: Are you well acquainted with the town over there?
Cauldwell: Yes sir.

Posey: Do you know the location of the different houses?
Cauldwell: I know the situation of a great many of them.

Posey: Is there any porch in front of the jail?
Cauldwell: Yes sir.

Posey: Where is it located?
Cauldwell: The porch runs along the front of the jail all the way along.

Posey: How long is the front of that building?
Cauldwell: I should judge some fifty feet.

Posey: How far is it from the front of the Court House or jail to the Plaza?
Cauldwell: It is not over a hundred yards, probably seventy-five yards.

Posey: Is the square in sight of the porch?
Cauldwell: You can go down on the lower side of the porch and see the Plaza.

Posey: You did not notice whether all the chambers of Allen's pistol was full or not?
Cauldwell: No, he had them in his hand.

Posey: He might have had some empty?
Cauldwell: Yes sir.

Posey: Might not that have been Allen's pistol that Rudabaugh loaded?

Cauldwell: They must have changed.

Posey: Might not Allen have passed his pistol back to Rudabaugh while you were driving?

Cauldwell: It might have been done.

Redirect by William Breeden

Wm. Breeden: You say Rudabaugh and Allen went off with your hack after coming out of Houghton's Hardware store?

Cauldwell: Yes sir.

Wm. Breeden: Did you see where they went?
Cauldwell: I was in sight of them for about twelve or fourteen miles.

Wm. Breeden: You kept in sight for about fourteen miles?
Cauldwell: From twelve to fourteen.

Wm. Breeden: Which way did they go?
Cauldwell: They went East.

Wm. Breeden: At what rate did they go?
Cauldwell: I don't know. They went pretty fast.

Wm. Breeden: When did you again see your hack?
Cauldwell: After I lost sight of it I did not see it again until after sundown.

Wm. Breeden: Where did you see it then?
Cauldwell: It was then about twenty four miles East of Vegas.

Wm. Breeden: Where did you again see Rudabaugh?
Cauldwell: I never saw him again until they brought him back to Vegas.

Wm. Breeden: Recently?
Cauldwell: Yes, within the last week.

Defense Witness - Prisoner William Mullen

William Mullen Sworn

Direct Examination by Mr. Posey

Posey: What is your name?
Mullen: William Mullen

Posey: Where do you live?
Mullen: I live in Santa Fe now.

Posey: Where were you on the second day of April 1880?
Mullen: In Las Vegas.

Posey: Where in Las Vegas?
Mullen: In jail.

Posey: You say you were in jail?
Mullen: Yes sir.

Posey: Will you state to the jury whether you saw Rudabaugh that day?
Mullen: Yes sir.

Posey: *Were you there when the jailer was killed?*
Mullen: *Yes sir.*

Posey: *Was Rudabaugh there?*
Mullen: *Yes sir.*

Posey: *State all you know about the circumstances connected with the killing.*
Mullen: *Rudabaugh and Allen came in there one afternoon abut two o'clock and had some tobacco and newspapers. They came in and Rudabaugh had his hand on the door of the cell. The first thing I heard was Allen saying "Give me those keys you son of a bitch." I don't know what the jailer said in Mexican. Then Allen shot him and ran behind and took the keys. And Rudabaugh ran out of the door.*

Posey: *Did Allen give the jailer any time to give up the keys?*
Mullen: *No sir. The pistol went off immediately.*

Posey: *What was Rudabaugh doing at that time?*
Mullen: *He had his hands up on the door talking to me and Webb.*

Posey: *Do you know what Rudabaugh came there for?*
Mullen: *No sir.*

Posey: *It was his habit to come there with papers?*
Mullen: *Yes sir. He came there two or three times a week.*

Posey: *What happened after the shot was fired and Rudabaugh ran out?*
Mullen: *Allen threw the keys down to Webb, and said "take these and unlock the door, I have to go."*

Posey: *Were there any of the jailers in sight?*
Mullen: *No sir. I believe there was one in the kitchen.*

Posey: *Did any of them come on the firing of the shot?*
Mullen: *Yes in two or three minutes.*

Posey: *Was Rudabaugh there when they came out?*
Mullen: *Yes sir.*

Posey: *How far were these men from you when the shooting took place?*
Mullen: *Not over two feet. Allen might have been four feet.*

Posey: *Where was the man who was shot?*
Mullen: *He was standing on the left side of Rudabaugh.*

Posey: *On which side of Rudabaugh was Allen standing?*
Mullen: *On the left.*

Posey: *What did the jailer do when he came out?*
Mullen: *I seen him run out of the kitchen with a pistol in his hand.*

Posey: *Did you see him point it at anybody?*
Mullen: *Yes sir.*

Posey: *How did this man get from the place where he was shot to the kitchen?*
Mullen: *Two prisoners carried him in.*

Posey: *Could you see this man where he fell from where you were in the cell?*
Mullen: *No sir. He fell backwards. I could see him after they picked him up and carried him to the kitchen.*

Posey: *Did Rudabaugh say anything when the shot was fired?*
Mullen: *I didn't hear him.*

Posey: *He ran out immediately?*
Mullen: *Yes sir.*

Posey: *Did Rudabaugh have a pistol in his hand.*
Mullen: *I didn't see any.*

Posey: *Could you have seen one?*
Mullen: *Yes sir.*

Posey: *When that shot was fired what was the position of his hands when the shot was fired?*
Mullen: *He had them on the cell door.*

Posey: *He was talking to you and Webb through the grating?*
Mullen: *He was asking us how we got along.*

Posey: *Did you hear any information from either Allen or Rudabaugh that they were coming that day?*
Mullen: *No sir.*

Posey: *As far as you know their coming there was not by appointment?*
Mullen: *No.*

Posey: *Did you hear any conversation between Rudabaugh and Webb at that time?*
Mullen: *No.*

Posey: *Did they have any private talk there?*
Mullen: *No.*

Posey: *You heard everything then said?*
Mullen: *Yes sir.*

Posey: *What was the substance of their conversation?*
Mullen: *They didn't stand there but a minute or two and shook hands with me and Webb and the next thing I heard was a shot.*

Posey: *The conversation was how you felt and if you wanted anything?*
Mullen: *Yes sir.*

Posey: *You could not see the man after he was shot and fell?*
Mullen: *I seen him about the time Allen pointed the pistol and he fell back.*

Cross Examination by William Breeden

Wm. Breeden: *What were you in jail for?*
Mullen: *Train robbery.*

Wm. Breeden: *What was Webb in for?*
Mullen: *Murder.*

Wm. Breeden: *You say Rudabaugh was in the habit of visiting you frequently?*
Mullen: *Yes sir, nearly every day.*

Wm. Breeden: *How long have you known Rudabaugh?*
Mullen: *I had known Rudabaugh four months.*

Wm. Breeden: *How long had you been in there?*
Mullen: *Somewhere between eight and ten months.*

Wm. Breeden: *He visited you all that time?*
Mullen: *Not every day.*

Wm. Breeden: *He is a friend of yours?*
Mullen: *Yes sir.*

Wm. Breeden: *As soon as the shot was fired Rudabaugh ran off?*
Mullen: *Yes sir.*

Wm. Breeden: *Turned and ran did he?*
Mullen: *Yes sir.*

Wm. Breeden: *How long did Allen remain there after Rudabaugh left?*
Mullen: *Two or three minutes, just long enough to –*

Wm. Breeden: *Never mind what he did, you answer my questions.*

Wm. Breeden: *Where did you say he got the keys?*
Mullen: *Out of the jailer's pocket.*

Wm. Breeden: *After he fell?*
Mullen: *Yes sir.*

Wm. Breeden: *How do you know he got them out of the jailer's pocket?*
Mullen: *I saw him come back with them.*

Wm. Breeden: *You did not see him take them out of the pocket?*
Mullen: *No sir.*

Wm. Breeden: *Can you swear positively that Rudabaugh did not take them?*
Mullen: *Yes sir.*

Wm. Breeden: *How can you swear?*
Mullen: *Because Rudabaugh was standing at the door when the shot was fired and turned and ran out.*

Wm. Breeden: *Rudabaugh was not at the door where the keys were taken out of the dead man's pocket?*
Mullen: *No sir.*

Wm. Breeden: *You could not see the dead man?*
Mullen: *No sir.*

Wm. Breeden: *Then you did not see who did take them out. How are you able to swear Rudabaugh did not?*
Mullen: *Because he was in that part of the jail. (gesture)*

Wm. Breeden: *How can you swear to that when you could not see the man when he fell?*
Mullen: *The jailer fell on that side and Rudabaugh was this way. (gesturing)*

Wm. Breeden: *How do you know Rudabaugh did not go back there where the dead man was?*
Mullen: *He did not came back there.*

Wm. Breeden: *How can you swear when you could not see that far?*
Mullen: *Simply because the jailer fell on this side and Rudabaugh ran out that way.*

Wm. Breeden: *You just swore that Rudabaugh did not do it and now you undertake to swear he did not do it when you did not see him.*
Mullen: *I saw Allen fire the shot.*

Wm. Breeden: *You said you could not see the dead man. Now how can you swear positively that Allen was the man who took the keys and not Rudabaugh?*
Mullen: *Allen jumped on top of he jailer and took the keys.*

Wm. Breeden: *How do you know he jumped on top of him when you couldn't see? You can swear positively to what you did not see? How do you manage to do that?*
Mullen: *The jailer fell on that side and Rudabaugh ran out on that side.*

Wm. Breeden: *Have you talked about his case before today?*
Mullen: *No sir.*

Wm. Breeden: *Tell anybody what you could testify?*
Mullen: *Yes sir.*

Wm. Breeden: *Tell Rudabaugh?*
Mullen: *No.*

Wm. Breeden: *When were you subpoenaed?*
Mullen: *This morning.*

Wm. Breeden: *You talked to these lawyers about it?*
Mullen: *I believe this gentleman called me outside and talked to me about it.*

Wm. Breeden: *Didn't you talk to Rudabaugh?*
Mullen: *No. I spoke to Mr. [Marshal] Breeden. The first time I spoke of it, I told them what I said here.*

Wm. Breeden: *How far around the placita was it?*
Mullen: *I should think about ten steps across it.*

Wm. Breeden: *You say Rudabaugh ran when he went?*
Mullen: *He ran right out of that room.*

Wm. Breeden: *He ran at the firing of the shot?*
Mullen: *Yes sir. Allen remained there until he had taken the keys from the dead man and attempted to unlock the door. He dropped the keys in front of the door and said, "take these and unlock the door. I have to go."*

Wm. Breeden: *Who was in the there beside you and Webb?*
Mullen: *The Stokes brothers [Joseph and William].*

Wm. Breeden: *And then Allen left?*
Mullen: *Yes. About two minutes behind Rudabaugh.*

Wm. Breeden: *All Rudabaugh said was, "how are you and do you want anything?"*
Mullen: *Yes sir.*

Wm. Breeden: *A minute?*
Mullen: *A minute or a minute and a half.*

Wm. Breeden: *What did Allen say?*
Mullen: *He did not speak at all.*

Wm. Breeden: *They came in together?*
Mullen: *Yes sir.*

Wm. Breeden: *Did Rudabaugh draw a pistol when he ran?*
Mullen: *No sir.*

Wm. Breeden: *Did you see that he had a pistol?*
Mullen: *I did not see any pistol about him.*

Redirect Examination by Posey

Posey: *Were these last charges against you dismissed at the last term of court?*
Mullen: *Yes sir.*

Posey: *You are not under indictment now?*
Mullen: *No sir.*

Posey: *Explain to me if you can the position of the door through which Rudabaugh went out of that placita or courtyard.*
Mullen: *There is a kind of a middle door and an outside door.*

Posey: *Did you see him come back?*
Mullen: *No sir.*

Posey: *If he had come back could you have seen him?*
Mullen: *Yes sir.*

Posey: *Did Rudabaugh go out of that courtyard or placita in the same direction that the jailer fell?*
Mullen: *Yes sir.*

Posey: *Which way did he go?*

Mullen: The jailer fell off that way and Rudabaugh went this way.

Posey: What did Allen do after he had fired the shot?
Mullen: He went toward this man after the keys.

Posey: Did he have the keys when he came back?
Mullen: Yes sir.

Defense Witness - Defendant David Rudabaugh

David Rudabaugh sworn

Direct Examination by Mr. Posey

Posey: What is your name?
Rudabaugh: David Rudabaugh.

Posey: You are the defendant in this cause?
Rudabaugh: Yes sir.

Posey: You were in Las Vegas in April 1880?
Rudabaugh: Yes sir.

Posey: You were present in the killing referred to?
Rudabaugh: Yes sir.

Posey: State to the jury how you came to be there?
Rudabaugh: I had been a police officer in Las Vegas prior to the killing of the jailer and was a personal friend of Webb who had got into a difficulty there and I used to go and see him and take him tobacco and newspapers and see how he was getting along. I was well acquainted with this jailer as well as the rest and was never refused admittance. I went over this day to the Sumner House in East Las Vegas. Allen went with me. We went to see a man who owed me some money. Mr. Allen wanted to go to the jail to see Webb, and I said I was going too.

The man I wanted to see was not at the Sumner House. This man was Tom Pickett. I went up where he lived. He was sick in bed and I went up to see him. I was there fifteen or twenty minutes and he said he was going down town and got into the hack and went with us to Menden Hall's stable. There he got out. I told the hack driver to drive us to the jail. I wanted to see Webb. When we got there I got out and knocked at the door. The jailer admitted us. He asked me if I wanted to see Webb. I said I did. He showed us the cell he was in. I had some newspapers which I gave them and asked them how they were getting along, and stood there talking to them. I was standing there with my hands crossed on the door and Allen shot the jailer. I turned around and said, "what did you do that for?" I looked round and saw the jailer fall. I started to go out when a jailer drew a pistol on me. I jumped out of range and pulled my pistol. By that time men were knocking at the front door. I opened the door and ran out. The hack I left at the door was gone. I ran down and overtook it in the Plaza, and asked him why he didn't wait. I never looked back.

By the time I got into the hack Allen was there. He got in the hack and told the driver to drive as fast as he could drive. On the way to the new town he tried to load his pistol but could not as he was under the influence of liquor. He gave me the pistol and asked me to load it and I loaded it. We drove over to the new town and I went into Goodlett's Saloon, where he told me there was a double-barrel shot gun belonging to him. Then we drove to Houghton's Hardware store and got these other guns. He brought them out, got into the hack and we left the town going in an Easterly direction. We drove about ten miles and gave the hack to two Mexican herders.

Posey: What did Allen do after the firing of the shot?
Rudabaugh: I don't know.

Posey: Why don't you know?
Rudabaugh: Because I left the jail.

Posey: How did you go?
Rudabaugh: I went pretty fast.

Posey: How came Allen to be with you going to the jail?
Rudabaugh: He said he would like to go in and see Webb and the Stokes. He said that he couldn't get in and knowing that I had admittance when I wanted to, asked me to take him in.

Posey: It is testified that on your way to the new town, Allen said to the driver of the hack, "I killed the son of a bitch" or words to that effect. Did you hear such a remark?
Rudabaugh: No sir.

Posey: How do you account for such a remark?
Rudabaugh: I think if he had said it, I should have heard it.

Posey: Did you [know] anything about it?
Rudabaugh: No sir.

Posey: Did you make any threats to any body?
Rudabaugh: None whatever.

Posey: And you only pulled your pistol when you were threatened by another jailer?
Rudabaugh: Yes sir.

Posey: Were you in the habit of carrying pistols?
Rudabaugh: Yes sir.

Cross Examination by Wm. Breeden

Wm. Breeden: Do you know Jesus Maria Tafoya?
Rudabaugh: I know him when I see him.

Wm. Breeden: Did you meet him at the doorway that day?
Rudabaugh: Not that I know of.

Wm. Breeden: Did you threatened him with a pistol?
Rudabaugh: No sir.

Wm. Breeden: Did you not point a pistol at him?
Rudabaugh: No sir.

> **Wm. Breeden:** *When did you see Allen again?*
> **Rudabaugh:** *When he got into the hack.*
>
> **Wm. Breeden:** *Was that the first time you saw him after the shot was fired?*
> **Rudabaugh:** *Yes sir.*
>
> **Wm. Breeden:** *What did you go the jail for?*
> **Rudabaugh:** *I went there to see Webb.*
>
> **Wm. Breeden:** *Didn't you go there to help Webb escape?*
> **Rudabaugh:** *No sir, I did not.*
>
> **Wm. Breeden:** *You say Allen went into Houghton's Hardware store after guns?*
> **Rudabaugh:** *Yes sir.*
>
> **Wm. Breeden:** *Are you not the man who went after the guns?*
> **Rudabaugh:** *No sir.*
>
> **Wm. Breeden:** *You did not go in?*
> **Rudabaugh:** *No sir.*

Instructions to the Jury:

The defendant by his attorneys asked that the following instructions be given to the jury:

> *"That if the jury believe from the evidence that the deceased just prior to his death from such shooting recognized that one Allen fired the shot that caused his death, and then and there, knowing his death to be close at hand, as stated, then they must find for the defendant."*

Which request for said instructions was denied by the Court, to which ruling of the Court the defendant by his Counsel excepts. The Court gave the following instructions to the jury:

Gentlemen of the Jury:

The defendant David Rudabaugh was indicted by the Grand Jury of San Miguel Co. together with John Allen for the murder of Antonio Lino Valdez at Las Vegas on April 5th, 1880. The defendant took a change of venue to this Court in order to obtain a jury entirely unprejudiced.

The evidence has been brief and the whole case has been brought before you within a shorter time than is usual in cases of such gravity so that the facts as testified to are all fresh in your memory.

Certain facts are undisputed and this simplifies your labors. It is undisputed that the deceased Valdez died from a wound received in the placita of the Las Vegas jail, on the day alleged in the indictment and that at the time of the firing of the pistol shot, the defendant and Allen were in such placita and soon after went out rapidly from the gateway thereof.

Here the indisputable evidence may be said to cease and you are to judge from all the evidence before you as to the other facts connected with the killing. You are first to decide whether the deceased was killed, and if you agree as to that, then as to who it was who killed him.

There is no evidence at all tending to show that the killing in any case was justifiable or excusable or that the circumstances existed to make such killing any degree of murder less than first.

The statuary definition of Murder in the First Degree is the unlawful killing of a human being perpetrated from a premeditated design to effect the death of the person killed and the penalty death.

It is a principle of law founded on reason, that if a felony is committed by one man and another is present, aiding and abetting such person in the commission thereof, the abettor is as guilty as the first. The act in such case is the act of both, and both are equally guilty.

If then, from all the evidence you are satisfied beyond a reasonable doubt that the defendant killed the deceased in such a manner as to constitute murder in the first degree, or that that crime was committed by Allen, the defendant now on trial, being present, aiding and abetting in the commission of such murder, it is your duty to find a verdict of Guilty of Murder in the First Degree.

If you do not so believe beyond a reasonable doubt, then it is your duty to acquit.

In this as in all criminal cases you are to remember that the law presumes every man to be innocent until he is found to be guilty. That the defendant is entitled to the benefit of every reasonable doubt and that unless you are satisfied of the guilt of the accused beyond such reasonable doubt, he is entitled to an acquittal.

A reasonable doubt, however, in the view of the law is a substantial doubt founded on the evidence, and not a mere fancy or the possibility of a doubt.

From various requests to charge, I give you the following, asked by the defendant's counsel:

If the jury believes that at the moment of the shooting the defendant was engaged in conversation with Mullen and Webb and was uninformed of any intent on the part of Allen to commit murder, then they must find for the defendant.

To all of which the defendant by his Counsel excepted. After the verdict had been rendered in the cause, the defendant by his Counsel moved the Court to set aside the verdict and grant him a new trial for the reasons set forth in said motion [see pages 79-80]. Which motion was overruled by the Court, to which ruling the defendant by his Counsel excepted.

The defendant now prays that his bill of acceptance may be signed and sealed by your honor and made a part of the record herein which is accordingly done.

L. Bradford Prince
Chief Justice of N. M.

Certification of Trial Record

Territory of New Mexico
County of Santa Fe

I, Clerk of the First Judicial District Court of said Territory in and for said County certify that the foregoing seventy three pages and nine lines contain a true copy of the record and of all the proceedings in the cause of Territory of New Mexico versus David Rudabaugh, as the same are of record in the my office.

Witness my hand and seal of said Court this 21th day of December, 1881.

R. W. Clancy, Clerk

Office a bill of exceptious, which said bill of exceptious is in the words and figures following, to wit:

Territory of New Mexico
County of Santa Fe
The Territory vs David Rudabaugh, Murder

Be it remembered that upon the trial of the above entitled cause at the April A.D. Term of the District Court for the County of Santa Fe, the following proceeding here had to wit:

The [preceding] evidence which was all of the evidence given in case was given upon the trial of the cause.

Appendix C | Rudabaugh's Death Photos

The pictures of Rudabaugh's decapitated head reproduced on pages 92-93 were taken by Albert W. Lohn, a nineteen-year-old, traveling, professional photographer who was in Parral the day Rudabaugh was killed.

> *"Shortly after the ferocious Dave quit breathing, Long [Lohn] got out his camera and took four pictures of the event. Two of the photographs were of better quality than the other two, so Long printed only the two best shots he obtained."*

When the governor of the Mexican State of Durango (the state located south of Parral) learned that Lohn was selling post cards of Rudabaugh's severed head, he demanded that the photos and negatives be turned over to him. Lohn acceded to the governor's request (order) and gave him the two negatives he had printed. He retained the negatives of the two poorer photographs, which he had not printed.

Lohn put the negatives away and totally forgot about them. In 1943, Fred W. Mazzulla, an avid collector of Western memorabilia, met Lohn in Nogales, Arizona, where Lohn was operating a photography studio. The two became good friends. During one of their conversations, Lohn mentioned that he had been present in Parral when Rudabaugh was decapitated and he had taken photos of the event. Prompted by Mazzulla's collector's interest, Lohn located the two negatives he had put away 57 years earlier and gave them to Mazzulla.

Of the two negatives, the one of the mob carrying Rudabaugh's head on a pole is dark (because it was taken at night) and poorly focused (but artfully composed). The one of a man, an unknown Mexican Rurales (Federal policeman), holding Rudabaugh's head is good. In this second photo, Rudabaugh has a black *"moustache, neatly trimmed and waxed,"* as described in the newspaper article about him two years earlier.

The beheading of Rudabaugh is known among Western History enthusiasts, but it is not the most famous beheading in Parral. On July 20, 1923, Mexican revolutionary Pancho Villa (birth name José Doroteo Arango Arámbula) was assassinated in Parral, where he had gone for a visit from his nearby ranchero. He was riding in a 1919 Dodge touring car. Near the city center, Villa and three of his entourage were ambushed by seven gunmen. Villa got one pistol shot off before dying of multiple wounds, killing one of his assassins.

On February 6, 1926, the *Arizona Daily Star* reported:

> *"The body of Francisco Villa, the late bandit chief, was exhumed and decapitated last night by a band of five men, according to reports reaching here from Parral."*

> *"The headless body was found near the grave this morning and nearby was a note saying the head would be sent to Columbus, N.M., which was raided by Villa's bandit band about ten years ago."*

Villa had been buried in the Parral city cemetery. After his body was dug up and beheaded, the recovered headless remains were reburied in a purposely-unmarked grave to prevent further desecration. In 1976, according to one account, they were dug up at the instigation of then Mexican President Luis Echeverría and moved to the Revolution Monument in Mexico City, Mexico.

Where Rudabaugh's body and head were buried is unknown, and almost certainly will remain unknown forever. -- *Editor*

Index

A

Abreu 86
Alkali Charlie 54
Allen, James "Jim" 51-52, 63, 69, 74, 77, 101-102
Allen, John J. 21, 52, 63-65, 67-69, 72, 84, 91, 93-94, 98, 127, 131, 136-144, 146, 148-149
Allison, Clay 5, 18, 22, 40-41, 55
Allison, William H. H. 93
Anaya, Pablo 84
Anderson, J. M. 32, 35
Arámbula, Jose Doroteo Arango 151
Ayers, George 115

B

Bacheco, Benito 93, 125
Baker, John 8, 63, 78
Barnes, Johnny 111-112
Barnes, Sidney M., Judge 62
Bass, Sam 29
Bassett, Charles E. 29
Bausman, Lou 85
Baxter, John 3, 73
Beaubien, Pablo 86
Behan, Johnny, Sheriff 108, 110-111
Bell, James W. 76
Bell, Jason B. 77
Bell, Mattie 61
Bemis, Leander, Captain 10
Benedict, Judge 99
Bennett 69
Berkeley, J. 3
Berkeley, R. J. 32
Bertie 25
Biersuth, R. A. 125
Billings, N. 32
Billy the Kid (William Henry McCarty, William Bonney) 6, 8, 18, 21-22, 29, 48, 51, 56, 63, 67-69, 71-73, 76-87, 90-91, 94-97, 102-105, 107, 112, 114-115
Bishop, Thomas 102
Blackington, C. F. 81-82
Blakes, F. A. 76
Blanchard, Judge 86, 122
Blanchard, W. F. 31, 33
Bliss 5
Born, Henry 55
Bowdre, Charles 18, 21-22, 69, 84, 88, 95
Bowers, Tol 19
Boyle, S. 52, 60-61
Branson, H. G. 10
Brazil, Manuel Silvestre 7

Breeden, Marshal A. 25, 93, 98-99, 126-129, 131, 134, 136-138, 143-144, 147
Breeden, William 93, 98, 125, 133, 140, 142
Brickley, William 60
Brito, Fabian 86
Brocius, William 107
Brooks, Charles 48
Brown, Frederick 13-14, 31, 61
Brown, Hoodoo (Hyman Graham Neill, "Santiago") 2, 48, 52-53, 55-58, 60, 62, 90-91
Brown, John 2
Brown, Randall 10, 57-58
Browne 86
Bull Shank Jack 54
Buntline, Ned 22
Burns 35
Burton, Al 82
Burtt, O. P. 75

C

Calamity Bill 32
Calborn, E. F. 106
Cale, James E. 82
Campbell, H. C. 74
Carbajal, Mercedes 86
Cardon 91
Carlyle, Jimmy 72, 78, 80, 83-84
Carr, John 10
Carrie 25
Carson, Joe 48-49, 53, 56-58, 72, 90-91
Carson, Mrs. Joe 54, 59, 61
Carter, T. J. 35
Cassidy, Butch 15, 107, 115
Catron, Thomas 65, 90, 99
Cauldwell, J. C. 36, 62, 64, 93, 137-139
Caypless, Edgar 90, 93
Cenci, Beatrice 39
Chambers, Lon 18, 85
Chapman, Mrs. 62, 69
Chavez, Herculano 101
Chavez, Miguel 86
Cherokee Bill 54
Chisum, John S. 84
Clancy, F. W. 93
Clancy, R. W. 150
Clanton, Bill 107
Clanton, Ike 7, 108
Cline, Captain 14
Clum, John P. 108-109
Clute 32
Cock-eyed Frank 54
Cockerall 19

154 ~ Index

Cody, William F. 54
Coffee, General 13
Collison, Frank 114
Cook, Joseph "Joe" 78
Cooke, P. St. George, Col. 14
Corn Hole Johnny 54
Cosgrove, Cornelius "Con" 71
Cosgrove, Michael "Mike" 71, 89
Courtright, Jim 5, 15, 20, 48, 55
Crocchiola, Stanley Francis Louis 1-3, 6
Crocchiola, Vincent 1
Cullen, Robert K. N. 67
Culley, John 2
Culp, John 8
Curly Bill 21, 72, 106-112, 114
Curry 56
Custer, General 55

D

Daley, Dan 48
Davidson, George 52, 63, 66, 70
Davis, George 52, 63, 68, 70, 76
De Remer, J. G. 40, 42, 44, 46-48
Dedrick, Dan 63, 68, 76
Dedrick, Mose 77-78
Deger, Larry
Dement, Dan 27-28, 30, 32, 35-37, 43, 121-123
Dettelback, A. M. 93, 125
Dewitt 35
Diaz the "Peeler" 56
Dixon, Billy 26, 55
Doan, Corvin 19
Dodge 48
Dold, Andrew 48
Dold, John 8
Dominguez, Juan Antonio 57-58
Donovan, Mike 19
Doolin, Bill 34
Dorsey, John 6, 57-58, 78
Dougherty, John, Sheriff 58
DuBois, L. P. 74
Duffy, James 35
Duffy, Thomas 101-102
Dugan, John 2
Duran, Benedicto 93
Duran, Facundo 93
Duran, Fasmundo 125
Dwyer, Matthew 104
Dwyer, Thomas 104

E

Eaker, John P. 80
Earp, Morgan 106, 110-111
Earp, Virgil 29, 55, 107-108
Earp, Warren 105
Earp, Wyatt 17-18, 19-21, 22, 24, 40, 42, 48, 55, 72, 105-112, 115

East, Jim 21-22, 71, 85
Echeverría, Luis 152
Edwards, Joseph M. "Bob" 78
Elkins, Stephen B. 65, 90
Emory, Thomas 18, 85

F

Felgard, G. 125
Filger, Simon 93
Finley, Jim 81-82
Finn Clanton 107
Fleming, Sheriff 19
Flores, Cypriano 86
Fly Spee San 54
Fogerty 102
Fowler, Joel 81-82
Francis of Assisi 7
Franklin, Deputy 102
Frost, Charles 74
Fuller, John, Sheriff 32-33

G

Gaines, George 77
Gallegos, Juan Luis 125, 93
Galleher, Paul 5
Garcia, Miguel 107
Garcia, Viscente 93, 125
Gardner, Fred 31-32, 122
Garrett, Patrick Floyd Jarvis "Pat" 21-22, 52, 56, 63-65, 68-69, 72, 76, 78-80, 84-90, 95-97, 102, 104, 115
Gay, George 77
Gerhardt, John 86
German, Joe 33
Giddings 86
Giovanni, Don 24
Glaze, Adam 8
Gonzalez, Antonio 65
Goodman, William 64, 102
Goodnight, Charles 23, 55
Gott, Thomas 27-30, 32, 35-36, 43, 121
Gould, Jay 48
Greathouse, James "Whisky Jim" 51, 63, 68, 72, 77, 79-84, 86, 89
Green, J. D. 21, 27-28, 30, 32, 35, 122-123
Griffin 102
Gross, Jacob 67
Gryden, Harry 33, 35
Grzelachowski, Alejandro 63-64, 85-87

H

Hall, Lee 85
Hallet, Judge 43
Hancock, Judge 106
Hardin, John Wesley "Wes" 29, 55
Harlin, J. J. 67

Hammond, James 35
Harrington 35
Harrison, Hank 78
Hart, S. S. 35
Haun, M. M., Rev. 17
Hawkins 9
Hayes, Rutherford B., President 83-84
Hedges, William 67
Henry, Tom "Dutch" 17, 48, 53-55, 69, 91
Henry, Tom 59
Herrington, B. F. 35
Hext 23
Hickok, James Butler "Wild Bill" 54
Hicks, Bill 111
Hicks, Milt 111-112
Hildago, Guadalupe 101
Hill, Anderson 8
Hoadley, C. B. 63
Holderman, E. R. 8
Holliday, John Henry "Doc" 17-18, 20-22, 24, 42, 44, 48, 55, 69, 107-108, 110-111, 115
Holmes, Rush J. 67
House, Thomas Jefferson 56-57
Hoyt, Walter V. 93, 125
Hubbs, C. L. 32
Hubbs, G. H. 32
Hudgens, John 7
Hudgens, William H. 74, 76-80, 112
Hughes, Jim 106
Hunt 47
Hunter, W. L. 35, 40
Huntley. Myrock 8
Hurd, A. A. 35
Hurley, John 80-81
Hurricane Bill 56

I

Indian Charley 110-111

J

James, Jesse 29, 32, 48, 114
Johnson, Archibald 8
Johnson, Jack 110
Johnston, J. E., Col. 14
Jones, John 112
Jordan, Oliver 4
Jordan, Oliver, Mrs. 67
Jose 115

K

Kay, Jim 81
Kearney, Frank 64, 102
Kearny, General 51
Kelley, Jim 18-20, 102
Kelliher, Michael 53-55, 60-62, 68
Kelly, Edward M. "Choctaw" 64, 97
Kendall, A. L. 35

Kenner, James 9
Ketchum, Thomas Edward "Black Jack" 15, 32, 115
Keyes 86
Kimbrell 72, 83, 85
Kincaid, Andrew 30-35, 122
King, Samuel 64
Kingfisher 18, 20
Kinnaman, Josiah 8
Kinnaman, William S. 8
Kistler, Russell A. "Russ" 53
Kozlowski, Martin 93 132
Kuch 80

L

Labadie 86
Lake, Stuart 18, 20, 106
Lamper, William J. 77-78
Lee 25
Leonard, Ira Edwin, Judge 83
Leyba, Marino 4
Light, Evander 37
Lillie 9
Linnenkohl, G. W. "Tom" 4, 67
Lipsey, J. J. 5
Livingstone 77
Llewellyn, John 62
Lockhart, James A., Col. 65-67
Lohn, Albert W. 151, 113-115
Long 99
Longworth, Thomas "Pinto Tom" 77-78
Love, A. G. 75
Lovell, Harry 32-33
Lovico, Rose 1
Lowe, James Anthony W. 56, 58-59
Luna, Jose 86
Lyle, Ed 111
Lyle, Johnny 111

M

MacArthur 35
Madrid, Francisco 71
Maguire, Don 55
Mallory, J. W. 31, 35
Manzanares 86
Mares, Florencio 101
Martin, Joseph 49, 59, 72, 90-91
Martindale, William 8
Martinez, Romulo, Sheriff 97, 103
Mason, Barney 63-64, 76, 85
Masterson, Ed 20, 29
Masterson, William Barclay "Bat" 17, 21-22, 25-27, 32-35, 44-48, 55, 63, 112
Mather, David Allen "Mysterious Dave" 5, 21, 29, 34, 48, 51-53, 56-57, 69, 71, 91
Maxwell, L. B. 65
Maxwell, Pete Menard 7, 72, 83, 86
Mayer, Mike 106

Mazzulla, Fred W. 113-115, 151
McArthur, J. E. 33
McCall, Jack 54
McCartney 9
McCause, Robert, Sheriff 26-27, 32-33, 35
McComb, Robert 32
McCurtrie, J. A.
McGuiness, Dick 77
McKinney, Thomas "Kip" 78
McLowery, Frank 107
McLowery, Tom 107
McManus, Jack 102
McMasters, Sherman 110-111
McMurtrie 40-42
Mcintyre, Jim 19-29, 48
Mead, S. G. 9-11
Mennet, Adolph 61
Mennet, Adolph, Mrs. 61-62
Miller 29
Mills, N. L. 35
Mitchell 75
Monta, Bob 56
Montoya, Antonio 65
Moody 23
Moore, Bill 18
Moore, Tom 104-105
Morehead, James 51-52, 63
Morley, Mrs. 41
Morley, William Ray 39, 40-41, 46-47, 90
Morris 25
Morrow, David 33
Morrow, Robert 14
Morse, Superintendant 33
Mullen, William 140, 49, 52, 59, 63, 67, 70, 72, 93-94, 135, 140-145
Murphy, A. 102
Murray, John 52, 63, 70, 93
Myer, Charlie 23

N

Neis, Anthony "Tony" 97
Nesper, Emma 25
Nieto 86
Nixon, Tom 34, 55
Noble, E. A. 32
Norton, Austin 8
Norton, Fred 8

O

O'Folliard, Thomas "Tom" 21, 69, 84, 88, 95
Old Man Clanton 107
One-Armed Kelley 54
Ortega 86
Ortiz 63
Otero, Miguel Antonio 40-41, 48, 51-52, 54, 61-63, 65-67, 86, 90-91
Otis, Judge 74

P

Pacheco, Pablito 86
Padilla 86
Palmer, C. 33
Palmer, Charles 35, 40-41, 47
Palmer, General 40, 45
Palmer, General 40, 45
Palmer, L. 33
Palmer, Thomas 35
Pancho Villa 151, 115
Pantele, Alberta, Mrs. 5
Parker, George 90
Parker, Quanah 55
Patterson, C. Ewing 74
Patterson, Frank 111
Patty, Mark
Peersons, Wesley 8
Peinold, P. A. 93
Perez, Demetrio 93
Peters, Judge 36
Peters, Tom 16
Pettibone, W. H. 35
Pickett, Thomas "Tom" 71, 76-77, 80, 83, 88-89, 94-96, 106, 112, 136-137, 139, 146,
Pierce, Franklin, President 7
Plummer, Henry 23, 60
Pock-Marked Kid 67
Poindexter, George 66-67
Polk, Cal 18, 85
Polly, E. E. 19
Pony Deal 111
Porter 56
Posey, George G. 93, 98, 125, 93, 128-129, 131-135, 138-142, 145-147
Prairie Dog Dave 54
Prather, Levi N. 9
Preston, Marshal 14
Prichard, G. W. 74
Prince, LeBaron Bradford, Chief Justice 21, 96-97, 99, 191, 125, 149
Pritchard, Col. 74

Q

Quantrill 10, 107
Quillan, Thomas 64, 102
Quinlan, Mrs. Thomas 102

R

Radenbaugh (Rudabaugh), Anne 2, 8
Radenbaugh (Rudabaugh), I. 2
Radenbaugh (Rudabaugh), J. 2
Radenbaugh (Rudabaugh), Z. 2
Raine 20
Ramirez 131, 134-135
Ramirez, Melquíades 86
Ramirez, Sisto 86
Randall, William 56-57

Rath, Charlie 25-26, 55, 121
Rattlesnake Bill Johnson 111
Reardon 97
Redmond, Jim 74, 76-78
Redpath, James 14
Reed, John 32
Reed, S. T. 35
Reid, John W. 14
Revere, Paul 41
Reynolds 9, 25
Ricker, Peter 8
Riley 33
Ringo, Johnny 21, 107-108, 110
Ritch, William G., Secretary 103
Roarke, Michael "Big Mike" 16, 18-19, 27, 28-32, 35-37, 43, 121-123,
Robinson 18, 40, 45-48
Robinson, A. A. 23, 46
Robinson, Bob 85
Robinson, Professor 75
Robley, Walter 33, 35
Rodenbaugh, James 2, 8
Rogers 102
Romero, Desiderio, Sheriff 63
Romero, Dolores 64
Romero, Francisco 63
Romero, Hilario, Sheriff 64-66, 89-91, 93, 96, 125-129, 133
Rosenstock, Fred 5
Ross, Charley 77
Roybal, Juan 86
Rudabaugh, David "Dave" 1-2, 5, 7-9, 11-12, 15-28, 30-37, 39, 42-44, 47-49, 51-53, 55-73, 76-81, 83-99, 101-115, 121, 125, 127, 131, 133, 136-140, 142-147, 150-152,
Rudolph, Charles Frederick 86
Ryan, Pat 30

S

Sandoval, Manuel 63, 93, 125
Saw Dust Charlie 67
Schroeder, S. 64, 102
Schunderberger, John "Dutchy" 48, 53-55, 57, 59-62
Scott, J. B. 10
Sena, Ignacio 5
Shannon, Governor 13-14
Shanssey, John 19-20
Shaughnassy 20
Sheeney, Frank 56
Sheldon, Lionel A., Governor 103
Sherman, John 7
Short, Luke 48, 55, 69
Shuler, Evelyn 5
Silva, Jesus 90
Silva, Vicente 51
Simpson, Peter 65

Siringo, Charles 85
Sitler, H. L. 23
Six-Shooter Bill 54
Slap Jack Bill 54
Slattery, John 35
Sligle, I. E.5
Slim Jim 54
Slit-Nose Red 54
Small, Schuyler Colfax 114-115
Smart, E. K. 32
Smith 81
Smith, General 13
Smith, Troy, Mrs. 5
Spence, Pete 107, 111
Spencer, Lon 81
Springer, A. G. 19, 23, 90
Starbird, Charles Nelson W. 63, 66-67
Starr, Charles 77
Steck, Joseph 78-80
Steele, Judge 54
Stephens, R. M. 93, 125
Stewart, Frank 85-89, 95
Stillwell, Frank 107-108
Stillwell, William H. 106, 110-111
Stockton, Ike 9, 81
Stoker, Joseph 93
Stokes, Joseph 49, 59, 64, 72, 92, 94, 145, 147
Stokes, William 49, 59, 64, 72, 92, 94, 145, 147
Straumer 76
Strong 46
Stubbs, Lawrence 13
Studer 23
Sturgis, Bvt. Col. 19
Suaso, Tomas 93
Summer, Edwin Vose Col. 13
Summer, Wayne 8
Sutton, M. W. 35, 53
Swape, H. F. 125
Sweet, Jim 74, 77
Swilling, Hank 108
Swope, H. L. 93

T

Tafoya, Jesus Maria 93-94, 129, 131-133, 147
Talbot, J. M. 62, 64
Tasker, Ben 55
Terrasas, Luis 112
Terry, W. D. 11
Texas Jack Vermillion 110
Thatcher, J. M., Captain 33
Thomas, David G. 3
Thompson, Ben 18, 20, 40, 44, 48, 55
Tilghman, William "Bill" 34
Tilghman, Zoe A.4
Tilton, Willis 5
Tomlinson, Judge 75
Torres, Jesus 93, 125

U

Tucker, David 9, 11
Tucker, Edwin 9

Updegraff, W. W. 14

V

Valdez, Antonio Lino 1, 49, 62-64, 66, 68, 71-72, 91-94, 96, 101-102, 125, 127, 133-134, 148
Vigil 63
Vining, D. 8

W

Waddingham, Wilson 71, 90
Wagner, Jack 29
Waldo, Judge 99
Walker, Alf 29
Wallace, Lew, Governor 62, 71, 82, 84
Walter, Edwin 10
Walters, Tom 35, 77
Waters, Capt. J. G. 35
Watson, William 74
Watts, Col. 74
Wear, George N. 35
Webb, John Joshua 17-18, 20-22, 25, 33, 37, 39, 42-44, 48, 51-53, 55-66, 68-72, 76, 93-94, 98, 101-104, 106, 136, 138, 141-143, 145-148
Weitbrec, Robert 45
Wells 32
West, Edgar J. 18, 27-30, 32-36, 82, 121-123
White, J. F. 35
White, Marshal Frederick 07
White, Martin, Rev. 14
Whitelaw, William 93
Whitfield, Col. 13
Wilcox, Thomas 87-88, 95-96
Wiley, Justice 34
Williams, George 85
Williams, William R. 104
Wilson, Billy (David L Anderson) 18, 52, 71, 76, 79-81, 83, 87-90, 95-97, 106, 112
Wilson, G. W. 35
Wilson, George 86
Wilson, H. S. 102
Wilson, John E. 3
Winters, Jack 73, 77
Winters, John V. 73
Wolcott, Royal 10
Woodson, Silas, Governor 14
Wooton, Dick 40, 48
Wright, Robert M. 25

Y

Young 23

Z

Zeigler, H. 33
Zimmerman 121
Zuber,, Hugo 84

Doc45 Publications

"Dirty Dave" Rudabaugh, Billy the Kid's Most Feared Companion

This book is about David Rudabaugh, a man whose life is both obscure and wildly mythologized.

Rudabaugh's obscurity begins with the spelling of his surname. In the only U.S. census in which he appears, his name is spelled Radenbaugh. His father, in his Civil War service record, spelled his name Rodenbaugh. Rodebaugh is the spelling David uses in his confession to an attempted train robbery. Yet, throughout his life, he answered to Rudabaugh, and was usually referred to as such in newspaper accounts and legal documents. That is also how most historians have chosen to spell his name. For these reasons, Rudabaugh is the spelling adopted in this book.

An off-repeated myth about Rudabaugh is that he was a *"nasty, treacherous bully"* who *"stole and killed and brutalized people... Dirty Dave would try anything, as long as it was crooked."* Not true. Another fictitious accusation is that Rudabaugh shot a jailer in cold blood. The true account of jailer Antonio Lino Valdez's fatal shooting is presented for the first time in this book, based on the never-before-published trial transcript. The unquestionable trial evidence shows that it was another man who shot the ill-fated jailer, not Rudabaugh.

Following the jailer's killing, Rudabaugh fled. Now a wanted man, Rudabaugh teamed up with Billy the Kid and participated prominently in Billy's final gun battles with authorities. Famously, Rudabaugh was captured along with Billy at Stinking Springs by Deputy Sheriff Pat Garrett and his posse.

After his capture, Rudabaugh was tried for Valdez's killing and sentenced to death by hanging. He escaped jail and went to Mexico.

On February 18, 1886, Rudabaugh was killed by a Winchester rifle shot to the chest in Parral, Mexico, by a grocery man named José. Following his killing, Rudabaugh was decapitated by José. His head was placed on a pole and paraded around the Parral plaza. Present at Rudabaugh's beheading was Albert W. Lohn, a nineteen-year-old photographer.

Lohn took four photographs of Rudabaugh's decapitated head. The two negatives he printed were confiscated by Mexican authorities. The other two negatives remained in Lohn's files for 57 years, entirely forgotten by him. The story of how these two negatives were acquired by an avid collector of Western memorabilia is given in the book.

Rudabaugh's life story is mesmerizing. It is as adventurous as that of any Wild West figure. The events of his life include being both a wanted man and a lawman, a failed train robbery, two successful stage hold-ups. being sentenced to death by hanging, an ingenious jail escape, and an eight-month association with Billy the Kid, an association that made him almost as famous in Wild West outlaw history as Billy.

Paperback, 194 Pages, ISBN 978-1-952580-20-8
Hardcover, 194 pages, ISBN 978-1-952580-21-5

Doc45 Publications

Killing Pat Garrett, The Wild West's Most Famous Lawman - Murder or Self-Defense?

Pat Garrett, the Wild West's most famous lawman – the man who killed Billy the Kid – was himself killed on leap day, February 29, 1908, on a barren stretch of road between his Home Ranch and Las Cruces, New Mexico.

- Who killed him?
- Was it murder?
- Was it self-defense?

No biographer of Garrett has been able to answer these questions. All have expressed opinions. None have presented evidence that would stand up in a court of law. Here, for the first time, drawing on newly discovered information, is the definitive answer to the Wild West's most famous unsolved killing.

Supplementing the text are 102 images, including six of Garrett and his family which have never been published before. It has been 50 years since a new photo of Garrett was published, and no photos of his children have ever been published.

Garrett's life has been extensively researched. Yet, the author was able to uncover an enormous amount of new information. He had access to over 80 letters that Garrett wrote to his wife. He discovered a multitude of new documents and details concerning Garrett's killing, the events surrounding it, and the personal life of the man who was placed on trial for killing Garrett.

- The true actions of "Deacon Jim" Miller, a professional killer, who was in Las Cruces the day Garrett was killed.
- The place on the now abandoned old road to Las Cruces where Garrett was killed.
- The coroner's jury report on Garrett's death, lost for over 100 years.
- Garrett's original burial location.
- The sworn courtroom testimony of the only witness to Garrett's killing.
- The policeman who provided the decisive evidence in the trial of the man accused of murdering Garrett.
- The location of Garrett's Rock House and Home Ranches.
- New family details: Garrett had a four-month-old daughter the day he killed Billy the Kid. She died tragically at 15. Another daughter was blinded by a well-intended eye treatment; a son was paralyzed by childhood polio; and Pat Garrett, Jr., named after his father, lost his right leg to amputation at age 12.

Garrett's life was a remarkable adventure. He met two United States presidents: President William McKinley, Jr. and President Theodore Roosevelt. President Roosevelt he met five times, three times in the White House. He brought the law to hardened gunmen. He oversaw hangings. His national fame was so extensive the day he died that newspapers from the East to the West Coast only had to write "Pat Garrett" for readers to know to whom they were referring.

2020 Will Rogers Medallion Award Finalist for Excellence in Western Media
2020 Independent Press Award Distinguished Favorite, Historical Biography
2019 Best Book Awards Finalist, United States History
2019 Best Indie Book Notable 100 Award Winner.

Doc45 Publications

The Trial of Billy the Kid

This book is about Billy the Kid's trial for murder, and the events leading to that trial. The result of Billy's trial sealed his fate. And yet Billy's trial is the least written about, and until this book, the least known event of Billy's adult life.

Prior biographies have provided extensive — and fascinating — details on Billy's life, but they supply only a few paragraphs on Billy's trial. Just the bare facts: time, place, names, result.

Billy's trial the most important event in Billy's life. You may respond that his death is more important — it is in anyone's life! That is true, in an existential sense, but the events that lead to one's death at a particular place and time, the cause of one's death, override the importance of one's actual death. Those events are determinative. Without those events, one does not die then and there. If Billy had escaped death on July 14, 1881, and went on to live out more of his life, that escape and not his trial would probably be the most important event of Billy's life.

The information presented here has been unknown until now. This book makes it possible to answer these previously unanswerable questions:

- What were the governing Territorial laws?
- What were the charges against Billy?
- Was there a trial transcript and what happened to it?
- What kind of defense did Billy present?
- Did Billy testify in his own defense?
- Did Billy have witnesses standing for him?
- Who testified against him for the prosecution?
- What was the jury like?
- What action by the trial judge virtually guaranteed his conviction?
- What legal grounds did he have to appeal his verdict?
- Was the trial fair?

Supplementing the text are 132 photos, including many photos never published before.

Available in both paperback and hardcover.

Paperback, 254 Pages, ISBN 978-1-952580024
Hardcover, 254 Pages, ISBN 978-1-952580048

2022 Will Rogers Medallion Award Finalist for Excellence in Western Media
2022 Pasajero Del Camino Real Award Winner.

Doc45 Publications

La Posta – From the Founding of Mesilla, to Corn Exchange Hotel, to Billy the Kid Museum, to Famous Landmark, David G. Thomas, paperback, 118 pages, 59 photos, e-book available.

"*For someone who grew up in the area of Mesilla, it's nice to have a well-researched book about the area – and the giant photographs don't hurt either.... And the thing I was most excited to see is a photo of the hotel registry where the name of "William Bonney" is scrawled on the page.... There is some debate as to whether or not Billy the Kid really signed the book, which the author goes into, but what would Billy the Kid history be without a little controversy?"* –Billy the Kid Outlaw Gang Newsletter, Winter, 2013.

Giovanni Maria de Agostini, Wonder of The Century – The Astonishing World Traveler Who Was A Hermit, David G. Thomas, paperback, 208 pages, 59 photos, 19 maps, e-book available.

"*David G. Thomas has finally pulled back the veil of obscurity that long shrouded one of the most enduring mysteries in New Mexico's long history to reveal the true story of the Hermit, Giovanni Maria de Agostini. ...Thomas has once again proven himself a master history detective. Of particular interest is the information about the Hermit's life in Brazil, which closely parallels his remarkable experience in New Mexico, and required extensive research in Portuguese sources. Thomas's efforts make it possible to understand this deeply religious man.*" – Rick Hendricks, New Mexico State Historian

Screen With A Voice - A History of Moving Pictures in Las Cruces, New Mexico, David G. Thomas, paperback, 194 pages, 102 photos, e-book available.

The first projected moving pictures were shown in Las Cruces 110 years ago. Who exhibited those movies? What movies were shown? Since projected moving pictures were invented in 1896, why did it take ten years for the first movie exhibition to reach Las Cruces? Who opened the first theater in town? Where was it located? These questions began the history of moving pictures in Las Cruces, and they are answered in this book. But so are the events and stories that follow.

There have been 21 movie theaters in Las Cruces – all but three or four are forgotten. They are unremembered no longer. And one, especially, the Airdome Theater which opened in 1914, deserves to be known by all movie historians – it was an automobile drive-in theater, the invention of the concept, two decades before movie history declares the drive-in was invented.

Billy the Kid's Grave – A History of the Wild West's Most Famous Death Marker, David G. Thomas, paperback, 154 pages, 65 photos.

"Quien es?"

The answer to this incautious question – "Who is it?" – was a bullet to the heart.

That bullet – fired by Lincoln County Sheriff Patrick F. Garrett from a .40-44 caliber single action Colt pistol – ended the life of Billy the Kid, real name William Henry McCarty.

But death – ordinarily so final – only fueled the public's fascination with Billy the Kid. What events led to Billy's killing? Was it inevitable? Was a woman involved? If so, who was she? Why has Billy's gravestone become the most famous – and most visited – Western death marker? Is Billy really buried in his grave? Is the grave in the right location?

These questions – and many others – are answered in this book.

Doc45 Publications

The Stolen Pinkerton Reports of the Colonel Albert J. Fountain Murder Investigation, David G. Thomas, editor, paperback, 194 pages, 28 photos.

The abduction and apparent murder of Colonel Albert J. and Henry Fountain on February 1, 1896, shocked and outraged the citizens of New Mexico. It was not the killing of Colonel Fountain, a Union Civil War veteran and a prominent New Mexico attorney, which roused the physical disgust of the citizenry - after all, it was not unknown for distinguished men to be killed. It was the cold-blooded murder of his eight-year-old son which provoked the public outcry and revulsion.

The evidence indicated that although Colonel Albert J. Fountain was killed during the ambush, his son was taken alive, and only killed the next day.

The public was left without answers to the questions:

- Who ambushed and killed Colonel Fountain?
- Who was willing to kill his young son in cold-blood after holding him captive for 24 hours?

The case was never solved. Two men were eventually tried for and acquitted of the crime.

The case file for the crime contains almost no information. There are no trial transcripts or witness testimonies. The only reports that exist today of the investigation of the case are these Pinkerton Reports, which were commissioned by the Territorial Governor, and then stolen from his office four months after the murders. These Reports, now recovered, are published here.

These Reports are important historical documents, not only for what they reveal about the Fountain murders, but also as a fascinating window into how the most famous professional detective agency in the United States in the 1890s - the Pinkerton Detective Agency - went about investigating a murder, at a time when scientific forensic evidence was virtually non-existent.

Paperback, 196 Pages, ISBN 978-0-9828709-6-9

Torpedo Squadron Four – A Cockpit View of World War II, Gerald W. Thomas, paperback, 280 pages, 209 photos, e-book available.

"This book contains more first-person accounts than I have seen in several years. ...we can feel the emotion... tempered by the daily losses that characterized this final stage of the war in the Pacific. All in all, one of the best books on the Pacific War I have seen lately." – Naval Aviation News, Fall 2011.

When New Mexico Was Young, Harry H. Bailey, paperback, 186 pages, 10 photos.

The autobiography of Harry H. Bailey (1868-1954) Mr. Bailey was a pioneer New Mexican who took a major role in the development of the Mesilla Valley. In 1900, he built the "Natatorium," the first public swimming pool in El Paso, Texas. Three years later, he built the Angelus Hotel. In 1906, part of the Angelus Hotel building became the Crawford Theatre. After leaving El Paso and returning to New Mexico, he helped develop Radium Springs as a health resort and built the hotel and baths there.

His autobiography contains many stories about the early-day Mesilla Valley settlers who were his companions. Among the individuals he knew were Sheriff Pat Garrett, Colonel Albert J. Fountain, Attorney Albert B. Fall, Oliver Milton Lee, Sheriff Mariano Barela, Demetrio Chavez, Humbolt Casad, and George Griggs. He was a close friend of Western author Eugene Manlove Rhodes. For almost a year, he lived in the courthouse building in Mesilla where Billy the Kid was sentenced to hang.

Paperback, 186 Pages, ISBN 978-1-952580-0-17

Doc45 Publications

Water in a Thirsty Land
by Ruth R. Ealy
David G. Thomas, Editor

"**Water in a Thirsty Land**" is a chronicle of Dr. Taylor Filmore Ealy's 1874 to 1881 sojourn as a medical missionary in Indian Territory (Oklahoma) and New Mexico Territory, compiled by his daughter Ruth R. Ealy.

Dr. Ealy's first assignment was Fort Arbuckle, Chickasaw Reservation, Oklahoma Territory. His second was Lincoln, New Mexico Territory. His final assignment was Zuni Pueblo, New Mexico.

Dr. Ealy's faithful accounts of his struggles and challenges at these — at the time — exotic locations make for fascinating reading. His daily records of eye-witnessed events in Lincoln are of exceptional historical value. He arrived in Lincoln on February 19, 1878, the day after John Henry Tunstall was murdered. The unprovoked, sadistic murder of Tunstall kicked off the bloody Lincoln County War. Dr. Ealy was present at Tunstall's funeral, the killing of Lincoln County Sheriff Brady and Deputy Hindman, and the five-day shootout that ended with the firing of Alexander McSween's home, and the heinous slaughtering of McSween and four others as they frantically fled the blazing conflagration.

There are many details about the Lincoln County War in Dr. Ealy's account not recorded in other sources. Here are examples:

- Tunstall's funeral was held at 3 pm. His bullet-holed, bloody clothes were lying on the dirty ground in McSween's back yard during the service.
- The book provides many details about Tunstall's store: *"The floors were good ones and the windows were large."* One room was *"12 feet high, 18 feet long, and 18 feet wide, with a huge window and a door with a large glass in it."* That room was *"large enough to hold three hundred people."* The store lot was five acres in size and fully fenced.
- When the McSween house was fired during that 5-day shootout, one of Elizabeth Shield's children stepped in the coal oil used to ignite the fire.
- Among the items in McSween's house destroyed by the fire were an elegant piano, a Brussels carpet, costly furniture, rich curtains, and fine paintings.
- After Taylor testified at the Dudley Court of Inquiry, he was warned by anonymous note that he would be killed before he got back to his home in Zuni (a "coffin note").

From Lincoln, Dr. Ealy went to Zuni Pueblo. His keen observations are one of the primary, early sources of halcyon life in Zuni in 1878.

The Editor has added an extensive introduction, contextual notes, footnotes, appendices, and an index to the text of this extremely rare book.

Paperback, 208 Pages, ISBN 978-1952580-10-9
Hardcover, 208 Pages, ISBN 978-1952580-11-6

Doc45 Publications

The Frank W. Angel Report on the Death of John H. Tunstall

"In the matter of the cause and circumstances of the death of John H. Tunstall...."

So begins the single most important contemporary document recounting the origins of the Lincoln County War. That document is the "Report of Special Agent Frank Warner Angel on the Death of John Henry Tunstall," known today to historians as the "Angel Report."

The 395-page, hand-written Report that Angel submitted on October 3, 1878, on Tunstall's unprovoked, sadistic murder is published for the first time in this book.

The Report documents the events leading to Tunstall's murder – the testimony of the men present at the brutal killing – including Billy the Kid's eye-witness account – and the violent consequences that followed.

It includes sworn accounts by William "Frank" Baker, Robert W. Beckwith, Henry N. Brown, James J. Dolan, William Dowlin, Pantaleón Gallegos, Godfrey Gauss, Florencio Gonzales, John Hurley, Jacob B. Mathews, Alexander A. McSween, John Middleton, Lawrence G. Murphy, John Wallace Olinger, Juan B. Patron, George W. Peppin, David P. Shield, Robert A. Widenmann, and 18 others.

Supplementing the Report are an extensive introduction, notes, contemporary documents, associated letters, biographical details, and a timeline.

The book also reveals the brazen attempt by two powerful politicians – Thomas Catron and Stephen Elkins – to destroy the Report, depriving history of its priceless contribution.

Forty three images, many never published before.

Available in both paperback and hardcover.

Paperback, 254 Pages, ISBN 978-1-952580079
Hardcover, 254 pages, ISBN 978-1-952580055

Doc45 Publications

Incident at Ple Tonan, An Imperial Japanese War Crime and the Fate of U.S. Navy Airmen in French Indochina

This book began 33 years ago, in early 1990, with a question posed to the author by his father. The author's father was just completing his memoir of his World War II military experiences and he was greatly troubled by not knowing the fate of two of his fellow fliers in his USS ESSEX based air squadron, Torpedo Four (VT-4). The two men whose fate still haunted the author's father 45 years after the fact were shot down in an air raid on Japanese-occupied French Indochina.

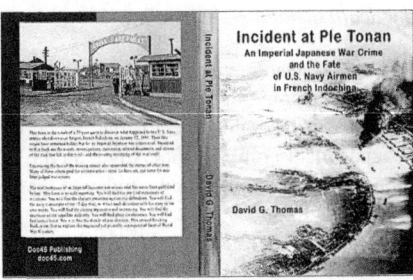

The answer to this question would have remained hidden but for an Imperial Japanese war crimes trial. In this book, you will find the events, investigations, statements, related documents, and stories of the men that led to that trial – and the riveting testimony of the trial itself.

Not surprisingly, uncovering the stories of the two missing squadron members' fates also uncovered the stories of other men. Many of these others, as disclosed in this book, paid the ultimate price – some for heroism, and some for acts later judged war crimes.

A courtroom criminal trial is unlike any other human institution. It is combat without physical weapons. And as in combat, the stakes can be as high as death.

Here you will find the statements and interrogations that led to the belief that multiple war crimes were committed at Ple Tonan in French Indochina on April 27, 1945. You will find the pre-trial statements of witnesses. You will find the charges presented against the defendants. You will find the daily transcripts of the 13 day trial. You will find the closing arguments and sentencing. You will find the decisions of the appellate authority.

You will find the pleas for clemency submitted for each defendant. You will find their last letters home to their families. You will find the details of their punishments.

A courtroom criminal trial can reveal a defendant's inner being in a way no other human institution can. A defendant that appears on the stand must try to explain and justify the actions for which the person is being tried. And that person must do so in an adversarial setting in which every assertion is open to challenge and refutation.

The men who appeared in the trial presented in this book all appeared on the stand in their own defense. This book is no cold reporting. With their trial testimony, each defendant got to explain and justify his actions. This book, based on the way in which it is presented, puts you in the position of, first, an investigator trying to determine whether a war crime was committed, and, second, a jury member who must decide the guilt or innocence of a defendant after hearing the evidence against the defendant.

59 images, many never published before.

Paperback, 320 Pages, ISBN 978-1-952580-14-7

Made in the USA
Middletown, DE
05 October 2024